REPRODUCTION Female bobcats usually have two, three, or four kittens every year.

HABITAT Bobcats live in many different places in Georgia, from rocky mountain slopes to thick forests to watery swamps.

Bobcats are mostly active at night. They rest for much of the day.

BEHAVIOR Bobcats are excellent climbers and can often be found in trees.

HSP Science

Georgia

Harcourt

SCHOOL PUBLISHERS

Visit *The Learning Site!*

www.harcourtschool.com

HSP Georgia Science

Bobcat

SCHOOL PUBLISHERS

Science and Technology features provided by

Printed in the United States of America

ISBN-13: 978-0-15-358540-1

ISBN-10: 0-15-358540-4

2 3 4 5 6 7 8 9 10 048 16 15 14 13 12 11 10 09 08

Series Consulting Authors

Michael J. Bell, Ph.D.
*Associate Professor of Early
   Childhood Education*
College of Education
West Chester University of
   Pennsylvania
West Chester, Pennsylvania

Michael A. DiSpezio
Curriculum Architect
JASON Academy
Cape Cod, Massachusetts

Marjorie Frank
*Former Adjunct, Science
   Education*
Hunter College
New York, New York

Gerald H. Krockover, Ph.D.
*Professor of Earth and Atmospheric
   Science Education*
Purdue University
West Lafayette, Indiana

Joyce C. McLeod
Adjunct Professor
Rollins College
Winter Park, Florida

Barbara ten Brink
Science Specialist
Austin Independent School
   District
Austin, Texas

Carol J. Valenta
Senior Vice President
St. Louis Science Center
St. Louis, Missouri

Barry A. Van Deman
President and CEO
Museum of Life and Science
Durham, North Carolina

Georgia Curriculum and Classroom Reviewers

Amy Benson
Tritt Elementary
Marietta, Georgia

Joyce Brooks
Alpharetta Elementary
Alpharetta, Georgia

Julie B. Burns
Blandford Elementary
Runcon, Georgia

Shelley Crittenden
Grantville Elementary
Grantville, Georgia

Calandra Eineker
Alpharetta Elementary
Alpharetta, Georgia

Jennie Haynes
A. B. Merry School
Augusta, Georgia

Gail Hines
A. B. Merry School
Augusta, Georgia

Dawn M. Hudson
Paulding County Schools
Dallas, Georgia

Valerie E. King
Big Shanty Intermediate
Kennesaw, Georgia

Sondra M. Lee
Grantville Elementary
Grantville, Georgia

Stacey N. Mabray
Augusta, Georgia

Heather L. Nix
Berrien Primary School
Nashville, Georgia

Lisa E. Reynolds
Holsenbeck Elementary
Winder, Georgia

Vicki Roark
Little River Elementary
Woodstock, Georgia

Karol H. Stephens
*Northeast High School/
Bibb County Board of Education*
Macon, Georgia

Karen W. Sumner
G.O. Bailey Primary School
Tifton, Georgia

Beth Thompson
Alpharetta Elementary
Alpharetta, Georgia

Gina A. Turner
Troup County Schools
LaGrange, Georgia

Nannette R. Ward
Lake Park Elementary
Albany, Georgia

Dianne Wood
Woody Gap School
Suches, Georgia

Dear Students and Parents,

The Georgia Performance Standards for Science (GPS), shown here for your reference, were designed to provide students with the knowledge and skills necessary for science proficiency at the third grade. Therefore, the GPS will drive science instruction. Since science is a way of thinking and investigating, as well as a body of knowledge, students need an understanding of both the Characteristics of Science and its Content. The GPS require that instruction treat these together, so they are shown here as co-requisites.

Georgia HSP Science was developed to provide complete coverage of the GPS. Throughout the book you will find exciting investigations, engaging text, and ties to Georgia people and places. These help ensure mastery of the GPS, while providing a rewarding science experience for all students.

Harcourt School Publishers

Co-Requisite—Characteristics of Science

Habits of Mind

S3CS1 **Students will be aware of the importance of curiosity, honesty, openness, and skepticism in science and will exhibit these traits in their own efforts to understand how the world works.**

a. Keep records of investigations and observations and do not alter the records later.

b. Offer reasons for findings and consider reasons suggested by others.

c. Take responsibility for understanding the importance of being safety conscious.

S3CS2 **Students will have the computation and estimation skills necessary for analyzing data and following scientific explanations.**

a. Add, subtract, multiply, and divide whole numbers mentally, on paper, and with a calculator.

b. Use commonly encountered fractions—halves, thirds, and fourths (but not sixths, sevenths, and so on)—in scientific calculations.

c. Judge whether measurements and computations of quantities, such as length, weight, or time, are reasonable answers to scientific problems by comparing them to typical values.

S3CS3 Students will use tools and instruments for observing, measuring, and manipulating objects in scientific activities utilizing safe laboratory procedures.

a. Choose appropriate common materials for making simple mechanical constructions and repairing things.

b. Use computers, cameras, and recording devices for capturing information.

c. Identify and practice accepted safety procedures in manipulating science materials and equipment.

S3CS4 Students will use ideas of system, model, change, and scale in exploring scientific and technological matters.

a. Observe and describe how parts influence one another in things with many parts.

b. Use geometric figures, number sequences, graphs, diagrams, sketches, number lines, maps, and stories to represent corresponding features

of objects, events, and processes in the real world.

c. Identify ways in which the representations do not match their original counterparts.

S3CS5 Students will communicate scientific ideas and activities clearly.

a. Write instructions that others can follow in carrying out a scientific procedure.

b. Make sketches to aid in explaining scientific procedures or ideas.

c. Use numerical data in describing and comparing objects and events.

d. Locate scientific information in reference books, back issues of newspapers and magazines, CD-ROMs, and computer databases.

S3CS6 Students will question scientific claims and arguments effectively.

a. Support statements with facts found in books, articles, and databases, and identify the sources used.

The Nature of Science

S3CS7 Students will be familiar with the character of scientific knowledge and how it is achieved.

Students will recognize that:

a. Similar scientific investigations seldom produce exactly the same results, which may differ due to unexpected differences in whatever is being investigated, unrecognized differences in the methods or circumstances of the investigation, or observational uncertainties.

b. Some scientific knowledge is very old and yet is still applicable today.

S3CS8 Students will understand important features of the process of scientific inquiry.

Students will apply the following to inquiry learning practices:

a. Scientific investigations may take many different forms, including observing what things are like

or what is happening somewhere, collecting specimens for analysis, and doing experiments.

b. Clear and active communication is an essential part of doing science. It enables scientists to inform others about their work, expose their ideas to criticism by other scientists, and stay informed about scientific discoveries around the world.

c. Scientists use technology to increase their power to observe things and to measure and compare things accurately.

d. Science involves many different kinds of work and engages men and women of all ages and backgrounds.

Co-Requisite—Content

EARTH SCIENCE

S3E1 **Students will investigate the physical attributes of rocks and soils.**

a. Explain the difference between a rock and a mineral.

b. Recognize the physical attributes of rocks and minerals using observation (shape, color, texture), measurement, and simple tests (hardness).

c. Use observation to compare the similarities and differences of texture, particle size, and color in top soils (such as clay, loam or potting soil, and sand).

d. Determine how water and wind can change rocks and soil over time using observation and research.

S3E2 **Students will investigate fossils as evidence of organisms that lived long ago.**

a. Investigate fossils by observing authentic fossils or models of fossils or view information resources about fossils as evidence of organisms that lived long ago.

b. Describe how a fossil is formed.

Rock City Gardens

PHYSICAL SCIENCE

S3P1 **Students will investigate how heat is produced and the effects of heating and cooling, and will understand a change in temperature indicates a change in heat.**

a. Categorize ways to produce heat energy such as burning, rubbing (friction), and mixing one thing with another.

b. Investigate how insulation affects heating and cooling.

c. Investigate the transfer of heat energy from the sun to various materials.

d. Use thermometers to measure the changes in temperatures of water samples (hot, warm, cold) over time.

S3P2 **Students will investigate magnets and how they affect other magnets and common objects.**

a. Investigate to find common objects that are attracted to magnets.

b. Investigate how magnets attract and repel each other.

LIFE SCIENCE

S3L1 **Students will investigate the habitats of different organisms and the dependence of organisms on their habitat.**

a. Differentiate between habitats of Georgia (mountains, marsh/swamp, coast, Piedmont, Atlantic Ocean) and the organisms that live there.

b. Identify features of green plants that allow them to live and thrive in different regions of Georgia.

c. Identify features of animals that allow them to live and thrive in different regions of Georgia.

d. Explain what will happen to an organism if the habitat is changed.

S3L2 **Students will recognize the effects of pollution and humans on the environment.**

a. Explain the effects of pollution (such as littering) to the habitats of plants and animals.

b. Identify ways to protect the environment.

    1. Conservation of resources

    2. Recycling of materials

Contents

UNIT B PHYSICAL SCIENCE 146

Big Idea
Many things can produce heat. Temperature can be measured by using a thermometer.

Big Idea
Magnets are attracted to objects with iron. Opposite ends of two magnets attract each other.

match burning

Big Idea
Certain body parts and behaviors can help plants and animals live in different places.

Big Idea
Georgia has many habitats. Each habitat contains different living things.

Chapter 8 Pollution and Conservation. 308

References

Big Idea
There are many ways to conserve resources and to protect the environment from harmful materials.

pine forest

Getting Ready for Science

 Georgia Performance Standards in This Chapter

Characteristics of Science

S3CS1 Students will be aware of the importance of curiosity, honesty, openness, and skepticism in science and will exhibit these traits in their own efforts to understand how the world works.

S3CS2 Students will have the computation and estimation skills necessary for analyzing data and following scientific explanations.

S3CS3 Students will use tools and instruments for observing, measuring, and manipulating objects in scientific activities utilizing safe laboratory procedures.

S3CS4 Students will use ideas of system, model, change, and scale in exploring scientific and technological matters.

S3CS5 Students will communicate scientific ideas and activities clearly.

S3CS6 Students will question scientific claims and arguments effectively.

S3CS7 Students will be familiar with the character of scientific knowledge and how it is achieved.

S3CS8 Students will understand important features of the process of scientific inquiry.

What's the Big Idea?

Scientists learn about the world by asking questions and doing investigations.

Essential Questions

 Go online ▶ for student eBook
www.hspscience.com

Science in Georgia

Chattahoochee National Forest

Dear Marcy,

Our field trip today was a lot of fun. We went hiking in the Chattahoochee National Forest and saw all kinds of plants and animals. A ranger answered a lot of my questions about the park. There were big waterfalls and lots of trees. We're taking pictures to show you!

See you next week,
Jason

How do you think scientists learn about the world around us? How do you think that relates to the **Big Idea?**

Characteristics of Science

S3CS1c Take responsibility for understanding the importance of being safety conscious.

S3CS3c Identify and practice accepted safety procedures in manipulating science materials and equipment.

S3CS7a Similar scientific investigations seldom produce exactly the same results, which may differ due to unexpected differences in whatever is being investigated, unrecognized differences in the methods or circumstances of the investigation, or observational uncertainties.

S3CS8c Scientists use technology to increase their power to observe things and to measure and compare things accurately.

Georgia Fast Fact

Measuring Up
The first humans probably used body parts for measuring tools! For example, the foot measurement was probably based on the length of a person's foot. In the Investigate, you will learn more about measurement.

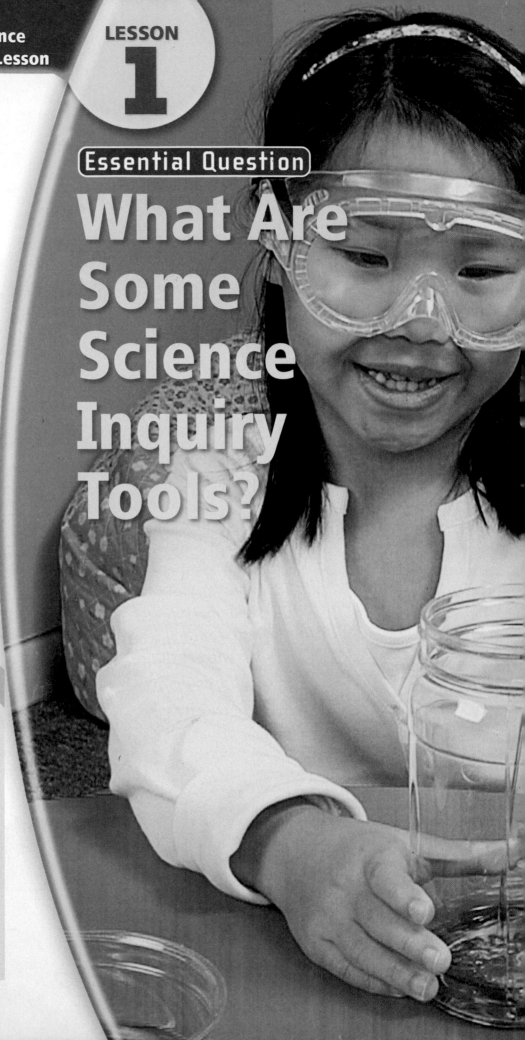

LESSON

1

Essential Question

What Are Some Science Inquiry Tools?

inquiry [IN•kwer•ee]
A question about
something or a close
study of it (p. 6)

accurate [AK•yuh•ruht]
Correct (p. 8)

thermometer
[ther•MAHM•uh•ter] A tool
that measures how hot or
cold something is (p. 9)

What are these
students doing?

Making Bubbles

Directed Inquiry

Start with Questions

Do you like to blow bubbles? Blowing bubbles is fun!

- Are all bubbles alike?

- What do bubbles look like up close?

Investigate to find out. Then read to find out more.

Prepare to Investigate

Inquiry Skill Tip

When you observe an object, you study it closely. You can observe size, shape, color, smell, sound, and any other information that comes to your senses.

Materials

- safety goggles
- metric measuring cup
- water
- large container
- dishwashing soap
- stirring stick
- small container
- straw
- hand lens

Make an Observation Chart

Bubble Observations	
Without Hand Lens	With Hand Lens

Follow This Procedure

CAUTION: Put on safety goggles.

1. Use the measuring cup to measure 1 L (1,000 mL) of water. Pour the water into a large container.

2. Measure 50 mL of dishwashing soap. Gently stir it into the water. Pour some of the liquid into a small container.

3. Use the straw to blow air into the liquid in the small container. Observe the bubbles. Record your observations.

4. Observe the bubbles with a hand lens. Record those observations.

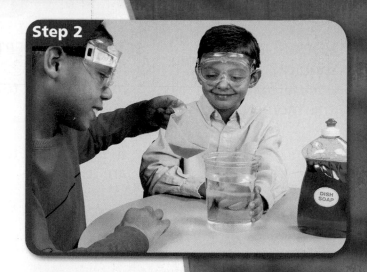

Step 2

Step 3

Draw Conclusions

1. How do hand lenses help you observe bubbles? **S3CS8c**

2. **Standards Link** In what ways were the bubbles you blew different from one another? What may have caused them to be different? **S3CS7a**

3. **Inquiry Skill** We often use our eyes to observe. How could you use a tool to observe something? **S3CS8c**

Independent Inquiry

Add 60 mL of glycerine and 8 mL of sugar to the liquid in the small container. Predict what the bubbles you will blow with this mixture will be like. Then blow some bubbles. How do your results compare with your prediction? **S3CS3c**

VOCABULARY
inquiry p. 6
accurate p. 8
thermometer p. 9

SCIENCE CONCEPTS
▶ what some measurement tools are
▶ how these measurement tools are used

Focus Skill MAIN IDEA AND DETAILS
Look for details about tools used for measuring things.

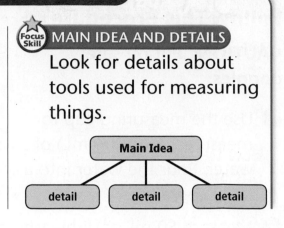

Main Idea

detail   detail   detail

Tools Used for Inquiry

A scientist tries to answer questions about how things work. An **inquiry** is a question that is asked about something or an organized study of something. Investigations and experiments are inquiries.

In most science inquiries, you use tools to collect data. These tools help you observe, measure, and compare objects. However, you must use these tools properly and safely so you don't get hurt.

 MAIN IDEA AND DETAILS What is an inquiry?

Hand Lens

What It Is: A hand lens is a tool that makes an object look bigger.

How to Use It: Hold a hand lens near the object that you want to observe closely. Look at the object through the lens. You can move the lens closer to or farther from the object to see it more clearly.

Safety: Be careful not to drop or scratch a hand lens.

Forceps

What They Are: Forceps are a tool that is used to pick up and hold on to small objects or objects that break easily.

How to Use Them: Place the tips of the forceps around the object you want to pick up. Squeeze the forceps' handles gently, and lift the object.

Safety: The tips of the forceps may be sharp. Always clean the forceps after you use them.

Dropper

What It Is: A dropper is a tool that picks up and releases small amounts of liquid.

How to Use It: Squeeze the dropper's bulb to get the air out. Keep squeezing as you place the end of the dropper in a liquid. Then stop squeezing. Some of the liquid will move up into the dropper. To release the liquid, squeeze the bulb again.

Safety: Droppers should be cleaned after each use.

Magnifying Box

What It Is: Like a hand lens, a magnifying box can magnify an object, or make it look bigger.

How to Use It: Place the object you want to observe inside the magnifying box. Look through the clear part of the box.

Safety: Some magnifying boxes have a glass lens. Be careful not to drop the box.

Insta-Lab

Use a Magnifying Box
Place a magnifying box on this page. Use it to look at the text and some of the photographs. What do you observe? Then look at other objects, such as leaves or paper clips.

Measuring Tools

The tools on this page can be used to take measurements in an inquiry. If you do not use a tool properly, your measurements will be wrong. You want your measurements to be **accurate**, or correct.

Using the right tool will make your measurements more accurate. You should also check each measurement more than once. Taking measurements two or three times can help you make sure they are accurate.

 MAIN IDEA AND DETAILS

Which tool would you use to measure how tall you are?

Measuring Cup

What It Is: A measuring cup measures volume, or the amount of space that something takes up. Measuring cups are usually used for liquids and for loose solids such as powders.

How to Use It: Carefully pour the substance you want to measure into the measuring cup. Use the marks on the outside of the cup to see how much is in it. To be accurate, bend down so that your eyes are at the same level as the marks on the cup.

Safety: Do not drop the measuring cup. Ask your teacher for help with spills.

Spring Scale

What It Is: A spring scale is a tool that measures an object's weight.

How to Use It: Attach the object you want to weigh to the hook at the bottom of the spring scale. Allow the object to hang as you hold the spring scale up. The scale will show the weight of the object.

Safety: Weigh objects on a spring scale only when your teacher asks you to do so.

Thermometer

What It Is: A **thermometer** is a tool that measures temperature, or how hot or cold something is.

How to Use It: Put the thermometer in the place where you want to measure the temperature. Wait about five minutes. Then find the top of the liquid in the thermometer's tube. Use the markings along the side of the tube to read the temperature.

Safety: If a thermometer breaks, do not touch it. Ask your teacher for help.

Ruler

What It Is: A ruler is a tool used to measure length, width, height, or depth.

How to Use It: Place the ruler against the object you want to measure. Use the markings on the ruler to see how long, wide, high, or deep the object is. To take accurate measurements, make sure the end of the ruler or the 0 mark is exactly at one edge of the object.

Safety: Do not use rulers to measure hot objects. You could get hurt or damage the ruler.

Measuring Tape

What It Is: A measuring tape is like a ruler, but it can measure curved objects.

How to Use It: Place the measuring tape along the object that you would like to measure. Use the markings on the tape to see how long, wide, high, or deep the object is.

Safety: Do not use plastic measuring tapes to measure hot objects.

Some Other Tools Used in Science

Many science tools have similar uses. For example, computers, tape recorders, and cameras can all record information. Measuring cups, measuring spoons, and graduated cylinders (GRA•joo•ayt•id SIL•uhn•duhrz) all measure how much space something takes up.

Your measurements will be more accurate if you use the proper tool. If you want to measure how much water is in a large bowl, for example, you would need a big enough tool. You would need a measuring cup, not a measuring spoon. Measuring spoons are only accurate for measuring small amounts.

 MAIN IDEA AND DETAILS **Why is it important to use the proper tool to measure something?**

Measuring Spoon

What It Is: A measuring spoon can be used to measure ingredients before combining them. The spoons come in a set.

How It Is Used: A measuring spoon can be used to measure powders or liquids. Choose the spoon that will measure the amount you need. Then pour the liquid into the spoon or dip the spoon into the powder.

Safety: Measuring spoons should not be used to measure hot liquids.

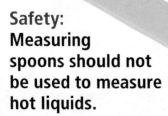

Graduated Cylinder

What It Is: Like a measuring cup, a graduated cylinder measures volume, or the amount of space that something takes up. A graduated cylinder is used to measure liquids.

How It Is Used: Pour the liquid into the graduated cylinder. To make an accurate measurement, bend down so that your eyes are even with the top of the liquid. Then read the measurement on the outside of the cylinder.

Safety: Handle glass graduated cylinders carefully so they do not break.

Pan Balance

What It Is: A pan balance is used to measure mass, or the amount of matter in an object.

How It Is Used: Make sure the pointer is in the middle. Place the object you want to measure in the left pan. Add standard masses to the right pan until the pointer comes back to the middle mark. Then add the numbers on the standard masses to find the mass of the object.

Safety: Use the pan balance only when your teacher asks you to do so.

Microscope

What It Is: A microscope is a tool that is used to make very small objects look larger. It helps you see details that are too small to see with just your eyes.

How It Is Used: Place the object on the platform under the lens. Look through the eyepiece. Turn the knob until you can see the object clearly.

Safety: Always use two hands when you carry a microscope. Do not touch the lenses with your fingers.

Essential Question

What are some science inquiry tools?

In this lesson, you learned about tools that can help you observe and measure things. Scientists use these tools in inquiries. It is important to be safe when using science tools.

1. (Focus Skill) MAIN IDEA AND DETAILS

Draw and complete a graphic organizer. Show details that support this main idea: *Many tools can be used in science inquiries.* **S3CS8c**

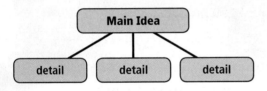

2. SUMMARIZE Make a table. List at least five of the tools named in this lesson. Tell a way you could safely use each tool.

S3CS1c

3. VOCABULARY Which of the following is **not** an inquiry?
A doing an investigation
B studying something closely
C cleaning a science tool
D asking a question **S3CS8a**

4. Critical Thinking You want to know whether a tiny animal you have found has six legs or eight. What tools could you use to help you find out? **S3CS8c**

CRCT Practice

5. Which should you always do to make accurate measurements?
A Use two kinds of tools.
B Take measurements twice to make sure they are correct.
C Copy the measurements that someone else made.
D Use a tool made of plastic instead of glass. **S3CS7a**

6. Which safety rule should you follow when using a thermometer?

A Ask for help if it breaks.
B Measure only cold liquids.
C Throw it out after you use it.
D Put it in your pocket. **S3CS3c**

 Writing ELA3W1c

Write a Paragraph

Choose a science tool that you have used. Write a **paragraph** about the tool you chose. Make sure your paragraph has a topic sentence and supporting details.

 Math M3M2d

Select Unit of Measure

Look at the photograph on the left. Make a list of five things that you could measure, using science tools. For each thing on your list, tell what tool you would use to measure it. Also name the units for each measurement on your list.

 Health

How Many Are Enough?

We should eat five servings of fruit and vegetables each day. One serving of dried fruit is $\frac{1}{4}$ cup. Ask a classmate to predict how many raisins are in $\frac{1}{4}$ cup. Then measure $\frac{1}{4}$ cup, and count to check the prediction.

 For more links and activities, go to **www.hspscience.com**

Characteristics of Science

S3CS1a Keep records of investigations and observations and do not alter the records later.

S3CS1b Offer reasons for findings and consider reasons suggested by others.

S3CS6a Support statements with facts found in books, articles, and databases, and identify the sources used.

S3CS8b Clear and active communication is an essential part of doing science. It enables scientists to inform others about their work, expose their ideas to criticism by other scientists, and stay informed about scientific discoveries around the world.

Essential Question

What Are Some Science Inquiry Skills?

Georgia Fast Fact

Blowing Bubbles
The longest bubble ever blown and measured was about 32 meters (105 ft) long! What shape do you think this huge bubble was? In the Investigate, you will learn about bubble shapes.

Wow! How can a bubble get so big?

Vocabulary Preview

predict [pree•DIKT]
To tell what you think
will happen in the future
(p. 20)

evidence [EV•uh•duhns]
Information collected in
a scientific inquiry (p. 23)

Cats are the best pets.

opinion [uh•PIN•yuhn] A
personal belief that is not
based on evidence (p. 23)

15

Shapes of Bubbles

Directed Inquiry

Start with Questions

Have you ever seen fancy-shaped wands for blowing bubbles? They look very interesting.

- Can you blow bubbles that have different shapes?

- Do bubble wands that have different shapes make bubbles that have different shapes?

Investigate to find out. Then read to find out more.

Prepare to Investigate

Inquiry Skill Tip

When you predict, you tell what you think will happen in an investigation. A prediction is not just a guess. Predictions should be based on what you know and have observed. You should always be able to tell why you made your prediction.

Materials
- safety goggles
- wire hangers
- aluminum pie pan
- bubble solution

Make an Observation Chart

Bubble Shapes		
Shape of Wand	Predicted Bubble Shape	Actual Bubble Shape

Follow This Procedure

CAUTION: Put on safety goggles.

1. Use the hangers to make bubble wands of different shapes.

2. Predict the shape of the bubbles that each wand will make. Record your prediction.

3. Pour some bubble solution into the pie pan. Dip a wand into the solution, and make bubbles. Observe and record their shapes. Repeat with all the wands. Try each wand at least twice.

Draw Conclusions

1. What information did you use to make your predictions?

2. **Standards Link** How did you know if your predictions were correct? **S3CS1a**

3. **Inquiry Skill** Use your observations to predict the shape of a bubble blown with a heart-shaped wand. Explain why you made the prediction you did. **S3CS1b**

Step 1

Step 3

Independent Inquiry

Your friend says that a bubble will be the same color as the wand. Plan an investigation to find out if she is correct. Try it. Did you gather evidence that supported her statement? **S3CS1b**

VOCABULARY
predict p. 20
evidence p. 23
opinion p. 23

SCIENCE CONCEPTS
▶ what some inquiry skills are
▶ how inquiry skills are used

Focus Skill MAIN IDEA AND DETAILS
Look for details about skills for science inquiry.

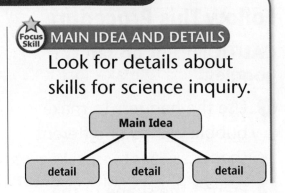

Skills Used for Inquiry

When scientists try to answer a question, they use thinking tools called inquiry skills. You have already used some of these skills. In the Investigates, you have observed, measured, recorded data, and compared.

You will probably use more than one skill in an investigation. That's because the inquiry skills work together. The skills that you use depend on what you are trying to find out.

Focus Skill MAIN IDEA AND DETAILS

Explain how you used two of the inquiry skills on the next page during the Investigate.

These students are setting up an investigation. They will need to use inquiry skills to complete the investigation. ▼

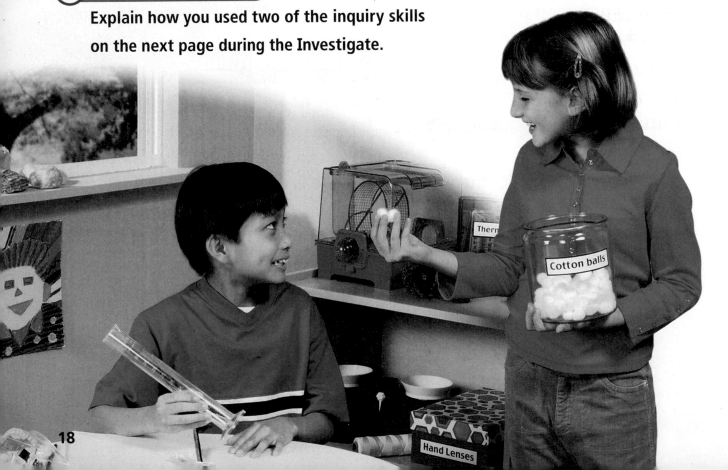

Observe

When you observe, you study something closely. You might observe the way something looks, smells, tastes, feels, or sounds. It is important to repeat your observations to make sure they are correct.

Infer

When you infer, you assume something that you did not actually observe. You might observe people wearing coats outside. You could infer that it is cold, but you could not be sure unless you went outside.

A ruler can be used to measure length.

Measure

You use numbers when you measure something. To take measurements, you use tools such as thermometers, spring scales, measuring tapes, and measuring cups.

Collect, Record, Analyze, and Display Data

When you measure or observe something, you are collecting data. Data is information. When you record data, you write it down. Recording data can help you *analyze*, or figure out, what the data is telling you. Data can be displayed in charts, tables, and graphs.

Communicate

Scientists communicate, or share information, with other people. Writing reports, telling others about results, and making web pages are all ways to communicate.

This student has collected data. He is making a bar graph to display it.

More Skills Used for Inquiry

Scientists want to learn new things. Inquiry skills help them make logical conclusions. A conclusion is logical if it is based on facts and makes sense.

You use inquiry skills in your life, too. For example, when you **predict**, you tell what you think will happen in the future. Predict what tomorrow's weather will be like. You are using an inquiry skill!

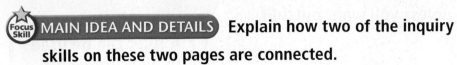 **MAIN IDEA AND DETAILS** Explain how two of the inquiry skills on these two pages are connected.

Compare
When you compare, you look to see how things are alike or different.

Classify/Order
To classify items, you group—or organize—them into categories. To order items or events, you place them in the correct sequence.

◀ This student is comparing different items and then classifying them into groups.

This student is using a stopwatch to time her classmate. She will use numbers—minutes and seconds—to tell how long something takes. Timing something involves using a time/space relationship. ▼

Use Time/Space Relationships
Where were you at noon yesterday? Every time that you identify where something is at a certain time, you are using a time/space relationship.

Predict
When you predict something, you use what you observe and what you know to tell what might happen in the future. Then you see what happens and compare your prediction with the actual result. What do you predict will happen to the water in the photograph?

Using Models

You might want to study something that is very big or very small, such as the solar system or an ant. Perhaps you want to learn about something that is dangerous, such as an earthquake.

You can use a model of what you want to study. A model can help you learn how something works. A good model works the same way as the thing that the model represents.

 MAIN IDEA AND DETAILS

Name two things that scientists might use models to study.

These students are learning more about volcanoes by building a model of one. ▼

Make a Model

Use modeling clay to make a model of a plant or an animal that interests you. How does your model compare to the real plant or animal?

Use Models

Models are often used in science to study things that are too big or too small to see easily in real life. Some models are made by computers. For example, computer models help people predict the weather.

Ashley records that the bug is pretty. Erin records that the bug has six legs. Which student is recording her opinion? Which student is recording evidence?

The bug is pretty.

The bug has 6 legs.

Evidence and Opinion

Evidence is information collected in a scientific inquiry. You know that evidence is true if the inquiry always has the same results. An **opinion** is a personal belief that is not based on evidence.

Scientists do not draw conclusions based on opinions. They use facts and evidence to understand the world.

MAIN IDEA AND DETAILS

Give an example of an opinion and an example of evidence about an apple.

Draw Conclusions

To draw conclusions, you think about everything you learned in an inquiry. Then you make a statement about it. Your conclusion should be based on data you gathered and information you already know. You can use facts from books and articles to help you draw a conclusion.

What are some science inquiry skills?

In this lesson, you learned how inquiry skills, or thinking skills, are important in science. Scientists use these skills to help answer their questions.

1. Focus Skill **MAIN IDEA AND DETAILS**
Draw and complete a graphic organizer. Show details that support this main idea: *Many skills can be used in science inquiries.* `S3CS8a`

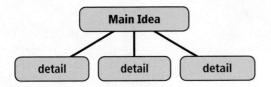

2. DRAW CONCLUSIONS
You want to find out how the heights of third graders differ from the heights of second graders. Which inquiry skills will you use? `S3CS1a`

3. VOCABULARY Describe how someone *predicts*, and give an example. `S3CS6a`

4. Critical Thinking Why is it important to keep records during an investigation? `S3CS1a`

CRCT Practice

5. Which of these is an opinion?
 A The weather is nice today.
 B Clouds are covering the sun.
 C It was 2°C colder yesterday.
 D It rained 6 cm today. `S3CS6a`

6. Pauline puts the results of her experiment on a website for others to see. Which inquiry skill is she using? **The Big Idea**
 A gather data
 B draw conclusions
 C use models
 D communicate `S3CS8b`

 Writing ELA3W1a

Write a Paragraph

Which do you think are the three most useful inquiry skills? Write a **paragraph** explaining your point of view. Tell how these skills can help scientists get accurate results in an investigation.

 Math M3D1a

Compare Data

Read question 2 in the Lesson Review again. Make a chart or table that would help you collect and record the heights of students in the second and third grades. Record at least 10 observations for each of the grades. Compare your observations of each grade.

 Language Arts ELA3R3d

Evidence or Opinion?

Someone says that peaches grown in Georgia have more juice than peaches grown in other states. Tell how you would find out whether this statement is a fact or an opinion. Which inquiry skills would you use?

 For more links and activities, go to **www.hspscience.com**

Characteristics of Science

S3CS2c Judge whether measurements and computations of quantities, such as length, weight, or time, are reasonable answers to scientific problems by comparing them to typical values.

S3CS4b Use geometric figures, number sequences, graphs, diagrams, sketches, number lines, maps, and stories to represent corresponding features of objects, events, and processes in the real world.

S3CS5c Use numerical data in describing and comparing objects and events.

Georgia Fast Fact

Number What?
Ancient Greeks used the first letter of words to stand for numbers. *Pente* means "five" in Greek, so *P* stood for 5. *Deka* means "ten," so *D* stood for 10. *DP* stood for 15. What did *DDDP* stand for?

LESSON 3

Essential Question

How Do We Use Numbers in Science?

data table
[DAY•tuh TAY•buhl] A display that organizes data into rows and columns (p. 32)

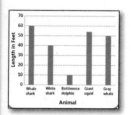

bar graph [BAR GRAF] A graph that uses bars to display data (p. 32)

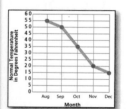

line graph [LYN GRAF] A graph that uses a line to display data (p. 33)

What makes some bubbles so large and others so small?

Numbers of Bubbles

Directed Inquiry

Start with Questions

A bubble bath is made when liquid soap is mixed with water in a bathtub.

- What happens if you add too much soap?

- What happens if you don't add enough soap?

- Does the amount of soap in the water make a difference?

Investigate to find out. Then read to find out more.

Prepare to Investigate

Inquiry Skill Tip

When you analyze your data, you look for a pattern. It might help to make a graph. A graph organizes your data and can help you see patterns.

Materials

- 3 plastic jars with lids
- marker
- water
- graduated cylinder
- dropper
- dishwashing soap
- ruler

Make a Data Table

Heights of Bubbles		
Jar	Height, Trial 1	Height, Trial 2
A		
B		
C		

Follow This Procedure

1. Mark the jars A, B, and C. Using the graduated cylinder, measure and pour 50 mL of water into each jar.

2. Use the dropper to put 5 drops of soap in Jar A, 10 drops in Jar B, and 15 drops in Jar C. Put the lids on the jars.

3. Shake Jar A five times. Use the ruler to measure the height of the bubbles. Record the number. Repeat with the other two jars.

4. Rinse the jars, and repeat Steps 1–3. Record your results.

Draw Conclusions

1. Which container had the most bubbles? The least?

2. **Standards Link** Use the data you collected to make a bar graph. **S3CS4b**

3. **Inquiry Skill** Analyze the data you collected. Use your graph to write a summary of your data. **S3CS8b**

Step 2

Step 3

Independent Inquiry

What do you think would happen if you shook the containers more than five times? Predict how the outcome of the investigation would change. Try it, and compare the results with the results of the original investigation. Was your prediction correct? **S3CS7a**

VOCABULARY
data table p. 32
bar graph p. 32
line graph p. 33

SCIENCE CONCEPTS
▶ how to use numbers to collect data
▶ ways to display data

MAIN IDEA AND DETAILS
Look for details about ways to use numbers.

Main Idea
detail   detail   detail

Using Numbers to Collect Data

How old are you? How tall are you? You can use numbers to measure yourself. You also use numbers to measure objects, count time, and compare things.

Without numbers, for example, we could not measure the distance to the moon. We would just have to say it is a long, long way from Earth.

This student is using a ruler to measure how long these roots are.

We can use minutes and seconds to measure how much time has gone by.

We also couldn't compare distances. We wouldn't know how much farther away the sun is than the moon. We couldn't measure temperatures, either. We would just say that the moon is cold and the sun is hot. We couldn't learn much without numbers!

One important way to compare numbers is to compare your measurements with measurements other scientists have made. This can help you decide whether your measurements make sense.

We can use degrees to measure temperature.

Focus Skill MAIN IDEA AND DETAILS

Explain three ways in which we use numbers.

We can use centimeters to compare two diameters.

Displaying Data

There are many ways to display the data you collect. A **data table** is a display that organizes data into rows and columns. A data table should have a title, and each column needs a heading.

You can also display data in graphs. Graphs need titles and labels. A **bar graph** is a graph that uses bars to display data. A bar graph works for data that is in categories.

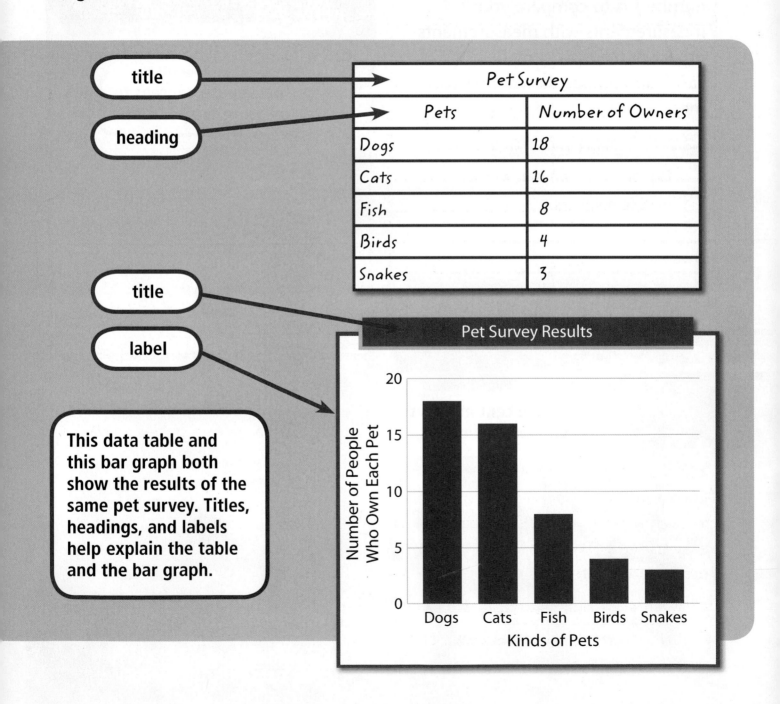

title

heading

Pet Survey

Pets	Number of Owners
Dogs	18
Cats	16
Fish	8
Birds	4
Snakes	3

title

label

This data table and this bar graph both show the results of the same pet survey. Titles, headings, and labels help explain the table and the bar graph.

Pet Survey Results

Average High Temperatures in Macon, Georgia	
Month	Temperature (°C)
January	14
February	16
March	20
April	24
May	29
June	32
July	33
August	33
September	30
October	25
November	20
December	15

This data table and this line graph both display the same data.

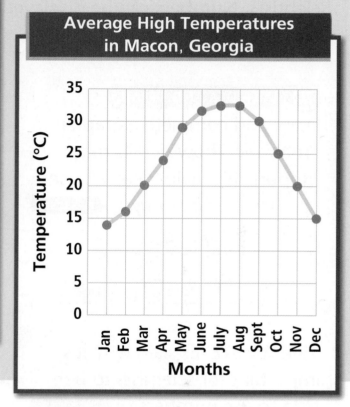

Average High Temperatures in Macon, Georgia

A **line graph** is a graph that uses a line to display data. The line graph above shows the average temperature in each month. Using the graph, it is easy to see how temperature and the month are related.

 MAIN IDEA AND DETAILS

What parts should all data tables and graphs have?

Make a Bar Graph
Go through this lesson, and count the number of times the words *measure* and *numbers* appear. Make a bar graph to show your data.

Essential Question

How do we use numbers in science?

In this lesson, you learned how numbers are used to measure and compare things. Scientists compare their measurements to measurements taken by other scientists. Numbers can be displayed in data tables and graphs.

1. (Focus Skill) MAIN IDEA AND DETAILS
Draw and complete a graphic organizer. Show details that support this main idea: *We use numbers in many ways.* **S3CS5c**

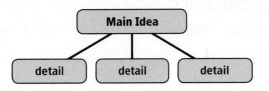

2. SUMMARIZE Explain why it's important for scientists to be able to use numbers. **S3CS5c**

3. VOCABULARY How is a line graph similar to a bar graph? How are they different? **S3CS4b**

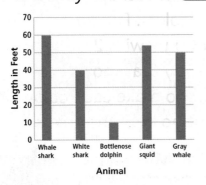

4. Critical Thinking Describe two ways in which your life would change if no one used numbers. **S3CS5c**

CRCT Practice

5. Jason read that the leaves of a red maple have three points. A tree in Jason's yard has red leaves with five points. What can Jason conclude?

A All leaves have points.

B His tree will lose its leaves.

C His tree is not a red maple.

D Red maples are red. **S3CS4b**

6. Which of these does **not** require using numbers?

A making data tables

B making observation charts

C making bar graphs

D making line graphs **S3CS4b**

The Big Idea

 Writing   ELA3W1g

Write a Narrative

Write a **short story** about a detective who measures the sizes of animal tracks to solve a mystery. Give details about where the mystery takes place and why solving it is important.

 Math   M3D1a

Make a Graph

Make a list of measuring tools that you often use. Include *ruler, measuring cup, thermometer, measuring tape,* and *clock or watch.* Next, ask 10 people which of the tools they have used this week. Then make a bar graph to display the data you have collected.

 Art

Paint by Numbers

Use a few colors of tempera paints to make many other colors. For example, mix 1 teaspoon of blue with 2 teaspoons of yellow. Make a key that shows how you used numbers to make each color. Then make a painting with the colors you made.

 For more links and activities, go to **www.hspscience.com**

Characteristics of Science

S3CS7a Similar scientific investigations seldom produce exactly the same results, which may differ due to unexpected differences in whatever is being investigated, unrecognized differences in the methods or circumstances of the investigation, or observational uncertainties.

S3CS8a Scientific investigations may take many different forms, including observing what things are like or what is happening somewhere, collecting specimens for analysis, and doing experiments.

S3CS8b Clear and active communication is an essential part of doing science. It enables scientists to inform others about their work, expose their ideas to criticism by other scientists, and stay informed about scientific discoveries around the world.

Essential Question

What Is the Scientific Method?

◤ Georgia Fast Fact

Bubble Art
These students added tempera paint to bubble solution to make art. Bubbles don't need paint added to them to be colorful, however. In the Investigate, you will observe bubble colors.

You can make a piece of art by adding paint to bubbles.

scientific method
[sy•uhn•TIF•ik METH•uhd]
An organized plan that scientists use to conduct investigations (p. 40)

investigation
[in•ves•tuh•GAY•shuhn]
A scientific study (p. 40)

hypothesis
[hy•PAHTH•uh•sis]
A possible answer to the question in an investigation (p. 41)

experiment
[ek•SPEHR•uh•muhnt]
A test done to find out if a hypothesis is correct (p. 41)

37

Bubble Colors

Directed Inquiry

Start with Questions

You probably have never seen bubbles that are different colors.

- Can you blow bubbles in different colors?
- Can you make bubbles change colors?

Investigate to find out. Then read to find out more.

Prepare to Investigate

Inquiry Skill Tip

To compare things, you name ways the things are the same and ways the things are different. In this investigation, you will do the same thing three times. Compare the results you get each time.

Materials
- safety goggles
- clear tape
- clear plastic lid
- flashlight
- cotton ball
- bubble solution
- spoon
- straw

Make an Observation Chart

Bubble Color Observations		
	Large Bubble	After Blowing
Observation 1		
Observation 2		
Observation 3		

Follow This Procedure

CAUTION: Put on safety goggles.

1. Tape the lid over the lit end of the flashlight.

2. Dip a cotton ball in bubble solution. Wipe it on the lid. Put a spoonful of solution on the lid.

3. Use a straw to blow a bubble. Turn off the lights. Record your observations of the bubble.

4. Dip the straw in solution. Then dip it in the bubble. Blow gently. Record your observations.

5. Break the bubble. Repeat Steps 3 and 4.

Draw Conclusions

1. Why was it important to wear safety goggles? **S3CS1c**

2. **Standards Link** What kinds of things might make each of your three observations turn out differently? **S3CS7a**

3. **Inquiry Skill** Compare the colors in the bubble when you first watched it to the color you saw right before the bubble popped. **S3CS8a**

Step 1

Step 4

Independent Inquiry

Predict how adding some tempera paint to the bubble solution would change your results. Plan and conduct a simple investigation to find out. How did your results compare with your prediction?

S3CS8b

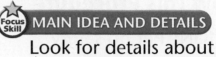

VOCABULARY
scientific method p. 40
investigation p. 40
hypothesis p. 41
experiment p. 41

SCIENCE CONCEPTS
▶ what the scientific method is
▶ how to use the scientific method

Focus Skill **MAIN IDEA AND DETAILS**
Look for details about how to use the scientific method.

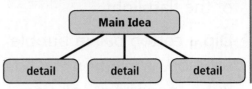

Planning an Investigation

How do scientists answer a question or solve a problem? They use an organized plan called the **scientific method** to conduct a study. A scientific study is called an **investigation**. In this lesson, you will learn how the scientific method can be used to plan an investigation to study bubbles.

 **Focus Skill** **MAIN IDEA AND DETAILS** **What plan do scientists use to help them answer questions?**

The student is observing the bubbles he has blown. ▶

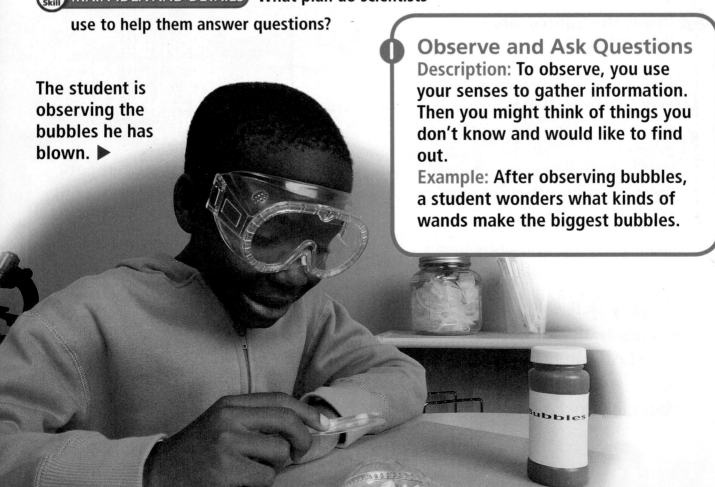

Observe and Ask Questions
Description: To observe, you use your senses to gather information. Then you might think of things you don't know and would like to find out.
Example: After observing bubbles, a student wonders what kinds of wands make the biggest bubbles.

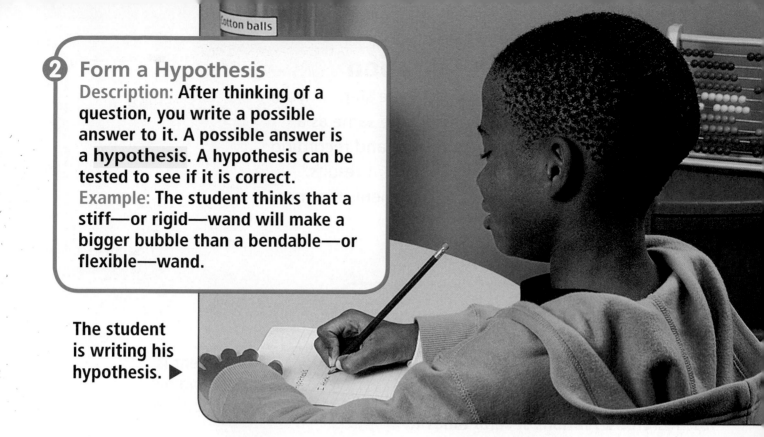

❷ Form a Hypothesis

Description: After thinking of a question, you write a possible answer to it. A possible answer is a **hypothesis**. A hypothesis can be tested to see if it is correct.

Example: The student thinks that a stiff—or rigid—wand will make a bigger bubble than a bendable—or flexible—wand.

The student is writing his hypothesis. ▶

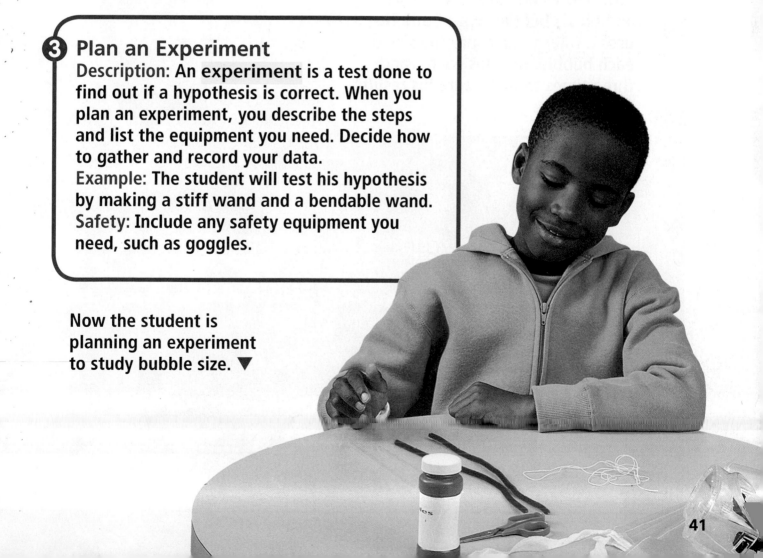

❸ Plan an Experiment

Description: An **experiment** is a test done to find out if a hypothesis is correct. When you plan an experiment, you describe the steps and list the equipment you need. Decide how to gather and record your data.

Example: The student will test his hypothesis by making a stiff wand and a bendable wand.

Safety: Include any safety equipment you need, such as goggles.

Now the student is planning an experiment to study bubble size. ▼

41

Conducting an Investigation

To conduct an investigation, follow the steps in your plan. Your results may not be exactly the same as a classmate's results. Using different tools and recording different observations can lead to different results. The more times you perform an experiment, the more accurate your observations will be.

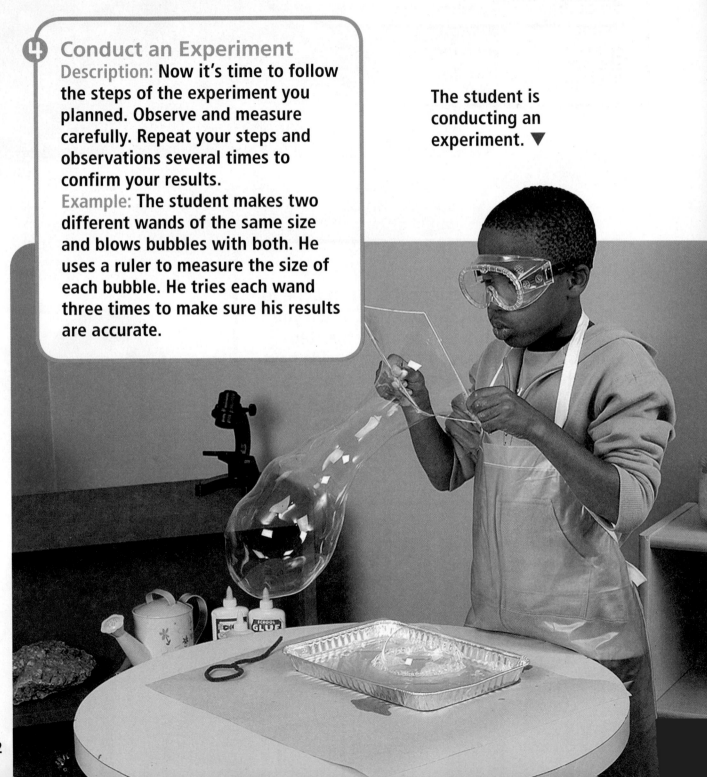

4 Conduct an Experiment

Description: **Now it's time to follow the steps of the experiment you planned. Observe and measure carefully. Repeat your steps and observations several times to confirm your results.**

Example: **The student makes two different wands of the same size and blows bubbles with both. He uses a ruler to measure the size of each bubble. He tries each wand three times to make sure his results are accurate.**

The student is conducting an experiment. ▼

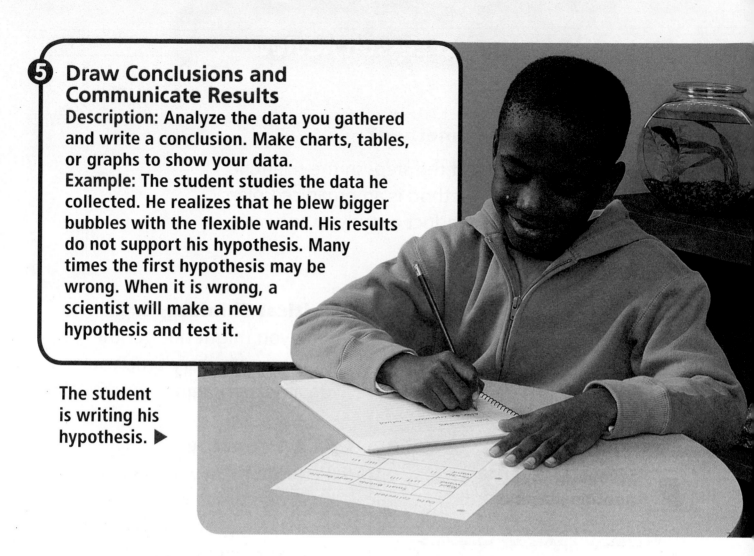

⑤ Draw Conclusions and Communicate Results

Description: Analyze the data you gathered and write a conclusion. Make charts, tables, or graphs to show your data.

Example: The student studies the data he collected. He realizes that he blew bigger bubbles with the flexible wand. His results do not support his hypothesis. Many times the first hypothesis may be wrong. When it is wrong, a scientist will make a new hypothesis and test it.

The student is writing his hypothesis. ▶

Next, you use your results to draw a conclusion. A conclusion is a decision based on what you know and on your results. Your results might show that your hypothesis was correct.

What if your results show that your hypothesis is wrong? You still learned something. Now you can write a new hypothesis. You can plan a new experiment to test it.

MAIN IDEA AND DETAILS

What information should you use to draw a conclusion?

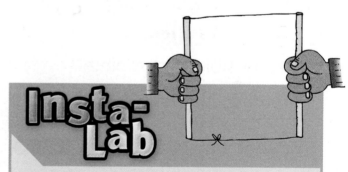

Insta-Lab

Blow a Super Bubble!

Thread a 90-cm string through two straws. Tie the ends of the string together to make a wand. Hold the straws so that the string is tight. Dip the wand in bubble solution, and blow bubbles. What do your bubbles look like?

Essential Question

What is the scientific method?

In this lesson, you learned the steps in the scientific method. The scientific method is an organized plan that you can follow to conduct a study or answer a question.

1. ⭐ **(Focus Skill) MAIN IDEA AND DETAILS**
Draw and complete a graphic organizer. Show details that support this main idea: *The scientific method has five main parts.* ◣ **S3CS8a**

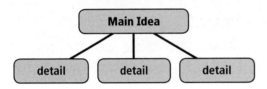

2. DRAW CONCLUSIONS
Is it possible to complete the steps in the scientific method in a different order? Why or why not? ◣ **S3CS7a**

3. VOCABULARY Explain how the terms *scientific method, hypothesis,* and *experiment* relate to each other. ◣ **S3CS8a**

4. Critical Thinking Explain why you might not get the same results every time you do an experiment. ◣ **S3CS7a**

CRCT Practice

5. Performing an experiment more than one time
  A makes your results confusing.
  B makes your results incorrect.
  C gives you practice for the real experiment.
  D helps you draw better conclusions. ◣ **S3CS8b**

6. How do scientists share information with each other?
  A They communicate results.
  B They repeat experiments.
  C They plan experiments.
  D They ask questions. ◣ **S3CS8b**

Make Connections

Writing   ELA3W1d

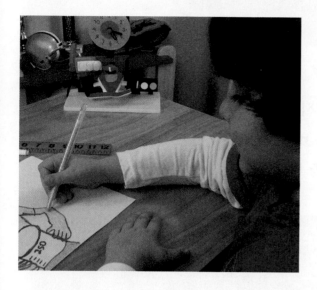

Write a Description

Write a **how-to booklet** about the scientific method. Before you begin writing, think about the best way to organize your booklet. Include illustrations and examples. Also, explain why scientists use the scientific method.

 Math   M3A1a

Wand Size	Bubble Size
1 cm	2 cm
2 cm	4 cm
3 cm	6 cm
4 cm	8 cm
5 cm	

Analyze Patterns

The table at the left shows the sizes of bubbles made by bubble wands of different sizes. Draw the table on a piece of paper. Look for a pattern among the numbers in the table. What size bubble will the 5-cm bubble wand make?

 Health

Getting Fit

Which exercise makes the heart beat faster, jumping jacks or sit-ups? Make a prediction. Then write a hypothesis to answer this question. Conduct an experiment to test your hypothesis. Compare your results to your prediction.

 For more links and activities, go to **www.hspscience.com**

CHAPTER 1

Wrap-Up

▶ Visual Summary

Tell how each picture helps explain the **Big Idea**.

The Big Idea Scientists learn about the world by asking questions and doing investigations.

Lesson 1 S3CS3, S3CS8

Aiming for Accuracy

To be accurate, scientists use tools, measure carefully, and repeat their observations. Following safety rules is important when using tools.

Lesson 2 S3CS1, S3CS5

Science Skills

Inquiry skills are used to study things in science. For example, scientists make predictions, compare things, and communicate their findings.

Lesson 3 S3CS2, S3CS4

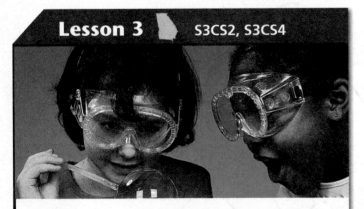

Using Numbers

Scientists use numbers to measure, to describe and compare objects, to put things in order, and to make graphs.

Lesson 4 S3CS6, S3CS7

How Scientists Work

Scientists use the scientific method to conduct investigations. They use the data from their investigations to draw conclusions.

Show What You Know

Chapter Writing Activity

Write About Famous Scientists/Informational

Choose a scientist, and learn more about him or her. For example, when and where did this person live? What was he or she interested in? What tools did he or she use? Did he or she make discoveries that are still important today? Write a report to share what you learned. Include a picture of the scientist.

ELA3W1j

Georgia Performance Task

Plan and Conduct an Investigation

Use the steps of the scientific method to plan and conduct an investigation. First, think of a question that interests you. For example, you might ask "What kinds of flowers do butterflies like?" or "What kind of soap works best?" Then follow the rest of the steps of the scientific method to answer your question.

S3CS8d

Georgia Performance Standards

Vocabulary Review

Use the terms below to complete the sentences. The page numbers tell you where to look in the chapter if you need help.

accurate (p. 8)   data table (p. 32)

predict (p. 20)   bar graph (p. 32)

evidence (p. 23)   scientific method (p. 40)

opinion (p. 23)   experiment (p. 41)

1. A tool that organizes data into rows and columns is a _____.   `S3CS4b`

2. A personal belief that is not based on evidence is an _____.   `S3CS6a`

3. Scientists use an organized plan called the _____.   `S3CS8a`

4. To _____, you tell what you think will happen in the future.   `S3CS1b`

5. A graph that uses bars to display data is a _____.   `S3CS4b`

6. Information collected in an inquiry is _____.   `S3CS1a`

7. Measuring more than once helps make sure the measurement is correct, or _____.   `S3CS7a`

8. To answer a question, you can conduct an _____.   `S3CS8a`

Check Understanding

Choose the best answer.

9. **MAIN IDEA AND DETAILS** Which tool is used to measure the length of an object? (p. 9)   `S3CS2c`
   A forceps   C measuring cup
   B balance   D ruler

10. What is the purpose of the tool in the picture? (p. 11)   `S3CS8c`
    A magnifying
    B measuring
    C predicting
    D weighing

11. Which of these statements is an opinion? (p. 23)   `S3CS6a`
    A The dog is brown and white.
    B The dog's name is Cody.
    C The dog is 45 centimeters tall.
    D The dog's color is beautiful.

12. Which inquiry skill would **most likely** be used with the tool shown below? (p. 10)   `S3CS8c`
    A classify
    B infer
    C predict
    D use numbers

13. Which of these should you **not** use when you draw a conclusion? (p. 23) `S3CS6a`
   A evidence   C observations
   B opinions   D facts

14. After you have the results of your investigation, what should you do first? (p. 43) `S3CS1b`
   A Think of a new question.
   B Conduct another experiment.
   C Communicate them to others.
   D Compare them to your prediction.

15. **MAIN IDEA AND DETAILS**
   Which of these is a prediction? (p. 21) `S3CS8c`
   A The ice melted in 4 minutes.
   B Only the temperature changed.
   C The ice in the sunlight will melt faster than the ice in the shade.
   D Each chunk of ice has the same shape.

16. Which of these statements about a conclusion is **true**? (p. 23) `S3CS6a`
   A It should be made at the beginning of an experiment.
   B It should match the prediction.
   C It should be an opinion.
   D It should be based on data from investigations.

Inquiry Skills

17. Use the numbers in the table below to make a bar graph that displays the data. `S3CS4b`

Eye Colors of Students in My Class	
Color	Number of Students
Brown	12
Green	4
Blue	6

18. Use the graph to predict how the temperature will change from December to August. `S3CS5c`

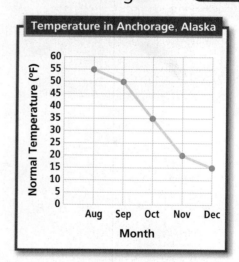

Critical Thinking

19. What tools could you use to measure the size of this book? Explain your answer. `S3CS8c`

20. Why do scientists follow the scientific method to answer their questions?

`S3CS8a`

49

UNIT A EARTH SCIENCE

Go online ▶ for student eBook
www.hspscience.com

Rocktown

This group of interesting rocks near Lafayette, Georgia is called Rocktown. Why aren't rocks like these found in other places?

Unit Inquiry

Soil Types and Plant Growth In this unit, you will learn about different kinds of soil. Will bean seeds grow better in certain types of soil? Is this true for all plants? Plan and conduct an experiment to find out.

Georgia Performance Standards in This Chapter

Content

S3E1 Students will investigate the physical attributes of rocks and soils.

S3E1a **S3E1b**
S3E1c **S3E1d**

This chapter also addresses these co-requisite standards:

Characteristics of Science

S3CS2 Students will have the computation and estimation skills necessary for analyzing data and following scientific explanations.

S3CS2a

S3CS4 Students will use ideas of system, model, change, and scale in exploring scientific and technological matters.

S3CS4b **S3CS4c**

S3CS7 Students will be familiar with the character of scientific knowledge and how it is achieved.

S3CS7a

S3CS8 Students will understand important features of the process of scientific inquiry.

S3CS8a **S3CS8c**

What's the Big Idea?

There are many kinds of minerals, rocks, and soils. Rocks and soils can be changed by wind and water.

Essential Questions

 GO online for student eBook
www.hspscience.com

Science in Georgia

Rock City Gardens

Dear Tony,

We took the most exciting field trip this week. We went to Rock City Gardens. From the overlook, I could see all the way to Tennessee and Alabama!

At Rock City Gardens, we saw some very interesting rocks. There were high cliffs, steep drop-offs, and narrow canyons! I found some black-and-white speckled rocks to add to my collection.

Your friend,
Kavita

USA

What did Kavita see and find on her field trip? How do you think that relates to the **Big Idea?**

Content

🔶 **S3E1a** Explain the difference between a rock and a mineral.

🔶 **S3E1b** Recognize the physical attributes of rocks and minerals using observation (shape, color, texture), measurement, and simple tests (hardness).

Characteristics of Science

🔶 **S3CS4b**   🔶 **S3CS8a**

🔶 **Georgia Fast Fact**

Minerals on Display At the Weinman Mineral Museum in Cartersville, you can see many kinds of minerals. The exhibits explain how each kind of mineral is different. Some minerals are hard enough to cut steel. Gypsum is so soft that you can scratch it with your fingernail.

LESSON

1

Essential Question

What Are Minerals and Rocks?

Gypsum Display at the Weinman Mineral Museum

mineral [MIN•er•uhl]
A solid object found in nature that has never been alive (p. 58)

hardness [HARD•nuhs]
The measure of how difficult it is for a mineral to be scratched (p. 60)

rock [RAHK] A naturally formed solid made of grains of one or more minerals (p. 62)

Testing Minerals

Guided Inquiry

Start with Questions

You use minerals every day. The salt in your kitchen is a mineral. So is the graphite in a pencil and the chalk you could use to draw on a sidewalk.

- Are all minerals the same color?

- How can you tell one kind of mineral from another kind?

Investigate to find out. Then read to find out more.

Prepare to Investigate

Inquiry Skill Tip

To put a set of objects in order, begin by placing two objects in order. Then fit another object in the sequence. Continue one object at a time.

Materials

- safety goggles
- hand lens
- minerals labeled A through G

Make a Data Table

Mineral Table			
Mineral To Test	Color of Mineral	Minerals It Scratches	Minerals That Scratch It
Sample A			
Sample B			
Sample C			
Sample D			
Sample E			
Sample F			
Sample G			

Follow This Procedure

CAUTION: Put on safety goggles.

1 A harder mineral can scratch a softer mineral. Try to scratch each mineral with Sample A. Record which minerals Sample A scratches.

2 A softer mineral can be scratched by a harder mineral. Try to scratch Sample A with each of the other minerals. Record the minerals that scratch Sample A.

3 Repeat Steps 1 and 2 for each mineral.

4 Using the information in your table, order the minerals from softest to hardest.

Draw Conclusions

1. Which mineral was hardest? Which was softest? How do you know?

2. Standards Link What properties other than hardness could help you identify the minerals? **S3E1b**

3. Inquiry Skill Scientists often put objects in order. How can putting minerals in order of hardness help you identify them? **S3CS4b**

Step 1

Step 4

Independent Inquiry

Test the hardness of each mineral again. This time, use a penny and your fingernail to scratch the minerals. Classify the minerals by what scratches them. **S3CS8a**

VOCABULARY
mineral p. 58
hardness p. 60
rock p. 62

SCIENCE CONCEPTS
▶ what minerals and rocks are
▶ what properties help identify minerals and rocks

MAIN IDEA AND DETAILS
Look for main ideas about minerals and rocks.

Minerals

You might know that minerals are found in some of the foods you eat. You may have even seen someone wearing minerals. A **mineral** is a solid object that is formed in nature and has never been alive.

There are many different minerals, and no two kinds are exactly alike. What differences can you see among the minerals on these pages? Minerals come in many shapes, sizes, and lusters. Gold, for example, is shiny. Other minerals are dull and dark. Some minerals can be shaped like cubes or pyramids!

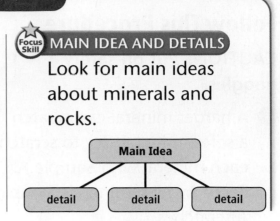
Mica

Garnet

◀ Garnet and amethyst are minerals that are used in jewelry.

Amethyst

Quartz

Gold

Graphite

People use these minerals every day.

Halite

Minerals have other properties, such as color, that can also help identify them. Some minerals can have more than one color, though. Quartz, for example, can be pink, purple, white, clear, or even black.

You use minerals every day. If you put salt on your food, you are using a mineral. Minerals are also in many of the things around you. For example, quartz is used to make glass in a window. Iron that is used in buildings comes from minerals, such as hematite.

 **MAIN IDEA AND DETAILS**

What are three ways minerals are used?

Ways to Identify Minerals

In the Investigate, you learned that some minerals are soft and other minerals are hard. Diamonds are so hard that people use them to cut steel. **Hardness** is the measure of how difficult it is for a mineral to be scratched. The hardness of a mineral can help you identify that mineral. The scale shown on this page is a tool scientists use to tell the hardness of a mineral.

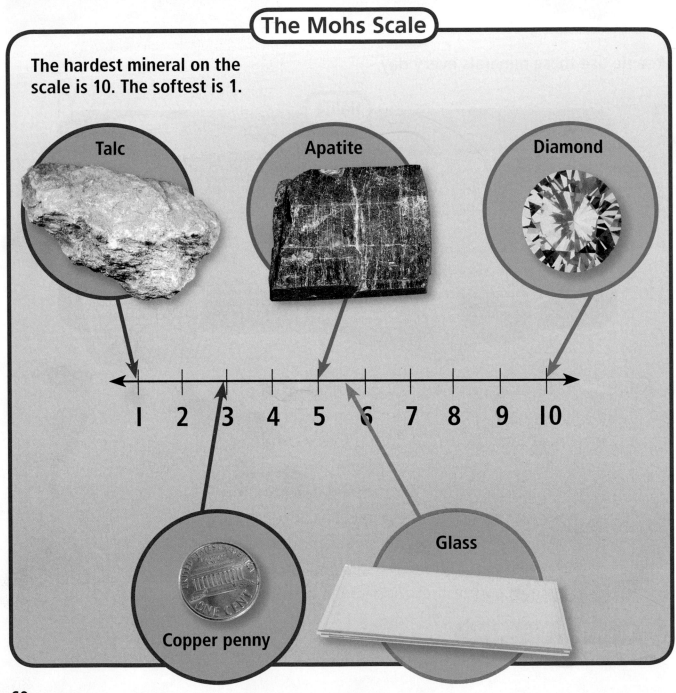

The Mohs Scale

The hardest mineral on the scale is 10. The softest is 1.

Talc

Apatite

Diamond

1 2 3 4 5 6 7 8 9 10

Copper penny

Glass

A streak test is one way to identify a mineral. ▼

Streak is another way to identify minerals. Streak is the color of the powder left behind by a mineral when it is rubbed against a rough white tile. The streak is usually the same color as the mineral. However, the streak can be a different color than the mineral's outside color.

MAIN IDEA AND DETAILS

What are two tests than can help you identify a mineral?

Insta-Lab

Streak It
Test the mineral hematite. Look at the color that is left behind. Compare the color of the streak to the color of the mineral. How could hematite's streak help identify it?

Rocks

What are hills, beaches, and the ocean floor all made of? Rocks! Rocks are found everywhere on Earth. You've probably seen many different kinds of rocks. All of them have one thing in common—minerals. A **rock** is a naturally formed solid made of grains of one or more minerals.

Look at the rock on this page. It is made of several minerals. Small grains of feldspar, quartz, and two kinds of mica make up the granite rock. Not all rocks are made of the same kinds of minerals. You can identify a rock by finding out which minerals it contains.

Savannah City Hall

▲ Builders use granite and limestone because they are common rocks that are very strong.

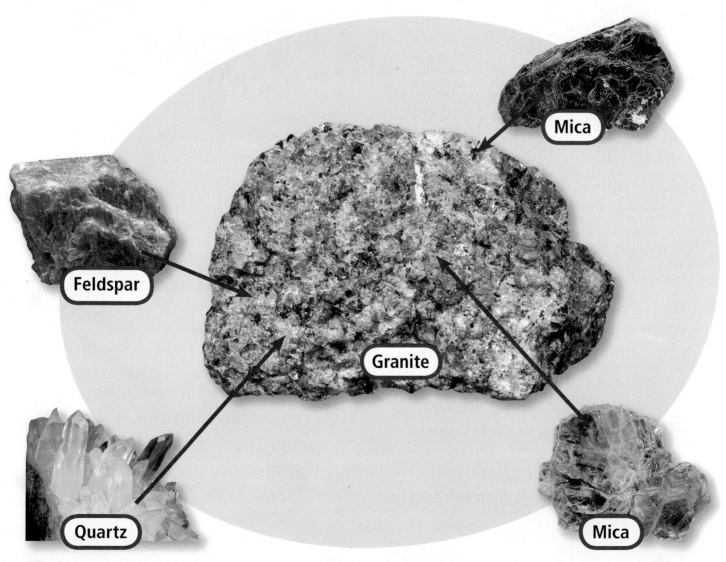

Mica

Feldspar

Granite

Quartz

Mica

Rock Textures

Siltstone has very small grains. It feels smooth when you touch it.

Sandstone has medium-sized grains. You can feel the grains when you touch the rock.

This rock is called conglomerate (kuhn•GLAHM•er•it). It has large grains that you can see and feel.

Just like minerals, rocks come in many shapes and colors. The size and shape of a rock's grains affect the rock's texture. Texture is how something feels when you touch it. Rocks can have smooth or rough textures.

 **MAIN IDEA AND DETAILS**

What is rock made of?

GPS Wrap-Up and Lesson Review

What are minerals and rocks?

Minerals and rocks are solids that are found in nature and have never been alive. Rocks are made of grains of one or more minerals. Minerals and rocks come in many shapes, sizes, and colors.

1. (Focus Skill) **MAIN IDEA AND DETAILS**
Draw and complete a graphic organizer. Show the details that support this main idea: Many properties can help identify minerals and rocks. **S3E1b**

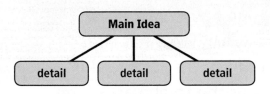

2. SUMMARIZE Write a summary that explains the difference between a rock and a mineral. **S3E1a**

3. VOCABULARY Write at least two sentences describing how to find a mineral's hardness. **S3E1b**

4. Critical Thinking Why is it better to identify a mineral by its hardness than by its color? **S3E1b**

CRCT Practice

5. Which is true of all minerals?
  A They are all hard.
  B They were never alive.
  C They are made of rocks.
  D They were once animals. **S3E1a**

6. Which statement is true of all rocks?
  A They all have the same texture.
  B They all contain quartz.
  C They all are made of minerals.
  D They all are very large in size. **S3E1a**

 Writing   ELA3W1f

Expository

Look at the rocks where you live. Choose one that looks interesting to you. Write a **description** of the rock. Make sure to tell about the color of the rock, how it feels, and what it looks like.

 Math   M3N3d

Gardening with Stones

Mr. Wells is building a wall out of stones. Each stone has a mass of 10 kilograms. Today, Mr. Wells has already moved 9 stones from his truck to the garden. What was the total mass of the stones he has moved?

 Social Studies   SS3E3d

Minerals in Money

The United States makes many different coins. Research the different materials the coins are made of. Find out what minerals those materials are obtained from. Make a poster to share your findings.

 For more links and activities, go to **www.hspscience.com**

Dahlonega Gold Museum

THE DAHLONEGA
Gold Museum Historic Site

Have you heard stories about the California Gold Rush? Starting in 1848, thousands of people moved to California in search of gold. However, California was not the only place that has had a gold rush. Twenty years earlier, gold was found in northern Georgia.

Thousands of miners rushed to northern Georgia. They set up small towns such as Dahlonega. *Dahlonega* is the Cherokee word for "gold."

At the Dahlonega Gold Museum Historic Site, you can see a gold nugget that weighs 141.7 grams (5 ounces).

DAHLONEGA COURTHOUSE GOLD MUSEUM

GEORGIA DEPT. OF NATURAL RESOURCES
PARKS & HISTORIC SITES DIVISION

OPEN TUES.-SAT. 9:00 A.M. - 5:00 P.M.
OPEN SUNDAY 2:00 P.M. - 5:30 P.M.
CLOSED MONDAYS

Panning for Gold

The first miners looked for gold that had been washed down mountainsides by streams. They used pans to scoop up gravel and water from the streams. Gold is heavy and shiny. Miners would swirl the water and gravel in their pans. Any gold in the pan sank to the bottom and glistened in the sun.

The miners found most of the gold that had been washed down the mountains. They also dug tunnels into the mountains. In these tunnels, they found chunks of quartz and gold mixed together.

The Rush Ends

In 1838, the Dahlonega Mint was started. It turned the miners' bits and chunks of gold into $6 million in gold coins. However, by 1861 the gold in Georgia had run out, so the mint closed. By then, most of the miners had already left for the new gold rush—in California.

The dome of Georgia's Capitol in Atlanta is made of gold mined in Dahlonega.

Think And Write

1. What is it about gold that enabled miners to identify it in a stream? `S3E1b`

2. Is gold mixed with quartz thought of as a rock or a mineral? Explain your answer. `S3E1b`

Visitors to Dahlonega can still pan for gold today.

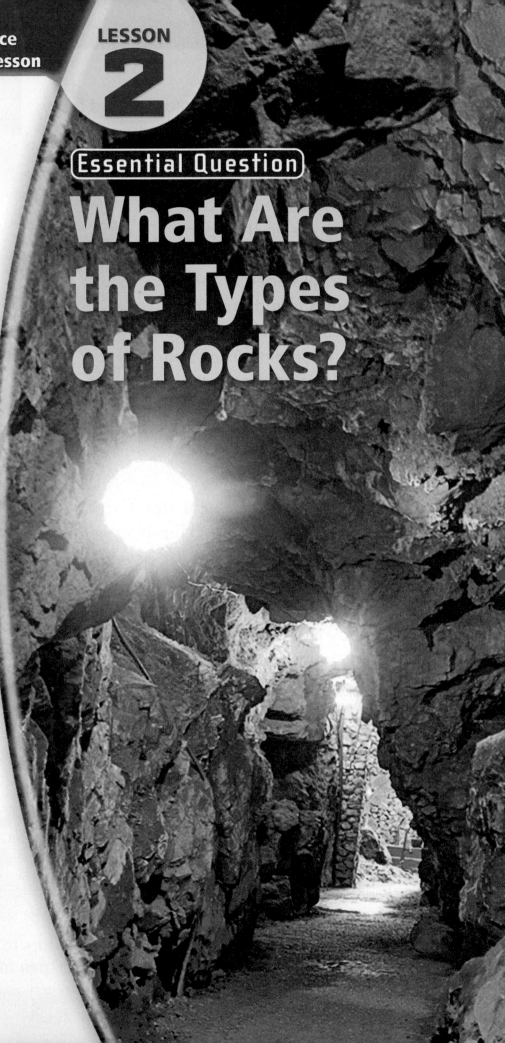

Content

S3E1b Recognize the physical attributes of rocks and minerals using observation (shape, color, texture), measurement, and simple tests (hardness).

Characteristics of Science

S3CS4c

Georgia Fast Fact

Journey into Earth Cave Spring is a small town near Rome in northwest Georgia. The town is known for its large cave, which cuts almost 92 meters (300 ft) into the limestone. More than 500 caves have been discovered in Georgia!

LESSON **2**

Essential Question

What Are the Types of Rocks?

Cave Spring, Georgia

igneous rock
[IG•nee•uhs RAHK] Rock that was once melted and then cooled and hardened (p. 72)

sedimentary rock
[sed•uh•MEN•ter•ee RAHK] Rock made when materials settle into layers and get squeezed until they harden into rock (p. 73)

metamorphic rock
[met•uh•MAWR•fik RAHK] Rock that has been changed by heat or pressure (p. 73)

Make a Model Rock

Guided Inquiry

Start with Questions

In Lesson 1, you learned that rocks are made of grains of minerals. In this lesson, you will find out that not all rocks were formed the same way.

- How do rocks form?

- How can you make a model of a rock?

Investigate to find out. Then read to find out more.

Prepare to Investigate

Inquiry Skill Tip

You can use a model to understand something that takes a long time to happen. After you observe the model, make a list of ways the model is different than the actual object.

Materials
- newspaper
- wax paper
- paper or plastic cup
- plastic spoon
- sand
- gravel
- white glue
- water
- hand lens

Make an Observation Chart

My Rock Observations	
Color	
Texture	
Hardness	
Drawing of Rock	

Follow This Procedure

1. Spread newspaper over your work area. Place a smaller sheet of wax paper on the newspaper.

2. Place 1 spoonful of sand and 1 spoonful of gravel in the cup.

3. Add 1 spoonful of glue to the cup. Stir the mixture until it forms a lump. You may need to add a little water.

4. Pour the mixture onto the wax paper, and let it dry. You have made a model of a rock.

Draw Conclusions

1. Use the hand lens to observe the dried mixture you made. What does the mixture look like?

2. **Standards Link** How do the rocks you made compare to the rocks in the photograph on page 70? **S3E1b**

3. **Inquiry Skill** Scientists often use models to understand processes they can't easily observe. One way rocks can form is when sand and gravel are pressed together. How is the model you made like a rock? **S3CS4c**

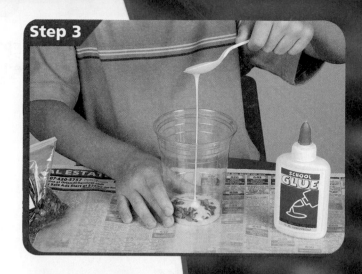
Step 3

Step 4

Independent Inquiry

Try to make models of rocks using different materials. Explore how changing the materials changes the rock. **S3CS4c**

VOCABULARY
igneous rock p. 72
sedimentary rock p. 73
metamorphic rock
p. 73

SCIENCE CONCEPTS
▶ what the three types
of rocks are
▶ how rocks form

(Focus Skill) **COMPARE AND CONTRAST**
Look for the words
alike and *different* when
reading about types of
rocks.

alike ——— different

Types of Rocks

Suppose you want to start a rock collection.
How would you group the rocks? By color, by
grain size, by whether they have layers? Rocks
can look very different, but there are just three
main types of rocks. The three types of rocks
are grouped by how they form.

Igneous (IG•nee•uhs) **rock** is rock that was
once melted and then cooled and hardened.
Some igneous rocks cool quickly and look like
glass. Other igneous rocks cool more slowly
and have large grains.

Igneous Rock

Obsidian (uhb•SID•ee•uhn)

Granite

72

Sedimentary Rock

Sandstone

Limestone

Gneiss (NYS)

Metamorphic Rock

Marble

Rock that forms from material that has settled into layers is called **sedimentary** (sed•uh•MEN•ter•ee) **rock**. The layers are squeezed together until they form rock.

The third type of rock is called metamorphic rock. **Metamorphic** (met•uh•MAWR•fik) **rock** is rock that has been changed by temperature and pressure.

COMPARE AND CONTRAST

How is metamorphic rock different from igneous rock?

Fizzy Rock

Calcite (KAL•syt) bubbles when it comes in contact with vinegar. Use a dropper to place several drops of vinegar on limestone and on sandstone. Which rock has calcite?

How Rocks Form

The three types of rock form differently. Melted rock can reach Earth's surface through a volcano. Then it cools and becomes igneous rock.

Sedimentary rock, by contrast, begins with the breaking of rocks. Wind and water break rock into bits. Then the wind and water carry the bits of rock and soil away. The bits settle into layers. After a long time, the layers harden into rock.

Metamorphic rock forms deep in Earth's crust in yet another way. The pressure and temperature there change rock into metamorphic rock.

Focus Skill COMPARE AND CONTRAST **Contrast the ways the three types of rock form.**

Volcanoes bring melted rock to the surface, where it cools. The cooled rock is igneous rock. ▶

▲ Wind and water carry small bits of rock. Layers of these bits of rock form and, under pressure, become sedimentary rock.

◀ Rocks inside Earth soften from Earth's high temperature. Pressure inside Earth then squeezes the rock. The rock changes into metamorphic rock.

The Rock Cycle

Over time, one kind of rock can become any other kind. The process of rocks changing from one kind of rock to another kind of rock is called the *rock cycle*. The diagram below shows this cycle.

Wind and water break down all kinds of rocks to form sedimentary rocks. Any kind of rock that melts and cools can become an igneous rock. Any rock can end up deep underground. That rock can be pressed and heated, which turns it into metamorphic rock.

COMPARE AND CONTRAST

How are all rocks alike and different?

▲ **Sand on a beach is made of pieces of larger rocks that were broken down by wind and water.**

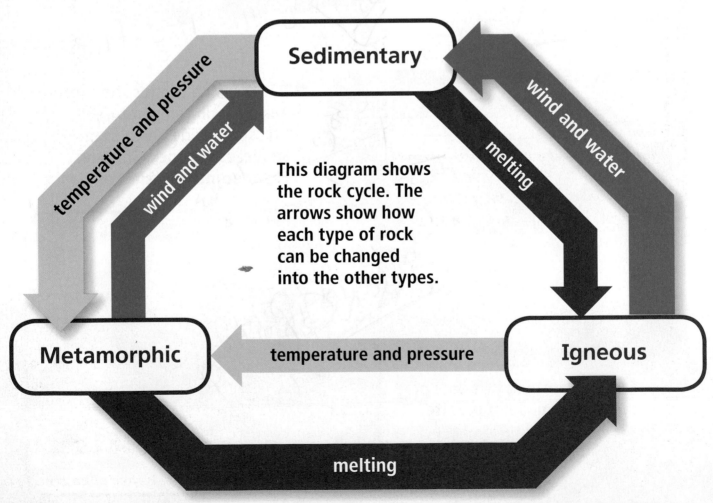

This diagram shows the rock cycle. The arrows show how each type of rock can be changed into the other types.

Sedimentary

Metamorphic

Igneous

temperature and pressure

wind and water

wind and water

melting

temperature and pressure

melting

The Rock Cycle

The rock cycle is an endless process in which rocks are changed from one type to another. The rock cycle never stops—rocks are constantly changing.

Changes to rocks usually do not happen quickly. Rocks change into other kinds of rocks over thousands or even millions of years. This diagram shows how granite can change to sandstone, which can then turn to quartzite.

Granite

▲ Granite is an igneous rock. It is formed when melted rock cools.

Sandstone

Quartzite

▲ Quartzite is a metamorphic rock. It forms when sandstone is placed under high temperature and pressure.

▲ Over time, granite breaks down into smaller pieces. Wind and water move the small pieces. Eventually, the pieces are cemented together and become sandstone.

Stone Mountain, just east of Atlanta, is made of granite.

For more links and animations, go to **www.hspscience.com**

Essential Question

What are the types of rocks?

The three types of rocks are igneous, metamorphic, and sedimentary. The three types of rocks form in different ways, and one type can change to the other types as part of the rock cycle.

1. **COMPARE AND CONTRAST** (Focus Skill)
   Draw and complete a graphic organizer. Show how the types of rocks are alike and different.
   S3E1b

   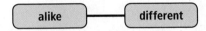

2. **DRAW CONCLUSIONS** Why are few sedimentary rocks found deep inside Earth? **S3E1b**

3. **VOCABULARY** Write one sentence that uses the terms *igneous rock* and *metamorphic rock*. **S3E1b**

4. **Critical Thinking** Suppose you're walking near a river. You see a tan rock that has light and dark layers. You pick up the rock and can scrape off small grains of sand. What type of rock do you think it is? Explain. **S3E1b**

CRCT Practice

5. Which of the following is a volcano most likely made of?
   A rocks without minerals
   B sedimentary rocks
   C metamorphic rocks
   D igneous rocks **S3E1b**

6. Which is **not** needed to form metamorphic rocks?
   A pressure
   B wind and water
   C an existing rock
   D high temperatures **S3E1b**

The **Big** Idea

 Writing ELA3W1d

Narrative

Write a **story** about the life of a rock. Include all the parts of the rock cycle in your story. Organize your story in the order that things happened to the rock. Make sure to describe changes that happened to the rock, and explain why the changes happened.

 Math M3N2a

Volcano Math

The melted rock leaving one volcano had a temperature of 806°C. After cooling for two hours, its temperature was 739°C. How much did the rock cool? After coming up with an answer, explain how you can check it to make sure you are correct.

I have stripes of thin brown bands made of tiny grains of sand.

 Language Arts ELA3W1n

Rock Riddles

Choose one rock from a collection. Write a rough draft of a riddle that describes the rock. After your teacher approves your draft, write a final copy on colorful paper. See if other people can pick out the rock based on your riddle.

 For more links and activities, go to **www.hspscience.com**

Content

S3E1c Use observation to compare the similarities and differences of texture, particle size, and color in top soils (such as clay, loam or potting soil, and sand).

Characteristics of Science

S3CS1a   **S3CS8c**

Essential Question

What Are Some Types of Soil?

Georgia Fast Fact

Slow-Forming Soil
It takes between 3,000 and 12,000 years to form soil that is good for farming. In Georgia, farmers grow crops on more than 5 million acres of land. Peanuts, cotton, peaches, and Vidalia onions all grow well in Georgia soils.

Farming in Georgia

humus [HYOO•muhs] The part of soil made up of broken-down pieces of dead plants and animals (p. 84)

sand [SAND] Soil with grains of rock that you can see with your eyes alone (p. 87)

silt [SILT] Soil with grains of rock that are too small to be seen with your eyes alone (p. 87)

clay [KLAY] Soil with very, very tiny grains of rock (p. 87)

loam [LOHM] Soil that is a mixture of humus, sand, silt, and clay (p. 89)

Observing Soil

Start with Questions

You might know that parts of Georgia are famous for their red soils. If all soils were the same, then the red soils in Georgia would not be special.

- In what ways are soils from two locations different?

- What does soil look like when viewed up close?

Investigate to find out. Then read to find out more.

Prepare to Investigate

Inquiry Skill Tip
When you compare two things, you tell how they are alike and how they are different. It is easier to compare things when you make careful observations. Write or draw as many details as you can.

Materials

- 2 soil samples
- microscope or hand lens
- small paper plates
- toothpick
- colored pencils

Make an Observation Chart

Soil Characteristics		
Characteristic	Sample 1	Sample 2
color		
shape		
size		
feel		

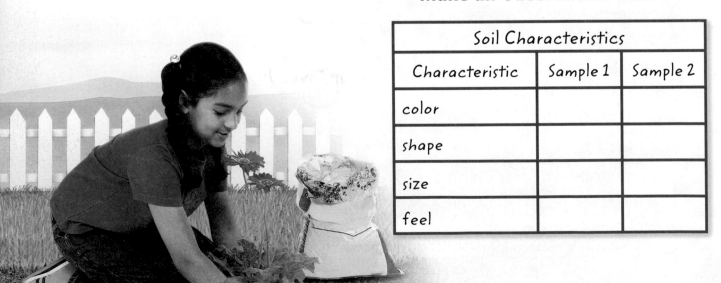

Follow This Procedure

1. Get a soil sample from your teacher. Place a few grains of the soil on a paper plate.

2. Using the microscope or hand lens, observe the soil. Use the toothpick to move the soil grains around. Notice the colors, shapes, and sizes of the grains. Record what you observe by drawing the soil grains.

3. Pick up some soil from the plate. Rub it between your fingers. How does it feel? Record what you observe.

4. Repeat Steps 1 through 3 with the other soil sample.

Step 2

Step 3

Draw Conclusions

1. What senses did you use to observe the soil?

2. **Standards Link** Scientists observe things so they can compare them. How were the soil samples alike, and how were they different? S3E1c

3. **Inquiry Skill** How did the observations you made using the microscope compare with the observations you made without the microscope? S3CS8c

Independent Inquiry

Which soil holds more water— potting soil or sandy soil? Write a hypothesis. Then plan and conduct an investigation to find out.

S3CS1a

VOCABULARY
humus p. 84
sand p. 87
silt p. 87
clay p. 87
loam p. 89

SCIENCE CONCEPTS
▶ how soil is layered
▶ how soils are different

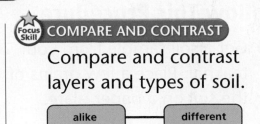

Focus Skill COMPARE AND CONTRAST

Compare and contrast layers and types of soil.

alike — different

Layers of Soil

You might not think of soil as a resource, but it is a very important one. Without soil, plants couldn't grow. Many animals wouldn't have places to live.

Soil is a mixture of many different things. Soil is made up of water, air, humus, and tiny pieces of rock. **Humus** is the part of soil that is made up of parts of dead plants and animals. For example, when a tree loses a leaf, the leaf falls to the ground. As the leaf breaks down into smaller parts, it becomes humus.

This plant's roots grow in soil. ▼

The soil close to the surface has a lot of humus. Soil that is deeper down has less humus and more small pieces of rock. If you cut into the soil, you would see different layers at different depths.

Focus Skill COMPARE AND CONTRAST How is soil close to Earth's surface different from the soil deeper below the surface?

Science Up Close

Soil Layers

Topsoil

Soil forms in layers. The top layer is called *topsoil*. Topsoil has a lot of humus. Many small animals, such as ants and earthworms, live in topsoil.

Subsoil

The layer underneath topsoil is called *subsoil*. Subsoil does not have a lot of humus, but it does have small rocks in it.

Bedrock

If you dig deep enough into soil, you will reach solid rock. This solid rock is called *bedrock*. Most small rocks in soil come from the bedrock underneath it.

For more links and animations, go to **www.hspscience.com**

Different Types of Soils

Not all soils are the same. In the United States alone, there are more than 70,000 different kinds of soils. Soils can have different colors. Some soils can hold more water than other soils.

Another difference among soils is the size of the rocks found in them. The rock sizes make the soils feel different.

This soil is made up mostly of sand. The sand grains are big enough to see without a hand lens. ▼

Georgia's famous red clay soils are made up of very tiny grains of rock. You need a microscope to see the grains. ▼

Soils that have small pieces of rock that you can see with your eyes alone are mostly **sand**. Soils with tiny grains of rock that are too small to see without a microscope are mostly **silt**. Soils with very, very tiny grains of rock are known as **clay** soils. When you rub clay between your fingers, you cannot feel the grains of rock.

The main difference between sand, silt, and clay soils is their grain size. These three types of soils can also be made up of different minerals.

Focus Skill COMPARE AND CONTRAST

Compare sand, silt, and clay soils.

Insta-Lab

Make a Soil Model

Put pieces of rock in the bottom of a plastic bottle. Then add a mixture of rock and humus. Finally, put humus and tiny pieces of rock on top. Label the layers. Is the soil in your top layer sand, silt, or clay?

The wet soils in Georgia marshes usually have a black color.

A person who studies soils is called a soil scientist. ▼

Water and Soils

Water is another important part of soil. Even soils that feel dry most likely have water. Plant roots take water from the soil.

Some soils can hold more water than other soils. Most soils that are bright in color drain water quickly. Air can then combine with iron in the soil, which makes a reddish color.

As humus breaks down, it is dark in color. Soils that hold more water are usually darker. This happens because humus does not break down as quickly in wet soils.

 COMPARE AND CONTRAST

How are wet soils and dry soils different?

The Importance of Soils

What would the world be like without soils? People couldn't make bricks, pottery, or other items that are made from clay soil. Many animals would have nowhere to live, and plants would not be able to grow.

Soils are very important to people for growing fruits and vegetables. The best kind of soil to use to grow fruits and vegetables is loam. **Loam** is a mixture of humus, clay, silt, and sand. Most soils found on farms are loam.

COMPARE AND CONTRAST

Contrast the ways people use different kinds of soils.

This woman is growing flowers and vegetables in loam. Sandy soil would dry out too quickly and the plants would die. ▼

Essential Question

What are some types of soil?

Soils are made of humus, water, and tiny grains of rock. One way to classify a soil is by the size of its rock grains. Soils can also be classified by their color.

1. **Focus Skill COMPARE AND CONTRAST**
Draw and complete a graphic organizer. Tell how all soils are alike, and tell ways that some soils are different. **S3E1c**

> alike ——— different

2. **SUMMARIZE** Write three sentences that tell what this lesson is mainly about. **S3E1c**

3. **VOCABULARY** Draw a graphic organizer that shows how humus, sand, silt, and clay are related to loam. **S3E1c**

4. **Critical Thinking** Robin wants to start a vegetable garden in her back yard. The soil in her back yard is mostly clay. What should Robin do before she plants her vegetable seeds? **S3E1c**

CRCT Practice

5. Where is most humus found in soil?
   A near the surface
   B in the bedrock
   C just above the bedrock
   D near plant roots **S3E1c**

6. Which of these soils has the smallest grains of rock?
   A red clay
   B silt from a river
   C sand at the beach
   D sand in a playground **S3E1c**

 Writing ELA3W1I

Persuasive

Suppose you are selling a type of soil. Write an **advertisement** that will persuade adults to buy your soil. Your advertisement should explain the best uses for the soil.

 Math M3M4c

Garden Grids

Doug designed an experiment to see how different plants grow in the soil in his garden. He divided his garden into sections that are each 1 square foot. Use the photograph on the left to find the total area of his experiment. Explain how you got your answer.

 Art

Colorful Soils as Art

You may have used colorful sand to make pieces of artwork in the past. Collect several soil samples that are different colors. Fill a clear plastic tube with layers of different colors. Place your artwork on display.

 For more links and activities, go to **www.hspscience.com**

Content

 S3E1d Determine how water and wind can change rocks and soil over time using observation and research.

Characteristics of Science

S3CS2a   **S3CS7a**

LESSON 4

Essential Question

How Do Rocks and Soil Change?

Georgia Fast Fact

Beach Erosion
Waves and wind move sand at the beach. Several inches of sand have washed away since this tree started growing on Wassaw Island. Millions of dollars have been spent to replace sand that has been washed away from beaches in Georgia.

weathering [WETH•er•ing]
The breaking down of rocks into smaller pieces (p. 96)

erosion [ih•ROH•zhuhn]
The movement of weathered rock and soil (p. 98)

Wassaw Island, Georgia

Water at Work

Guided Inquiry

Start with Questions

Rocks can be found in many shapes and sizes. Some rocks have sharp edges while others are rounded.

- Does the size or shape of a rock change over time?

- Does water affect the size or shape of rocks?

Investigate to find out. Then read to find out more.

Prepare to Investigate

Inquiry Skill Tip

When you interpret data, you explain the results of your investigation. To do this, think about which step of the procedure explains why the data came out the way it did.

Materials
- balance
- water
- small pieces of brick
- extra masses for the balance
- clear jar with lid

Make a Data Table

How Water Affects Brick	
Date	Mass of Brick
Day 1	
1 Week Later	

Follow This Procedure

1. **Measure** the mass of the brick pieces. Record your results.

2. Fill the jar three-fourths full of water.

3. Put the brick pieces into the jar of water. Put the lid on the jar.

4. Take turns with a partner to shake the jar for 10 minutes. Do this three times a day for one week. Then take the brick pieces out of the jar, and let them dry. **Measure** and **record** the mass of the brick pieces.

Draw Conclusions

1. What happened inside the container as you shook it?

2. **Standards Link** Do the brick pieces look different after a week of shaking them? If so, how are they different?

   S3E1d

3. **Inquiry Skill** Scientists **interpret** data to understand how things work. Use your data to calculate how much the mass of the brick pieces changed. What caused the change in mass? **S3CS2a**

Step 3

Step 4

Independent Inquiry

Do large pieces of rock weather faster than small ones? **Plan and conduct an investigation** to test your prediction. **S3CS7a**

VOCABULARY
weathering p. 96
erosion p. 98

SCIENCE CONCEPTS
▶ what weathering does
▶ what erosion does

Focus Skill SEQUENCE
Look for the steps that lead to erosion.

How Rocks Are Broken Down

Earth's surface is rock. Rock wears down and breaks apart. The way rocks are broken down into smaller pieces is called **weathering** (WETH•er•ing).

Water causes weathering. Wind also breaks rock down. It picks up sand and then smashes it against rocks. This chips the rocks slowly. Ice breaks down rock in a different way. You can see how it does this on the next page. Plant roots can grow in cracks in rock and widen them, too.

Weathering happens slowly. It can take thousands of years for rocks to be broken down to become sand and soil.

Focus Skill SEQUENCE How does wind break down rocks?

Water flows through cracks in rock. It slowly wears down the rock edges into rounded shapes.

Weathering has cracked this rock. The layers on the surface have broken off.

How Ice Cracks Rock

Water in the form of ice can break down rock and concrete.

1 Water goes into a crack.

2 The water freezes and becomes ice. Frozen water takes up more space than liquid water. It pushes against the sides of the crack.

3 The crack becomes wider and breaks the concrete or rock.

 For more links and animations, go to **www.hspscience.com**

How Rock Pieces Move

After rocks are broken down, erosion moves the pieces. **Erosion** (ih•ROH•zhuhn) is the movement of weathered rock. Creep is a very slow type of erosion that moves rocks and soil. It can bend fences and walls over time.

Moving water is the cause of much erosion. Rainfall loosens sand and rock. It carries the sand and weathered rocks into rivers. The rivers carry the materials downstream.

When the water's flow slows down, the materials drop. Rivers drop sand along their banks. This is one way the shape of a river can change.

Plants help hold soil in place. They keep water from washing the sand away from farmlands.

Rivers drop sand and rock at their mouths. The sand and rock build up to form a landform called a delta. ▼

Rivers erode soil along their banks. This muddy river is carrying a lot of soil. ▼

Wind erosion blows sand into huge mounds called dunes. Dunes form in deserts and along sandy coasts.

The layers of this rock are made of different materials. The bottom layers have weathered faster than the top layers, making the rock larger on top.

Wind causes erosion, too. The stronger the wind, the more soil it can carry. When the wind slows down, the soil drops and makes landforms.

In deserts, wind forms big piles of sand called dunes. Sand dunes can be taller than a 20-story building.

Erosion is often slow. It can take hundreds or even thousands of years to change the land.

 **SEQUENCE** What must happen before rock can be eroded?

Growing Ice

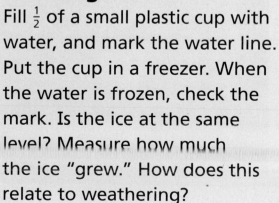

Fill $\frac{1}{2}$ of a small plastic cup with water, and mark the water line. Put the cup in a freezer. When the water is frozen, check the mark. Is the ice at the same level? Measure how much the ice "grew." How does this relate to weathering?

Essential Question

How do rocks and soil change?

Rocks are broken down into smaller pieces in the process of weathering. Wind and water move soil and small rocks in the process of erosion.

1. (Focus Skill) **SEQUENCE** Draw and complete a graphic organizer. Show what happens as a rock is broken down. **S3E1d**

2. **DRAW CONCLUSIONS** Would a tree root pushing up and cracking a sidewalk be an example of weathering or of erosion? Explain. **S3E1d**

3. **VOCABULARY** Draw a picture of erosion. Then write a caption that explains what erosion is. **S3E1d**

4. **Critical Thinking** Jamie visits her grandmother every summer. She sees that the stream in her grandmother's back yard has gotten wider. Explain how this may have happened. **S3E1d**

CRCT Practice

5. Which of the following would cause the **most** erosion?
   A a light summer breeze
   B a winter snowfall
   C a drizzle of rain
   D a flooding river   **S3E1d**

6. Which of these is **not** an example of erosion?
   A Ice cracks a rock.
   B A river carries soil away.
   C Wind blows sand from a sand dune.
   D The ocean knocks over a sand castle.   **S3E1d**

The **Big** Idea

 Writing ELA3W1j

Expository

Interview someone who studies weathering and erosion or someone who works with rocks and minerals. Find out what he or she does. Write a **report** about what you learn, and share your report with the class.

 Math M3N3g

Solve Problems

Every day, a river erodes 18 cm of soil and rock from its bank. How many centimeters will have been eroded after 12 days? Show your work.

 Social Studies SS3H1a

Crumbling Buildings

Find out about an ancient building in Greece. Write a few sentences about what the building was used for. Research what materials the building was made from. Explain why some of the materials are weathered.

 For more links and activities, go to **www.hspscience.com**

Dorothy Nickerson

▶ **DOROTHY NICKERSON**
▶ Soil scientist
▶ Helped develop a chart of soil colors

What's the color of dirt? Brown right? Not always!

In the early 1900s a scientist named Dorothy Nickerson helped scientists who test soil. Nickerson helped to make standards that scientists can use when they study dirt and rocks.

As part of her work, Nickerson worked with Albert H. Munsell. Munsell had invented a color chart system. Nickerson worked with Munsell so that the chart could be used for describing soil color.

Why is studying dirt important? Experts use the Munsell color chart and color names when surveying soil. The surveys show scientists what kind of soil exists in our country. Then scientists can decide the best way to use the soil.

✎ Think and Write

❶ What properties of soil did Dorothy Nickerson study? **S3E1c**

❷ Dorothy Nickerson studied soils almost 100 years ago. Do you think her work is still important today? Explain. **S3CS7b**

Soil colors depend on what materials the soil is made of.

Miguel Cabrera

Dr. Miguel Cabrera knows a lot about soils. He knows that plants need nutrients from the soil to grow and stay healthy. He also knows that droppings from animals help plants grow.

Cabrera studies the effects of adding animal droppings to soil on farms and pastures. He tests the soil before and after adding the droppings. He measures how much better the plants grow.

▶ **DR. MIGUEL CABRERA**

▶ Professor of Crop and Soil Sciences, University of Georgia
▶ Studies fertilizers

However, if the droppings aren't used in the right ways, they run off the land during rainstorms and pollute streams, rivers, and lakes. Cabrera wants to find ways to help plants grow and to protect the environment at the same time.

 ## Think and Write

❶ Why do some farm soils need fertilizers?　　S3E1c

❷ Why is Dr. Cabrera concerned about erosion in fields with fertilizer?　　S3E1d

Chicken and turkey droppings add nutrients to the soil on this farm.

Wrap-Up

Visual Summary

Tell how each picture helps explain the **Big Idea**.

The Big Idea There are many kinds of minerals, rocks, and soils. Rocks and soils can be changed by wind and water.

Lesson 1 — S3E1a, S3E1b

Identifying Rocks and Minerals
You can tell minerals apart by their color, hardness, streak, and luster. Rocks are made of grains of one or more minerals.

Lesson 2 — S3E1b

Three Kinds of Rocks
The kinds of rocks—sedimentary, igneous, and metamorphic—form in different ways. One kind can be changed into another kind.

Lesson 3 — S3E1c

Soil Parts
Soil is made of humus, tiny grains of rocks and minerals, and water. Soils differ in their colors and textures.

Lesson 4 — S3E1d

Weathering and Erosion
Rocks are broken down in the process called weathering. Erosion is the movement of rocks and soil by wind and water.

Show What You Know

Chapter Writing Activity

Writing About Rocks and Soil/Informational

Draw a diagram that shows a change happening to a rock or to soil. Write a paragraph to explain your diagram. Think about ways to organize your writing. You could write about the steps of the change in the order that they happen, or you could explain the causes and effects of the change. You could also compare the rock or soil before and after the change. **ELA3W1d**

Georgia Performance Task

Rocks and Soil All Around You

Collect rock and soil samples from locations near your home. Record the properties, such as color and texture, of each sample. Use the rocks you collected to make a rock collection in egg cartons. Place the soil samples in clear containers. Make a label for each sample. Compare your collection with the collections of your classmates and of other students in Georgia. **S3E1b** **S3E1c**

Vocabulary Review

Use the terms below to complete the sentences. The page numbers tell you where to look in the chapter if you need help.

mineral p. 58   humus p. 84

hardness p. 60   clay p. 87

rock p. 62   weathering p. 96

igneous rock p. 72   erosion p. 98

1. Rock formed when melted rock cools is _____.   **S3E1b**

2. A rock is made of at least one kind of _____.   **S3E1a**

3. The movement of rock and soil by wind or water is _____.   **S3E1d**

4. Pieces of dead plants and animals in soil is called _____.   **S3E1c**

5. When you scratch a mineral, you are testing its _____.   **S3E1b**

6. Soil with the smallest grains of rock is _____.   **S3E1c**

7. The breaking down of rocks into smaller pieces is _____.   **S3E1d**

8. A solid made of one or more minerals is a _____.   **S3E1a**

Check Understanding

Choose the best answer.

9. **CAUSE AND EFFECT**
   Which of these is an effect of weathering? (p. 96)   **S3E1d**
   A Mountains are built.
   B Rocks are split.
   C Water freezes.
   D Volcanoes erupt.

10. Which does **not** describe minerals? (p. 58)   **S3E1a**
    A are solid
    B were formed in nature
    C are all the same color
    D have never been alive

11. Why does the rock in the drawing below have layers of different colors? (p. 73)   **S3E1b**
    A Layers of different sediments were pressed together.
    B A volcano erupted many times.
    C Wind and water changed the color of the rock.
    D The rock is from deep inside Earth.

12. Which does **not** cause erosion or weathering? (p. 98) `S3E1d`

  A ice   **C** water
  B volcano   **D** wind

13. MAIN IDEA AND DETAILS
Which describes how some metamorphic rocks form? (p. 75) `S3E1b`

  A Water freezes in cracks in rocks.
  B Melted rock cools and hardens.
  C Pressure changes a rock.
  D Rock pieces pile up in layers.

14. Which is **not** a way to identify a mineral? (pp. 60–61) `S3E1b`

  A by its hardness
  B by its outside color
  C by soaking it in water
  D by doing a streak test

15. Which of the following is needed for a sedimentary rock to form? (p. 76) `S3E1a`

  A high temperature and pressure
  B wind and water
  C melted rock
  D a volcano

16. What is the hardest mineral on the Mohs scale? (p. 60) `S3E1b`

  A talc
  B copper
  C apatite
  D diamond

Inquiry Skills

17. Your teacher asks you to compare two different soils. What are three possible differences that you should look for? `S3E1c`

18. Suppose you need to identify three minerals. Explain how you could order the minerals by their hardness. `S3CS4b`

Critical Thinking

19. Why is most metamorphic rock harder than the sedimentary rock from which it formed? `S3E1b`

20. This graph shows what a sample of loam is made of. How could you divide the red part of the graph into three smaller categories? `S3E1c`

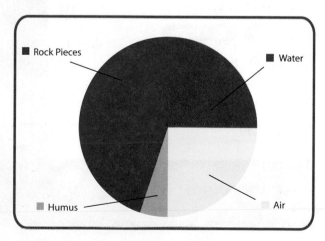

Georgia Performance Standards in This Chapter

Content

S3E2 Students will investigate fossils as evidence of organisms that lived long ago.

S3E2a   **S3E2b**

This chapter also addresses these co-requisite standards:

Characteristics of Science

S3CS4 Students will use ideas of system, model, change, and scale in exploring scientific and technological matters.

S3CS4c

S3CS5 Students will communicate scientific ideas and activities clearly.

S3CS5b   **S3CS5c**

S3CS6 Students will question scientific claims and arguments effectively.

S3CS6a

What's the Big Idea?

Fossils help scientists learn about plants and animals that lived long ago.

Essential Questions

GO online for student eBook www.hspscience.com

St. Marys River

Dear Nelly,

This morning I got to see teeth from the largest sharks to ever swim in the ocean! A researcher came to our class and showed us two shark teeth.

One was from a great white shark that is alive today. The other tooth was from a shark that lived more than a million years ago. The researcher found the fossil tooth in the St. Marys River.

Your Friend,
Marvin

USA

What could Marvin learn from the shark teeth he saw? How does this relate to the **Big Idea?**

Content

S3E2a Investigate fossils by observing authentic fossils or models of fossils or view information resources about fossils as evidence of organisms that lived long ago.

S3E2b Describe how a fossil is formed.

Characteristics of Science

S3CS4c   **S3CS5b**

LESSON 1

Essential Question

What Are Fossils?

Georgia Fast Fact

Learning from the Past
Animals like this one no longer exist. At the Fernbank Museum of Natural History in Atlanta, you can learn about unusual plants and animals that lived millions of years ago.

fossil [FAHS•uhl]
The hardened remains of
a plant or an animal that
lived long ago (p. 114)

Fernbank Museum of
Natural History in Atlanta

Make a Model Fossil

Guided Inquiry

Start with Questions

Scientists want to learn about plants and animals that lived long ago. Scientists can do this by looking at fossils. These are the remains of plants and animals that lived long ago.

- What do fossils look like?

- How do fossils form?

Investigate to find out. Then read to find out more.

Prepare to Investigate

Inquiry Skill Tip
Using models is a good way to learn about things that would be hard to study directly. It is hard to study how fossils form because the process takes a long time. When you make a model, it should be as much like the real thing as possible.

Materials

- seashell
- petroleum jelly
- small plastic bowl or paper plate
- white glue
- modeling clay

Make an Observation Chart

My Fossil Models	
Kind of Fossil	Description
Modeling Clay Fossil	
Glue Fossil	

Follow This Procedure

1. Coat the outside of the seashell with a thin layer of petroleum jelly.

2. Press the seashell into the clay to make a model of a fossil.

3. Remove the seashell carefully from the clay.

4. Place the clay with the seashell's shape in the plastic bowl.

5. Drizzle white glue into the imprint. Fill it completely. This also makes a model of a fossil.

6. Let the glue harden for about a day. When it is hard, separate the hardened glue from the clay.

Step 2

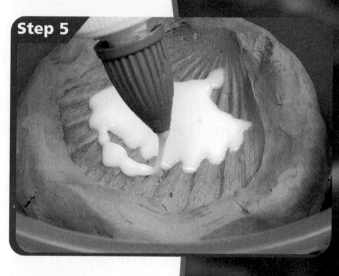
Step 5

Draw Conclusions

1. How do you think pressing the seashell into the clay models how some fossils form? **S3E2b**

2. **Standards Link** You made two models of fossils. How do the fossils compare? **S3E2a**

3. **Inquiry Skill** Scientists use models to better understand how things happen. Why was clay a good material to use for your model? **S3CS4c**

Independent Inquiry

Use at least four other once-living materials such as fallen leaves to make models of fossils. Draw a conclusion about which materials make the best fossils. **S3CS5b**

VOCABULARY
fossil p. 114

SCIENCE CONCEPTS
▶ what fossils are
▶ how fossils form

Focus Skill MAIN IDEA AND DETAILS
Look for information about different kinds of fossils.

Main Idea

detail   detail   detail

Fossils

Think about the "fossils" you made in the Investigate. Did they look like the shell you used? How were they different from the shell? A **fossil** is a trace or the remains of a living thing that died a long time ago. There are many different kinds of fossils.

Some fossils, such as bones and teeth, look like the actual parts of animals. Slowly, minerals replaced the bones.

Other fossils, such as dinosaur tracks in mud, are only marks left behind. These marks are called trace fossils. The mud hardened, and in time it changed to rock.

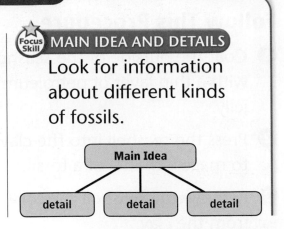

This fossil shows a trilobite (TRY•luh•byt), an animal that lived more than 200 million years ago.

Dinosaur tracks give clues to the animal's size and shape.

A mold is the shape of a once-living thing left in sediment when the rock formed. The living thing that made the mold breaks down, leaving only a cavity shaped like the plant or animal.

A cast forms when mud or minerals later fill a mold. The cast has the actual shape of the living thing. You made a model of a fossil mold and a fossil cast in the Investigate.

Plant fossils are not as common as animal fossils. That's because the soft parts of plants are easily destroyed as rocks form.

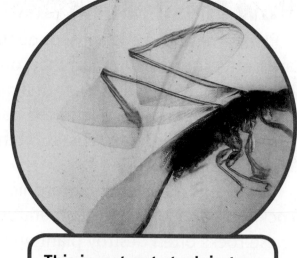

This insect got stuck in tree sap. The sap hardened and became amber.

MAIN IDEA AND DETAILS

What are three kinds of fossils?

Petrified (PEH•truh•fyd) wood is another type of fossil. The soft parts of a once-living plant were replaced by hard minerals. ▶

Cast

Mold

How Fossils Form

Places that have a lot of sedimentary rocks are better for fossil hunting than other places. Why? It's because what's left of a once-living thing is sometimes buried in the particles that form sedimentary rock. Fossils often form in limestone and shale.

Few fossils form in metamorphic and igneous rock. The pressures and temperatures that form these rocks often destroy plant and animal parts before they can become fossils.

Science Up Close

How a Fossil Forms

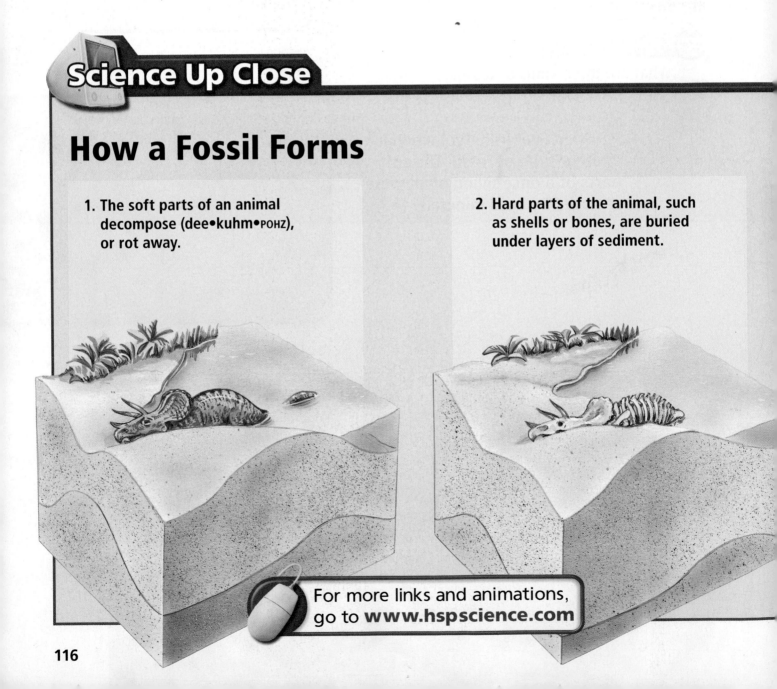

1. The soft parts of an animal decompose (dee•kuhm•POHZ), or rot away.

2. Hard parts of the animal, such as shells or bones, are buried under layers of sediment.

For more links and animations, go to **www.hspscience.com**

The Science Up Close shows how a fossil might have begun forming millions of years ago. After dying, the animal was quickly covered by layers of sediment. If the animal had not been covered quickly, another animal might have eaten it. After millions of years, the layers of sediment became sedimentary rock. What was left of the animal is now a fossil.

Focus Skill MAIN IDEA AND DETAILS **Why are more fossils found in sedimentary rocks than in other rocks?**

This photo shows a triceratops (try•SAIR•uh•tahps) fossil. ▼

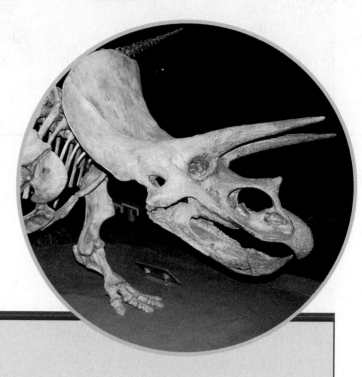

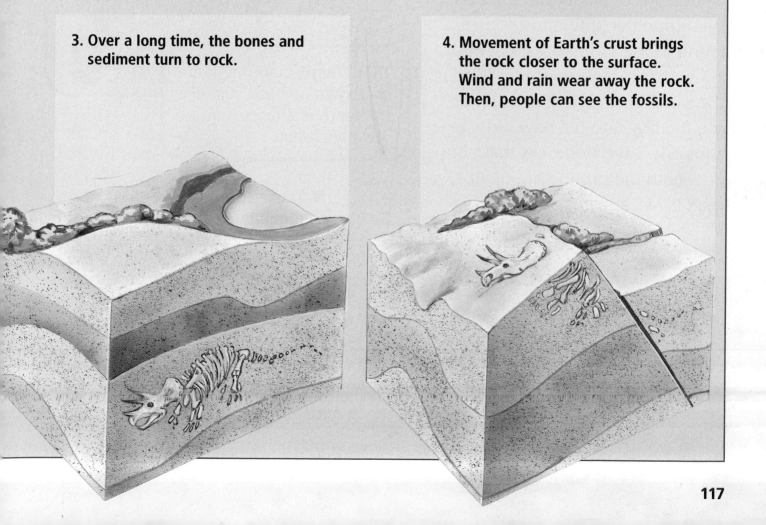

3. Over a long time, the bones and sediment turn to rock.

4. Movement of Earth's crust brings the rock closer to the surface. Wind and rain wear away the rock. Then, people can see the fossils.

117

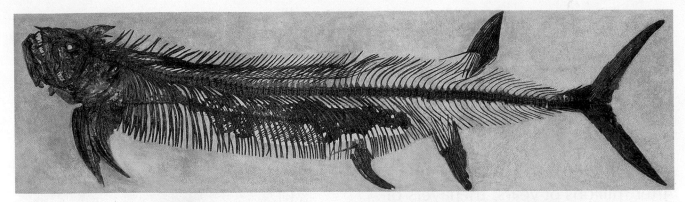

▲ Scientists can tell what kind of food this fish ate.

Learning from Fossils

Scientists today study fossils to learn about animals and plants that no longer exist. For example, scientists learn what kind of foods animals ate by looking at the shapes of fossil teeth. Animals that eat meat usually have sharp teeth.

Scientists also use fossils to tell what kinds of plants and animals lived together. If two fossils are found in the same rocks, scientists know that those two things lived at the same time. Scientists can also use the layers to tell how old a fossil is. Layers of rocks that are deeper in the ground are older than layers above.

These fossil shark teeth are sharp and pointed, just like the teeth of sharks that are alive today.

▼ These scientists are digging fossils from the same layer of rock.

Sand dollars live in the ocean. This sand dollar fossil was found in Georgia. The fossil is evidence that parts of Georgia used to be under water.

Living sand dollar

Did you know that there are clam fossils in Georgia? Fossils help scientists know what a place was like long ago. Much of what is now southern Georgia was under an ocean. In some parts of southern Georgia, you can find fossil whale bones and shark teeth.

The oldest fossils in Georgia can be found in the mountains. Some plant fossils found there are more than 300 million years old! In fact, coal from Georgia mountains formed from the remains of plants that lived long ago.

★ **MAIN IDEA AND DETAILS**

What can scientists learn from fossils?

Insta-Lab

Fossil Find
Press a hard object, such as a paper clip, into a ball of clay. Then remove the object. Trade clay imprints with a partner. Don't tell what object you used to make your imprint. Try to tell what object your partner used to make his or her imprint.

Essential Question

What are fossils?

In this lesson, you learned that the hardened remains of plants and animals that lived long ago are fossils. Different kinds of fossils form in different ways.

1. **(Focus Skill) MAIN IDEA AND DETAILS**
   Draw and complete a graphic organizer. Show details that support this main idea: *Fossils are the remains of plants and animals from long ago.* **S3E2a**

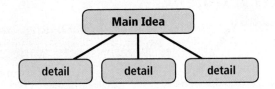

2. **SUMMARIZE** Explain how a fossil forms in a rock. **S3E2b**

3. **VOCABULARY** Write a sentence that describes a *fossil*. **S3E2a**

4. **Critical Thinking** After walking in his tennis shoes through mud, Kyle notices an imprint of his shoe. What kind of fossil is formed this way? **S3E2b**

CRCT Practice

5. Which is one thing scientists learn from fossils?
   - **A** how rocks form
   - **B** what sediments are
   - **C** what animals are like today
   - **D** about once-living things that no longer exist **S3E2a**

6. Which is **not** a fossil?
   - **A** petrified wood
   - **B** the footprint of a dinosaur
   - **C** a 300 million-year-old rock
   - **D** the imprint of a fern in a piece of coal **S3E2a**

The **Big** Idea

 Writing ELA3W1c

Narrative Writing

Research a kind of fossil found in Georgia. Write a **story** about what life was like for the living thing that made the fossil. Include information about where the plant or animal lived, its size, and what it ate. Tell how the living thing died and became a fossil.

 Math M3A1b

Write Word Problems

Write two word problems using information from this table. Trade with a classmate and solve each other's problems. Make sure to show how you got your answer.

Lengths of Dinosaurs	
Dinosaur	**Length (in meters)**
Stegosaurus	12
Tyrannosaurus	14
Brachiosaurus	25

 Language Arts ELA3R2e

What's in a Dinosaur's Name?

The word *triceratops'* is a combination of Greek root words. *Tri* means "three," *ceras* means "horn," and *ops* means "face." Make a list of dinosaurs, and research the root words in their names.

 For more links and activities, go to **www.hspscience.com**

GEORGIA SOUTHERN UNIVERSITY'S HALL OF
Natural History

Vogtle whale fossil

What's 78 million years old, nearly 10 meters (30 feet) long, and lived in the ocean when the dinosaurs lived on land? If you said a *Mosasaur* (MOH•suh•sawr), you're right. You can see the fossil skeleton of a *Mosasaur* in the Hall of Natural History at Georgia Southern University.

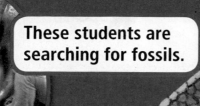

These students are searching for fossils.

Mosasaurs had flexible tails for moving through the water.

Oceans in Georgia

Mosasaurs were strong, meat-eating reptiles that lived in the oceans millions of years ago. At that time, ocean water covered most of what is now southern Georgia. *Mosasaurs* had large teeth and flexible lower jaws, like today's snakes. They moved their tails from side to side to swim.

More Fossil Finds

Mosasaurs aren't the only fossils on display. A few years ago, a rare whale fossil was found near the Vogtle power plant in Waynesboro, Georgia. Now called the Vogtle whale, it is the oldest whale fossil ever found in North America. The animal lived about 40 million years ago. Like today's whales, the Vogtle whale whipped its tail up and down to swim.

In another part of the hall, you can see fossils of animals that lived from 2 million to 5 million years ago. You can see ancient shells of scallops, clams, and oysters and the teeth of mako, tiger, and great white sharks.

✎ Think and Write

❶ *Mosasaurs* lived in the ocean. Why are their fossils found on dry land in Georgia? **S3E2a**

❷ Could you find whale fossils and dinosaur fossils in the same rocks? Explain. **S3E2b**

Content

 **S3E2a** Investigate fossils by observing authentic fossils or models of fossils or view information resources about fossils as evidence of organisms that lived long ago.

Characteristics of Science

S3CS5c **S3CS6a**

Essential Question

What Can We Learn from Fossils?

Georgia Fast Fact

Studying Fossils
The Macon Museum of Arts and Sciences has a collection of fossils. One of the most interesting fossils at the museum is a 40-million-year-old whale fossil that people named Ziggy. The fossil was found with the fossil remains of a shark in its rib cage, which helped scientists learn what the whale ate.

The Macon Museum of Arts and Sciences

extinct [ek•STINGT]
Describes a kind of living
thing that is no longer
found on Earth (p. 132)

Animals from Long Ago

Guided Inquiry

Start with Questions

How do living things of the past compare with living things today? To answer this question, scientists use evidence from fossils.

- Did the plants and animals of long ago look like those we see today?

- Were there living things long ago that did not look like any plants or animals living today?

Investigate to find out. Then read to find out more.

Prepare to Investigate

Inquiry Skill Tip

There are many ways to make observations. One way to improve your observation skills is by using numbers. Analyzing the data you collect can help you draw conclusions.

Materials
- shell fossil
- modern-day shell
- ruler
- elephant picture card
- woolly mammoth picture card

Make an Observation Chart

My Animal Observations		
	Alike	Different
Shell fossil and modern-day shell		
Woolly mammoth and elephant		

Follow This Procedure

❶ Observe the shell fossil and the modern-day shell. Record your observations.

❷ Use the ruler to measure the width and length of each shell. Record your measurements.

❸ Now observe the picture cards for the elephant and the woolly mammoth. Compare the two animals, and record your observations.

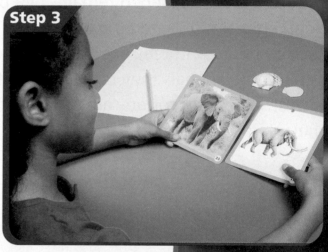

Draw Conclusions

1. How are the elephant and the woolly mammoth alike? How are they different?

2. Standards Link Do some shells from long ago look like ones we see today? If so, in what ways are they alike? **S3E2a**

3. Inquiry Skill Use numbers to compare the shell fossil and the modern-day shell. Do you think the kinds of animals that lived in the shells have changed much over time? Explain. **S3CS5c**

Independent Inquiry

Use books, magazine articles, or the Internet to research the size of the imperial mammoth. Then, on a flat surface outdoors, use a meterstick to mark its length and height. Draw its outline with chalk. Do the same for a present-day elephant. How do the sizes of these two animals compare?

 S3CS6a

VOCABULARY
extinct p. 132

SCIENCE CONCEPTS
▶ how some things that lived long ago have disappeared
▶ how some things living today look like some that lived long ago

Focus Skill COMPARE AND CONTRAST
Look for ways living things of long ago are like those of today.

[alike]——[different]

Animals Then and Now

A fossil is the hardened remains of a plant or an animal that lived long ago. Some fossils, such as bones and teeth, look like the actual parts of the animals they came from. Other fossils, such as footprints, are only marks that the animals left behind.

Tyrannosaurus rex was about 4.5 meters (15 ft) tall and had teeth as big as bananas.

Modern-day camel

Small camel fossil

How much taller were large camels of long ago than camels are today?

Camel Heights

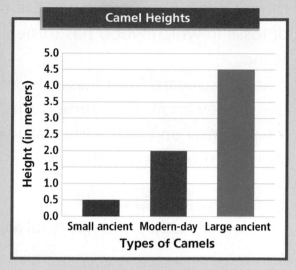

▲ Camels lived in North America many years ago. Fossils tell us that some of these camels were about the size of a rabbit. Others were about 4.5 meters (15 ft) tall.

Fossils show how animals have changed. There are no animals alive today that look like *Tyrannosaurus rex*. On the other hand, camels have not changed much. Camels of long ago were different in size, but they looked like the camels of today.

COMPARE AND CONTRAST

How are footprint fossils different from bone fossils?

Scientists thought the kind of fish shown in this fossil no longer lived on Earth, until a live one was caught by a fisherman.

129

Plants Then and Now

Plant fossils are not as common as animal fossils. That's because the soft parts of plants are easily destroyed.

Some plant fossils are leaf prints in mud. Others are *petrified wood,* a type of fossil in which wood has turned to stone.

Scientists learn from fossils. From them, they know that some plants no longer grow on Earth. Other plants look like those we see today.

COMPARE AND CONTRAST

How are fossil plants like fossil animals?

Making Fossils

Gather leaves and other plant parts. Press them into a flat piece of modeling clay. Look at the prints you made. What would they tell future scientists about the plants in your area?

Scientists can see how ferns have changed by comparing fossil ferns with modern-day ferns. ▼

Fern fossil

Modern-day fern

The ginkgo tree is often called a living fossil because it has not changed much in 100 million years.

Ginkgo leaves

Ginkgo leaf fossil

Modern-day ginkgo tree

Like ginkgo trees, there were bristlecone pine trees 100 million years ago. Fossils show that these trees have changed little over time. ▶

Bristlecone pinecones

Fossil pinecones

Bristlecone pine tree

131

Extinct Plants and Animals

Many kinds of plants and animals are extinct. **Extinct** means a kind of plant or animal is no longer living. When the last *Tyrannosaurus rex* died, that animal became extinct.

Living things become extinct for many reasons. When an environment changes, some living things can change and stay alive. Others find new places in which to live. Some cannot change, and they die.

The last great auk died in 1844. These birds are now extinct. ▼

◀ **Saber-toothed cat fossil**

Saber-toothed cats were about 30 centimeters (12 in) shorter than today's lions. However, they were twice as heavy.

North America has had many Ice Ages. During these times, huge sheets of ice covered much of the land. Many plants and animals became extinct because they could not live in the cold weather.

People can cause living things to become extinct. They cut down forests and drain swamps. Plants and animals may lose their homes and become extinct.

▲ Woolly mammoths lived during the last Ice Age. However, they died when the weather became warmer after the Ice Age.

(Focus Skill) **COMPARE AND CONTRAST**

How was the weather during an Ice Age different from the weather today?

An Ice Age lasts for millions of years. This map shows areas that were covered by ice in the last Ice Age.

PACIFIC OCEAN

ATLANTIC OCEAN

Essential Question

What can we learn from fossils?

In this lesson, you learned that living things have changed over time. Some living things today look like things that lived long ago. Some things that lived long ago have died out.

1. (Focus Skill) **COMPARE AND CONTRAST**
   Draw and complete a graphic organizer to compare and contrast an elephant and a woolly mammoth. **S3E2a**

   [alike]——[different]

2. **DRAW CONCLUSIONS** Suppose you found a fossil. Why should you be careful with it? **S3E2a**

3. **VOCABULARY** Explain how the words *fossil* and *extinct* are related to each other. Use both words in your answer. **S3E2a**

4. **Critical Thinking** You read a report that says "Woolly mammoths were larger than today's elephants." Explain how you could use numbers to make the statement more exact. **S3CS5c**

CRCT Practice

5. Which of these is **not** extinct?
   - **A** saber-toothed cats
   - **B** *Tyrannosaurus rex*
   - **C** *Triceratops*
   - **D** pine trees **S3E2a**

6. Which is **not** something you can learn by looking at a fossil leaf?

   The **Big** Idea

   - **A** how big the leaf was
   - **B** what color the leaf was
   - **C** what shape the leaf was
   - **D** how wide the leaf was **S3E2a**

Writing — ELA3R3h

Write a Description
Find a picture of a fish that lives today. Compare it to the photograph of the fish fossil on the left. Write three **paragraphs**. Describe ways the two fish are the same and ways they are different. Explain whether you think the fish in this photo is a fossil of the living fish.

9÷3 Math — M3N4c

Sharks Then and Now
Megalodon is an extinct shark. It was closely related to the great white shark, which is alive today. *Megalodon* was three times longer than a great white shark. *Megalodon* was 16 meters long. About how long is a great white shark?

Social Studies — SS3CG1c

Endangered Species
Living things that may become extinct are said to be endangered species. Research the Endangered Species Act. Write a report about how the law helps protect a Georgia plant or animal. Tell which branch of government wrote the Endangered Species Act.

For more links and activities, go to **www.hspscience.com**

Edward Chatelain

▶ **DR. EDWARD CHATELAIN**

▶ **Associate Professor at Valdosta State University**

▶ Studies fossils

Have you ever heard of ammonoids (AM•uh•noydz) or gastroliths (GAS•truh•liths)? Does either term stump you? They don't stump Dr. Edward Chatelain. He's been studying ammonoids and gastroliths since the 1980s.

An ammonoid was a soft-bodied sea animal with tentacles. It looked like an octopus, but it lived in a coiled, chambered shell. Ammonoids became extinct 65 million years ago.

Gastroliths are stones that some animals swallow. The stones help them grind up tough plant foods. Dr. Chatelain studies the gastroliths of some dinosaurs.

Think and Write

❶ Why do most ammonoid fossils look like shells, not like animals with tentacles? **S3E2a**

❷ How might Dr. Chatelain tell the difference between a gastrolith and an ordinary stone? **S3E2a**

Gastroliths are stones that were swallowed by animals long ago.

Ammonoid fossils

Lisa White

You would probably be excited to find a fossil of a dinosaur. Would you be as excited to find a fossil that is so small that you can barely see it?

Dr. Lisa White studies fossils of tiny living things in the oceans, such as diatoms. After ancient diatoms died, they sank to the ocean floor and became fossils. Even though the fossils are small, Dr. White can find out a lot about diatoms that lived long ago.

Millions of diatoms still live in the oceans. They are an important source of food for fish. Lisa White can compare diatoms living today with the fossils of diatoms she studies.

▶ **DR. LISA WHITE**

▶ **Associate Professor of Geology, San Francisco State University**

▶ Studies tiny fossils

✎ Think and Write

1 How can Lisa White learn about diatoms that lived long ago? **S3E2a**

2 What tools might Dr. White use to study diatom fossils? **S3CS8c**

Diatoms have many different shapes. Some are quite beautiful.

CHAPTER 3

Wrap-Up

→ Visual Summary

Tell how each picture helps explain the **Big Idea**.

The Big Idea Fossils help scientists learn about plants and animals that lived long ago.

Lesson 1 S3E2b

Fossil Formation

Fossils are evidence of plants and animals that lived long ago. Some fossils form over thousands of years when a dead plant or animal is covered with sediment. Other fossils, such as petrified wood, form when hard minerals replace parts of a once-living thing.

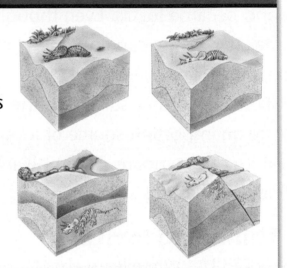

Lesson 2 S3E2a

Extinction Is Forever

When a kind of animal no longer lives on Earth, it is said to be extinct. Scientists learn about extinct plants and animals by studying fossils. Some plants and animals from long ago were like plants and animals living today.

Show What You Know

Write About Finding a Fossil/Narrative

Write a story about finding a dinosaur fossil. Include descriptive words that tell what the fossil looks like and how you found it. Tell what you would do with the fossil. Use words that describe the people in the story and the place where the story happens.

ELA3W1h

Georgia Performance Task

Designing Dinosaur Displays

Design an exhibit about fossils or extinct animals to display in a natural history museum. Your display could show the life cycle of an extinct animal or how tall different kinds of dinosaurs were. You could make a model of dinosaur bones out of paper. Invite other classes to see your exhibits. Explain your display, and answer questions that others may have.

S3E2a **S3E2b**

Vocabulary Review

Match the terms to the definitions below. The page numbers tell you where to look in the chapter if you need help.

fossil p. 114   **extinct** p. 132

1. Trace or remains of a living thing that died long ago **S3E2a**

2. Describes a living thing that is no longer found on Earth **S3E2a**

Check Understanding

Write the letter of the best choice.

3. Where are most fossils found? (p. 116) **S3E2a**
   A in amber   **C** in rocks
   B in bones   **D** in mud

4. Which of these is formed when mud or minerals fill in a mold? (p. 115) **S3E2b**
   A skeleton   **C** cast
   B wood   **D** sap

5. What animal today is similar to the triceratops? (p. 117) **S3E2a**
   A rhinoceros   **C** hippopotamus
   B elephant   **D** camel

6. What is petrified wood made of? (p. 115) **S3E2b**
   A amber   **C** wood
   B minerals   **D** mud

7. Which happens first when a fossil forms? (p. 116) **S3E2b**
   A Soil and other sediments cover the remains of a living thing.
   B Scientists dig up a fossil.
   C A living thing becomes extinct.
   D A living thing dies.

8. **COMPARE AND CONTRAST** How are casts different from molds? (p. 115) **S3E2b**
   A Molds are made when materials fill up a cast.
   B Casts are plant fossils. Molds are animal fossils.
   C Casts are fossils. Molds are not.
   D Casts are made when materials fill up a mold.

9. What do the drawings show? (p. 116) **S3E2b**

   A how environments change
   B how a mineral forms
   C how animals go extinct
   D how a fossil forms

10. Which of the following groups is extinct? (p. 132) `S3E2a`

   A dinosaurs   **C** plants
   B insects   **D** fish

11. MAIN IDEA AND DETAILS Which type of fossil is most common? (p. 115) `S3E2b`

   A animal   **C** mineral
   B amber   **D** plant

12. How do scientists know that animals have changed over time? (p. 129) `S3E2a`

   A They compare fossils with animals that live today.
   B They know the names of bones.
   C They look in old science books.
   D They use a field guide.

13. What can a footprint tell you about the animal that made it? (p. 114) `S3E2a`

   A what color the animal was
   B the exact age of the animal
   C the animal's size
   D what the animal ate

14. What can you infer about a place that has fish fossils? (p. 119) `S3E2a`

   A The place was once land.
   B That place is now a sea.
   C That place was once under a sea.
   D The fish did not live in water.

15. What can scientists learn from fossils? (p. 128) `S3E2a`

   A which plants will go extinct
   B what sound animals in the past made
   C the kinds of animals that lived on Earth in the past
   D how Earth formed

16. Which of these fossils is a trace fossil? (p. 114) `S3E2b`

   A an insect trapped in sap
   B a dinosaur footprint
   C a dinosaur bone
   D a petrified tree

Inquiry Skills

17. Describe one way you could make a model of a fossil. `S3E2b`

18. A scientist digs up two fossils. How can he or she tell which fossil is older? Use time/space relationships to explain. `S3E2a`

Critical Thinking

19. A scientist finds a dinosaur tooth that is sharp, like a shark tooth. What kind of food did the dinosaur eat? Why? `S3E2a`

20. Do all extinct animals look like animals that are alive today? Explain how scientists know. `S3E2a`

The Big Idea

1. Why is quartz a mineral?

A. It is a solid and has never been alive.

B. You can find it anywhere.

C. It's used to make glass.

D. It's made of rocks. **S3E1a**

2. Why is granite a rock?

A. It's beautiful and very strong.

B. It's made of several minerals.

C. It's used in buildings.

D. It can be carved into statues.

S3E1a

Use the diagram below to answer question 3.

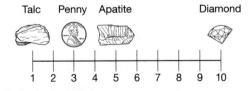

Talc   Penny   Apatite   Diamond

1 2 3 4 5 6 7 8 9 10

3. What does this scale help you know about a penny?

A. A penny is not heavy.

B. A penny is brown and shiny.

C. A penny is softer than most minerals.

D. A penny is harder than most minerals. **S3E1b**

Use the drawing below to answer question 4.

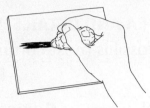

4. What is being tested here?

A. hardness

B. shape

C. weight

D. streak color **S3CS8a** **S3E1b**

5. Which rock has the smoothest texture?

A. a rock made of very large grains of minerals

B. a rock that is not made of minerals

C. a rock made of very small grains of minerals

D. a rock made when pressure and temperature change it

S3CS1 **S3E1b**

Use the drawing below to answer question 6.

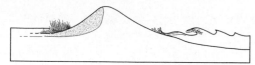

6. **Which sentence tells about the type of soil shown above?**

   A. It contains a lot of humus.

   B. The grains of rock in it are too small to see with the eyes.

   C. The grains of rock in it can be seen clearly.

   D. It can hold more water than most soils. **S3E1c**

7. **You examine soil from Georgia that is red in color. The soil feels smooth when you rub it between your fingers. You can't feel any grains of rock in the soil. The soil has a lot of**

   A. sand.

   B. silt.

   C. clay.

   D. erosion. **S3E1c**

8. **Which property should NOT be used to identify a mineral?**

   A. hardness

   B. shine

   C. taste

   D. color **S3CS3c** **S3E1b**

9. **Which type of soil contains pieces of rock in many different sizes?**

   A. sand

   B. loam

   C. silt

   D. clay **S3E1c**

Use the diagram below to answer question 10.

10. **Look at this diagram of a stream. What is happening to the soil?**

   A. Water is weathering the soil.

   B. Wind is weathering the soil.

   C. Water is eroding the soil.

   D. Wind is eroding the soil. **S3CS4b** **S3E1d**

11. How does erosion change soil?

   A. Erosion breaks soil into smaller pieces.

   B. Erosion carries soil from one place to another.

   C. Erosion causes cracks that break rocks into small pieces.

   D. Erosion helps clean soil.

 S3E1d

12. The banks of a river are much wider than they used to be. What probably caused this change?

   A. weathering by water

   B. weathering by wind

   C. erosion by water

   D. erosion by wind

 S3E1d

Use the diagram below to answer question 13.

13. What happened to the rock?

   A. It was weathered.

   B. It was eroded.

   C. It became a fossil.

   D. It became a metamorphic rock.

S3CS4b   S3E1d

Use the drawing below to answer question 14.

14. How did this fossil form?

   A. Parts of an organism were slowly replaced by minerals.

   B. An organism died, was buried, and decayed. A mold of it was left behind.

   C. Mud filled a mold left by an organism. The mud turned to rock.

   D. An animal made tracks in mud. The mud dried and hardened into rock.

 S3E2b

15. How are fossil imprints formed?

   A. Parts of an organism are slowly replaced by minerals.

   B. An organism dies, is buried in mud, and decays. A mold of it is left behind.

   C. Mud fills a mold left behind by an organism. The mud turns to rock.

   D. An animal makes tracks in mud. The mud dries and hardens into rock.

S3E2b

Use the drawing below to answer question 16.

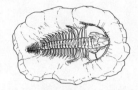

16. **What does this fossil prove?**

  A. This animal is now extinct.

  B. This animal lived long ago.

  C. This animal still lives on Earth.

  D. This animal has not changed much since ancient times.

 S3E2a

17. **Which of these is NOT a fossil?**

  A. a cast of a seashell

  B. a footprint of a dinosaur

  C. a chunk of petrified wood

  D. a bone of an elephant

 S3E2a

18. **What might scientists learn from a fern fossil?**

  A. what color the fern was

  B. which animals ate the fern

  C. how ferns have changed

  D. which other plants lived at the same time

S3E2a

Use the drawing below to answer question 19.

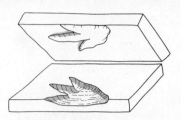

19. **Which statement about the fossils is NOT correct?**

  A. They both were made from the same animal.

  B. They both were made when mud hardened into stone.

  C. They are both very old.

  D. They both were made when minerals replaced bits of an animal. S3CS4c S3E2b

20. **How could you make loam?**

  A. by mixing sand, silt, and clay

  B. by mixing sand, silt, clay, and humus

  C. by taking large pieces of rock out of some soil

  D. by breaking bedrock into tiny pieces and adding clay and silt

 S3E1c

PHYSICAL SCIENCE

Sledding in Atlanta

Chapter 4 Heat
Chapter 5 Magnets

for student eBook
www.hspscience.com

People enjoy sledding on cold winter days. How cold does it need to be to snow? How warm does it need to be for the snow to melt?

Unit Inquiry

Keeping Food Cold
To keep food cold in the hot sun, you use a cooler. Coolers are containers made of materials that don't allow heat to quickly pass through. What materials make the best coolers? Plan and conduct an experiment to find out.

Georgia Performance Standards in This Chapter

Content

S3P1 Students will investigate how heat is produced and the effects of heating and cooling, and will understand a change in temperature indicates a change in heat.

S3P1a   **S3P1b**
S3P1c   **S3P1d**

This chapter also addresses these co-requisite standards:

Characteristics of Science

S3CS1 Students will be aware of the importance of curiosity, honesty, openness, and skepticism in science and will exhibit these traits in their own efforts to understand how the world works.

S3CS1b

S3CS4 Students will use ideas of system, model, change, and scale in exploring scientific and technological matters.

S3CS4b

S3CS8 Students will understand important features of the process of scientific inquiry.

S3CS8b

Many things can produce heat. Temperature can be measured by using a thermometer.

Essential Questions

GO online ▶ for student eBook
www.hspscience.com

Science in Georgia

Lake Lanier

Dear Rick,

We spent the weekend at Lake Lanier. Did you know that the lake is 23 miles long? It formed when Buford Dam was built on the Chattahoochee River.

It was very hot during the day today. To cool off, we stayed in the shade and swam in the lake water. Mom made me wear sunscreen to protect my skin from the sun.

See you soon,
Phyllis

What produced the heat that made Phyllis warm? How does this relate to the

Big Idea?

Georgia Performance Standards in This Lesson

Content

S3P1c Investigate the transfer of heat energy from the sun to various materials.

S3P1d Use thermometers to measure the changes in temperatures of water samples (hot, warm, cold) over time.

Characteristics of Science

S3CS4b   **S3CS8b**

Essential Question

What Is Heat and How Is It Measured?

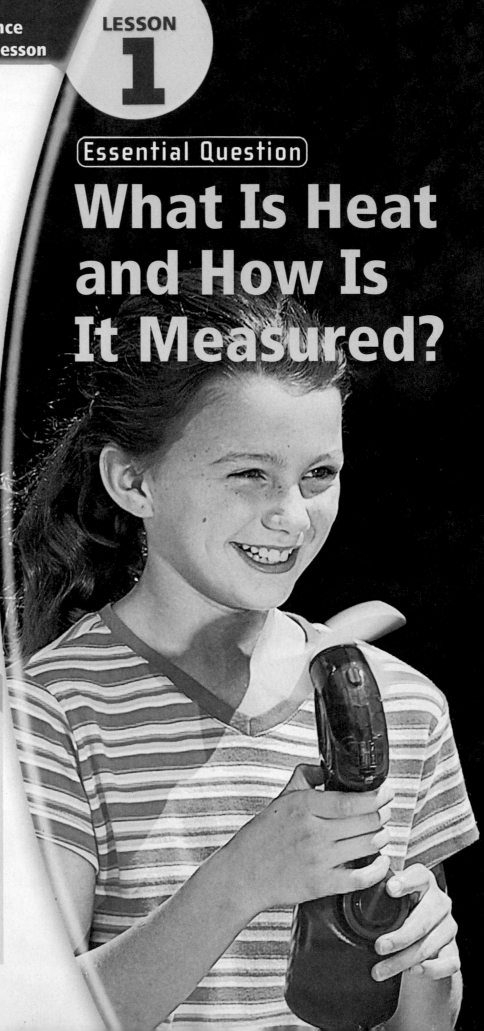

Georgia Fast Fact

Hot Times
On average, the hottest days in Georgia are in July and August. The coldest days are in January. The hottest temperature ever recorded in Georgia was 44°C (112°F), in Louisville, in 1952.

Fans provide relief from Georgia heat.

Vocabulary Preview

temperature
[TEM•per•uh•cher] The measure of how hot or cold something is (p. 154)

Celsius [SEL•see•uhs] The metric scale for measuring temperature (p. 155)

thermal energy
[THER•muhl EN•er•jee] The form of energy that moves particles of matter (p. 156)

heat [HEET]
The movement of thermal energy from hotter to cooler objects (p. 156)

Measuring Temperature

Guided Inquiry

Start with Questions

Liquid nitrogen is so cold that you can't touch it.

- What happens when a cold object touches something warm?

- What happens to a glass of liquid water when ice cubes are added?

Investigate to find out. Then read to find out more.

Prepare to Investigate

Inquiry Skill Tip
There are many ways to record data. You might use a data table or an observation chart. You communicate data by sharing it with others.

Materials

- metric measuring cup
- hot water
- plastic jar or beaker
- thermometer
- 3 ice cubes of the same size
- plastic spoon

Make a Data Table

Water Temperatures		
	Temperature (°C)	Other Observations
Warm tap water		
After first ice cube		
After second ice cube		
After third ice cube		

Follow This Procedure

1 Measure 200 mL of warm tap water. Pour it into the jar or beaker.

2 Use the thermometer to measure the temperature of the water. Record the data.

3 Add an ice cube to the water. Stir. Record what you observe.

4 Measure the temperature of the water again. Record the data.

5 Repeat Steps 3 and 4 twice.

Draw Conclusions

1. What happened to the ice cubes in the water?

2. **Standards Link** What happened to the temperature of the water each time you added an ice cube? Why do you think this happened?

   S3P1d

3. **Inquiry Skill** One way scientists communicate data is in a bar graph. Make a bar graph to communicate what happened to the temperature in this activity. **S3CS8b**

Step 2

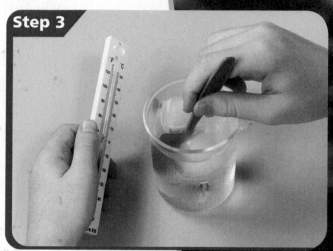
Step 3

Independent Inquiry

Think about the data you collected during this investigation. How might the data be different if you put 100 mL of water in a pan in a freezer? Measure the temperature of the water every 10 minutes. Interpret the data, and draw a conclusion that explains why the water changed. **S3CS4b**

VOCABULARY
temperature p. 154
Celsius p. 155
thermal energy p. 156
heat p. 156

SCIENCE CONCEPTS
▶ what heat is
▶ how temperature is measured

MAIN IDEA AND DETAILS
Look for details about heat and temperature.

Main Idea

detail | detail | detail

Measuring Temperature

Has anyone ever taken your body temperature? Have you ever checked the temperature outside? **Temperature** is the measure of how hot or cold something is. Temperature can be measured with a thermometer.

On these pages, you can see different types of thermometers. Many thermometers used today have equal divisions printed on them, much as rulers do. Instead of centimeters, degrees are used to divide thermometers. Two scales can be used on a thermometer, Fahrenheit or Celsius.

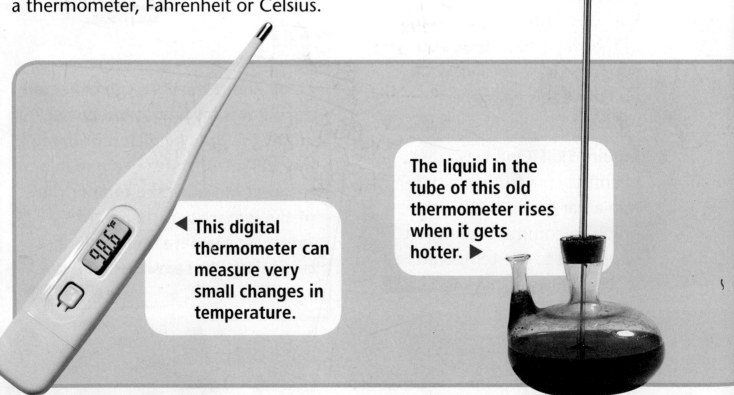

◀ This digital thermometer can measure very small changes in temperature.

The liquid in the tube of this old thermometer rises when it gets hotter. ▶

Scientists usually use the Celsius scale. **Celsius** is the metric temperature scale. On this scale, water boils at 100°C. It freezes at 0°C. You may be more familiar with the Fahrenheit temperature scale.

It's important to record the scale that is used to measure temperature. This way, temperature information can be shared and compared. Suppose one scientist sent data about temperatures to another scientist without telling which scale was used. What might happen?

MAIN IDEA AND DETAILS

What tool do you use to measure temperature?

Math in Science
Interpret Data

How Fast Does It Chirp?

The speed at which a cricket chirps depends on the temperature. Look at the table. As the temperature goes up, does a cricket chirp more quickly or more slowly?

Cricket Chirps	
Chirps Per Second	**Temperature**
1	11°C
2	19°C
3	28°C

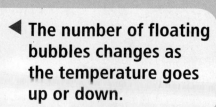

◀ This outdoor thermometer has big numbers that you can read through the window.

The numbers on this meat thermometer go up to 200°F! ▶

◀ The number of floating bubbles changes as the temperature goes up or down.

Thermal Energy and Heat

Think about sitting outside on a sunny day. The warmth from the sun might cause your skin temperature to go up.

Like all matter, your skin is made up of tiny particles. These particles are always moving. Temperature measures how fast the particles are moving. If the particles are moving very fast, the temperature is high. When the temperature is high, the particles have more energy.

The form of energy that moves particles of matter is called **thermal energy**. The movement of thermal energy is called **heat**. Thermal energy naturally flows from hotter to cooler objects.

When you sit outside on a sunny day, the thermal energy moves from the sun to your skin. The particles in your skin move faster. You feel this as warmth.

◄ The particles in melted glass move freely. The man can change the shape of the hot glass.

What happens to the particles in an ice cube when you heat it? The energy from the heat makes the particles move faster. The temperature goes up. Next, the ice cube melts. After the ice becomes a liquid, the particles move even faster, and they are farther apart. If you keep heating the water, the particles will move so fast that they fly apart. The water then becomes a gas.

MAIN IDEA AND DETAILS

What is heat?

Insta-Lab

How Hot?

Make a list of 5 items outside. After your teacher checks your list, touch the 5 items. Rank the items according to their temperature.

When the glass cools, its particles move slowly. It becomes a solid with a fixed shape. ▶

Controlling Thermal Energy

Have you ever gotten cold right after you stopped running? As the sweat on your skin begins to change into a gas, it carries heat away from your body. This makes you feel cooler.

If you get too cold, you might shiver. The motion warms your body. People sweat and shiver to help control their body temperature.

People control the temperature outside their bodies, too. People use a *thermostat* to control the temperature in a room. It turns the heater or air conditioner off or on as the temperature in the room changes.

MAIN IDEA AND DETAILS

How does your body control its temperature?

These runners in the Peachtree Road Race are cooling down by running through mist.

How a Thermostat Works

Inside the thermostat is a coil. It's made of strips of two different metals. Both strips expand as they get warmer. The strip on the inside of the coil expands faster. That makes the coil uncurl.

1 When the coil uncurls far enough, it flips a switch. The switch turns the heater off or the air conditioner on.

2 As the room cools, the coil contracts. This moves the switch to the other position.

3 As the temperature in a room changes, the thermostat turns heating or cooling devices on or off.

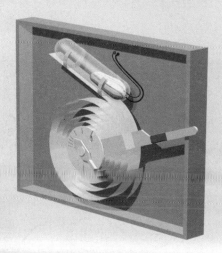

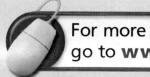

For more links and animations, go to **www.hspscience.com**

Essential Question

What is heat and how is it measured?

In this lesson, you learned that heat is the movement of thermal energy from hotter to cooler objects. You use a thermometer to measure temperature.

1. **Focus Skill** MAIN IDEA AND DETAILS
Draw a graphic organizer that shows details about the two scales used to measure temperature. **S3P1d**

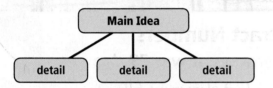

2. DRAW CONCLUSIONS What would happen if you left a glass of cold water outside on a sunny summer day? **S3P1c**

3. VOCABULARY Write a definition of each vocabulary term in your own words. **S3P1c**

4. Critical Thinking Why is it important to know which scale someone used to measure a temperature? **S3P1d**

CRCT Practice

5. Which of the following is a source of thermal energy?
A a thermostat
B a thermometer
C the sun
D a cooler **S3P1c**

6. Which tool is most useful for finding the temperature at which water freezes?
A a thermometer
B a graduated cylinder
C a balance
D a ruler **S3P1d**

The Big Idea

Writing
ELA3W1g

Narrative

Write a personal **story** about a time you learned how warm the sun's rays can be. Maybe you were on a picnic with your family or you found out that crayons melt when they are left in sunlight too long. Develop the characters in your story by telling what happened to them or what they said and thought.

Math
M3N2c

Add/Subtract Numbers

One fall afternoon, it was 79 degrees Fahrenheit in the shade in Albany, Georgia. The air temperature in the sun was 91 degrees Fahrenheit. What was the difference in temperature between a sunny and a shaded location?

Social Studies
SS3H1a

Research Olympic Sports

Make a list of sports that are part of the Olympic Games. Sort the sports into winter and summer games. Tell which sports rely on certain temperatures. Find out which games on your list were part of the first Olympic Games in ancient Greece.

For more links and activities, go to **www.hspscience.com**

161

Content

S3P1b Investigate how insulation affects heating and cooling.

Characteristics of Science

S3CS1b

Essential Question

How Does Thermal Energy Move?

Georgia Fast Fact

Up and Down
Each lava lamp has a light bulb in its base. Heat from the bulb warms the goo, which rises. When the goo cools at the top, it falls. That's one way thermal energy moves from one place to another.

Lava lamps

conduction
[kuhn•DUHK•shuhn]
The movement of heat between objects that are touching each other
(p. 167)

conductor [kuhn•DUHK•ter]
An object that heat can move through easily
(p. 167)

insulator [IN•suh•layt•er]
An object that doesn't conduct heat well (p. 168)

insulation
[in•suh•LAY•shuhn]
Material used to slow the movement of heat
(p. 169)

Getting Warmer?

Start with Questions

While playing outdoors on a sunny day, you may have noticed that some objects are warmer than other objects.

- Do some materials get warm faster than other materials?

- What materials are good at slowing down the movement of heat?

Investigate to find out. Then read to find out more.

Prepare to Investigate

Inquiry Skill Tip
If you have trouble drawing a conclusion, try drawing a picture! You can use a drawing or a diagram to summarize the results of an investigation and better understand what happened.

Materials
- safety goggles
- hot water
- wooden spoon
- metal spoon
- plastic spoon
- 3 plastic foam cups
- ceramic mug with handle
- plastic mug with handle
- metal mug with handle

Make a Data Table

Temperatures of Objects			
	Wooden Spoon	Plastic Spoon	Metal Spoon
Dry			
After 1 min			
	Ceramic Mug	Plastic Mug	Metal Mug
Dry			
After 30 sec			
After 60 sec			
After 90 sec			
After 120 sec			

Follow This Procedure

CAUTION: Wear safety goggles. Be careful with hot water.

1. Touch the three spoons. Record your observations.

2. Fill three foam cups with hot water. Place one spoon in each cup. Wait 1 minute.

3. Gently touch each spoon. Record your observations.

4. Touch the three mugs. Record your observations. Then fill each mug with hot water. Carefully touch each handle every 30 seconds for 2 minutes. Record what you observe.

Draw Conclusions

1. Why was it important to touch the spoons and the mugs before adding the hot water?

2. **Standards Link** Compare your observations of the spoons and the mugs before and after the water was used. **S3P1b**

3. **Inquiry Skill** What conclusion can you draw about the way thermal energy travels through different substances? Write your conclusion down and compare it with a classmate's.

    S3CS1b

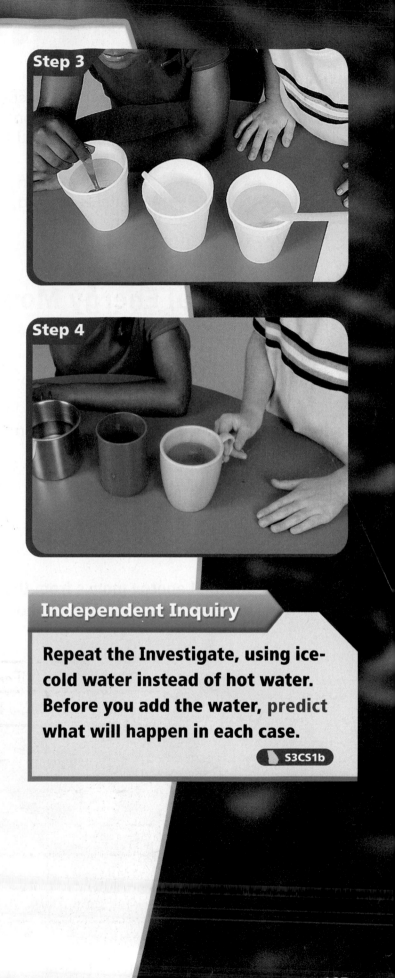

Step 3

Step 4

Independent Inquiry

Repeat the Investigate, using ice-cold water instead of hot water. Before you add the water, predict what will happen in each case.

S3CS1b

VOCABULARY
conduction p. 167
conductor p. 167
insulator p. 168
insulation p. 169

SCIENCE CONCEPTS
▶ how thermal energy moves from one place or object to another
▶ how insulation affects heating and cooling

MAIN IDEA AND DETAILS

Look for details about the movement of thermal energy.

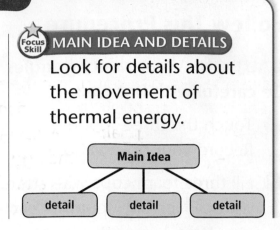

Ways Thermal Energy Moves

In the last lesson, you learned that heat is the movement of thermal energy. There are three ways thermal energy can move.

Sometimes, thermal energy travels from particle to particle in a solid. Or, particles of a gas or liquid can carry it from one place to another. It can even move through empty space. That's how heat from the sun reaches Earth.

MAIN IDEA AND DETAILS

What are the three ways thermal energy can move?

Thermal energy moves from the fire through the air to cook the hot dogs. ▼

Conductors

To cook an egg, you put it in a pan and turn on the stove. The heat from the burner makes the pan hot. Soon, the thermal energy moves through the hot pan to the cold egg. The egg gains thermal energy from the pan. Eventually, the egg and the pan are the same temperature. The movement of thermal energy between objects that touch each other is **conduction**.

A pan is used for cooking because it is made of metal, such as iron or copper. Thermal energy moves easily through most metals. An object that thermal energy can move through easily is called a **conductor**.

 **MAIN IDEA AND DETAILS**

What are two materials that are good conductors?

Which of these items are good conductors?

Heat moves from the burner to the pan to the food by conduction.

Insulators

To pick up a hot pan, you use a potholder. It keeps thermal energy from moving to your hand. The potholder is an **insulator**—an object that doesn't conduct heat well. Wood, cloth, and plastic are good insulators.

Air is an insulator, too. Some winter jackets have air spaces in their stuffing. The air keeps thermal energy from moving away from your body. When birds fluff up their feathers, they make air spaces. The air spaces keep the birds warm.

▲ The cover wrapped around this pot is an insulator.

Focus Skill MAIN IDEA AND DETAILS

What are two examples of good insulators?

Water seeps in between the wet suit and the surfer's skin. This water warms up and acts as an insulator, along with the wet suit.

This worker is adding insulation to the walls and ceiling of a house.

Insulation

Materials that are good insulators are used to make insulation. **Insulation** is a material that is used to slow the movement of heat. You can find insulation in the walls of your home, in a thick jacket, or in a thermos or cooler.

You know that thermal energy moves from warmer objects to cooler objects. In winter, insulation helps keep warm air inside a home. In summer, insulation helps keep hot air from getting into the home.

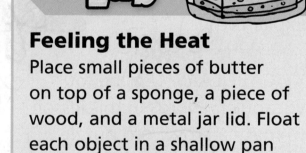

Feeling the Heat
Place small pieces of butter on top of a sponge, a piece of wood, and a metal jar lid. Float each object in a shallow pan of hot water. What happens to the butter? Why?

 MAIN IDEA AND DETAILS

Why do people add insulation to their homes?

Essential Question

How does thermal energy move?

In this lesson, you learned that thermal energy moves from warmer objects to cooler objects. Insulation helps slow the movement of thermal energy.

1. **(Focus Skill) MAIN IDEA AND DETAILS**
   Draw and complete a graphic organizer. Show details that support this main idea: *Thermal energy moves through solids, liquids, gases, and space.* **S3P1b**

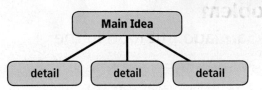

2. **DRAW CONCLUSIONS** Tasha had a foam cup of hot cocoa. The cocoa stayed hot, and the cup didn't get too hot to hold. Explain why. **S3P1b**

3. **VOCABULARY** Use the four vocabulary words in this lesson to make a crossword puzzle. **S3P1b**

4. **Critical Thinking** Make a list of 10 different kitchen items. Next to each item, write whether the item is a good conductor or not. **S3P1b**

CRCT Practice

5. What could the owner of a house do to keep the house cool on a hot day and save money?
   - **A** Turn the thermostat to a cooler setting.
   - **B** Add insulation to the walls of the house.
   - **C** Paint the house a dark color.
   - **D** Keep the refrigerator door open. **S3P1b**

6. Which is a good insulator?
   - **A** silver spoon
   - **B** aluminum foil
   - **C** stainless steel spoon
   - **D** wooden spoon **S3P1b**

The **Big** Idea

Make Connections

Narrative

Write a **description** of how it feels to be outside in cold weather. Include adjectives to describe your experience. Tell what you do to stay warm in the cold weather.

 Math   M3M1

Solve a Problem

At 5:45 P.M., Santiago put food in the oven. Santiago took the food out of the oven at 6:15 P.M. How many minutes did the food cook? What fraction of an hour does that equal?

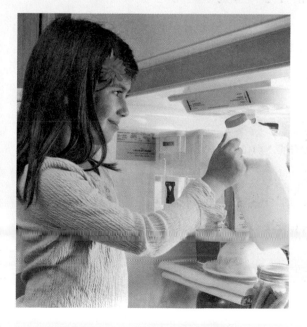

 Health

Keeping Food Safe

Refrigerators keep food from spoiling quickly. Research ways people kept food from spoiling before refrigerators were invented. Write a report to share with the class.

 For more links and activities, go to **www.hspscience.com**

Technology Delivers
HOT PIZZA

You know that thermal energy always moves from hot objects to cold objects. This means thermal energy moves from a hot pizza to the cooler air around it. In the process, the hot pizza gets cold. And who wants cold pizza?

We Want It Hot

A recent survey found that more than half of all take-out food was delivered to homes rather than picked up. Keeping pizza hot while the delivery person finds the right house is sometimes a problem. Customers want their food delivered fast, and they want it to arrive piping hot. Companies that deliver cold pizzas are soon out of business. So it's good news that science is helping pizza companies deliver your pizza hot to your door.

Keeping Thermal Energy In

The hot bag is made with three layers of material. The inside liner, made of nylon and vinyl, reduces condensation. It also has a shiny silver color to reflect the heat of the food back inside the container.

The middle layer is a dense foam. This layer is the insulator for the bag. Thermal energy doesn't move easily through the foam. That means the heat is trapped inside the bag. The foam also prevents air from moving into or out of the bag. Even though the inside of the bag is hot, the outside of the bag remains cool and easy to handle.

The outside of the bag is made of heavy vinyl. This makes the bag waterproof. The bag can be closed and sealed shut, keeping even more thermal energy in. The hot bag also has two small openings that allow steam to escape. They keep the pizza crust from becoming soggy on its trip to your home.

Think and Write

1. Is foam a good insulator or a good conductor? Why? **S3P1b**

2. Would these bags be helpful for delivering ice cream? Explain. **S3P1b**

Find out more. Log on to **www.hspscience.com**

Content

S3P1a Categorize ways to produce heat energy such as burning, rubbing (friction), and mixing one thing with another.

Characteristics of Science

S3CS1b   **S3CS8a**

Essential Question

How Is Thermal Energy Used?

Georgia Fast Fact

Heating Up Things
Evenings can get cool in any part of Georgia. Heaters like these let people eat outside even if it is chilly. In the Investigate, you'll find out about other ways to "heat up" things.

friction [FRIK•shuhn]
A force between two moving objects that slows the objects and produces heat (p. 178)

Where's the Heat?

Guided Inquiry

Start with Questions

Even on a cold winter day, the hood of a car gets warm after the car has been driven.

- What are some things that cause objects to get warm?

- What can you do to warm yourself on a cold winter day?

Investigate to find out. Then read to find out more.

Prepare to Investigate

Inquiry Skill Tip
Remember that a hypothesis is an educated guess that tries to explain an event. You can use observations, facts, data, and past experiences to help you make a hypothesis.

Materials
- metal button
- wool
- penny
- paper

Make an Observation Chart

Temperatures of Objects		
Objects	Hypothesis	Observations
Hands held together		
Hands rubbed together		
Button and wool rubbed together		
Penny and paper rubbed together		

Follow This Procedure

1. Hold the palms of your hands together for 10 seconds. Do your hands feel warm or cold, dry or damp? Record what you observe.

2. Hypothesize what you would feel if you rubbed your hands together. Test your hypothesis. Record what you observe.

3. Hypothesize what would happen if you rubbed a button and a piece of wool together.

4. Rub a button and a piece of wool together for 10 seconds. Touch the button. Touch the wool. Record what you observe.

5. Repeat Steps 3 and 4, using a penny and a sheet of paper.

Step 2

Step 4

Draw Conclusions

1. What kind of changes did you observe in each step?

2. **Standards Link** What do you think caused the changes in this investigation? **S3P1a**

3. **Inquiry Skill** What knowledge and experiences did you use to help you hypothesize? **S3CS8a**

Independent Inquiry

How does the amount of time you rub things together affect the outcome? Plan and conduct a simple investigation to find out.

S3CS1b

VOCABULARY
friction p. 178

SCIENCE CONCEPTS
▶ how heat can be produced

Focus Skill **COMPARE AND CONTRAST**
Compare different ways to produce heat.

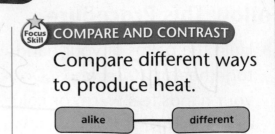

alike — different

Ways to Make Things Hot

How can you warm something up? You might put it near a campfire, place it in an oven, or set it in the sun. What happens if you need something heated up that can't go in an oven, such as your hands? What if it isn't a sunny day? There are many other ways thermal energy can be produced.

In the Investigate, you produced thermal energy by using friction. **Friction** is a force between moving objects. Friction slows the moving objects and produces heat.

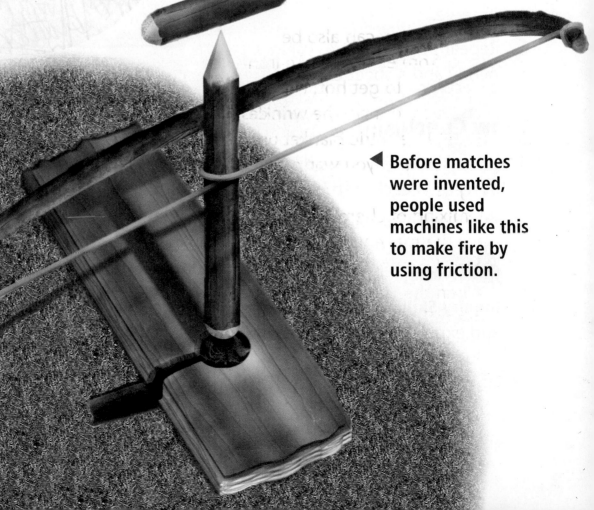

◀ **Before matches were invented, people used machines like this to make fire by using friction.**

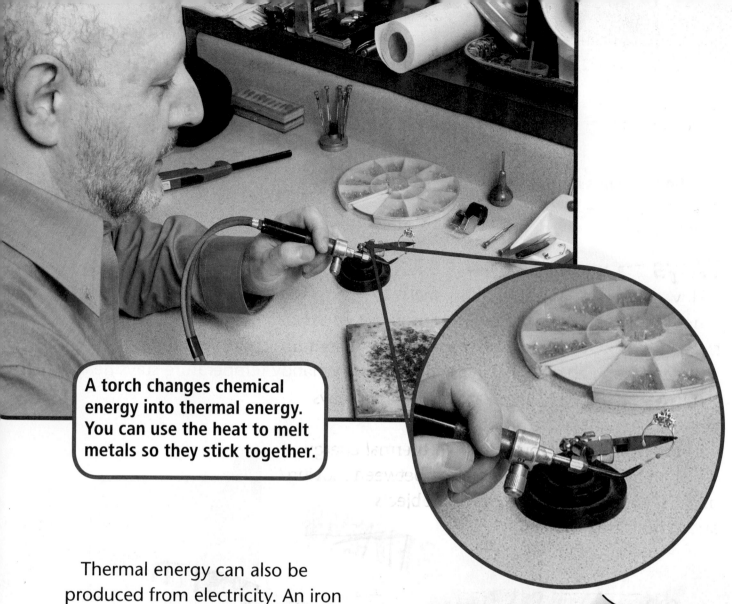

A torch changes chemical energy into thermal energy. You can use the heat to melt metals so they stick together.

Thermal energy can also be produced from electricity. An iron uses electricity to get hot. Heat from the iron helps remove the wrinkles in clothes. An electric blanket uses electricity to keep you warm during cold nights.

The mixing of chemicals can also produce thermal energy. Some heat packs produce thermal energy in this way. When the chemicals in the pack are mixed, the pack gets warm and is ready to be used.

 COMPARE AND CONTRAST

Compare and contrast how irons and heat packs work.

Insta-Lab

Heat It Up

Rub a block of wood with a piece of cloth for 30 seconds. Touch the wood. Record how hot the wood feels. Now rub the wood with sandpaper for 30 seconds. Touch the wood. Compare how the wood felt when rubbed with the cloth and the sandpaper.

Ways to Use Thermal Energy

People have used thermal energy for thousands of years. Before ovens were invented, people used fire to cook food. Today, some stoves burn natural gas to produce heat. Cars burn gasoline in order to run.

You use thermal energy, too. If you have ever sat by a fire to get warm, you have used thermal energy. When you take a warm bath or shower, thermal energy is used to heat the water. Your body produces its own thermal energy so your body temperature stays near 37°C (98.6°F).

The machines on this page produce thermal energy. ▼

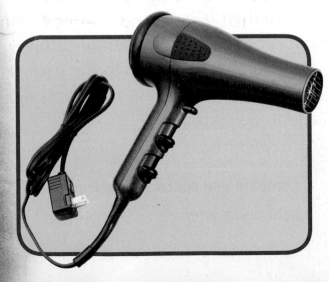

This solar panel uses the sun's energy to heat water. ▼

An ice pack gets colder when the substances inside are mixed. ▶

You learned that the sun is a source of heat. Some people use solar panels to heat the water used in their homes. Other people use boxes called solar cookers to cook food in places without electricity.

You learned that mixing chemicals can produce heat. Did you know some chemicals absorb heat when they are mixed? That's how ice packs get cool. Air conditioners and refrigerators also use chemicals that absorb heat.

Focus COMPARE AND CONTRAST

How do the ways people use thermal energy today contrast with the ways people used it in the past?

Essential Question

How is thermal energy used?

People use thermal energy in many ways. The sun, friction, burning, electricity, and the mixing of certain chemicals are sources of thermal energy.

1. **Focus Skill** COMPARE AND CONTRAST

Draw and complete a graphic organizer. Show ways thermal energy can be produced and used. **S3P1a**

alike —— different

2. DRAW CONCLUSIONS
Why was fire important to people before electricity was discovered? **S3P1a**

3. VOCABULARY Make a list of words and phrases that come to mind when you think about friction. Choose two of the words or phrases and explain how they relate to friction. **S3P1a**

4. Critical Thinking Every few months, a car needs an oil change. Oil is used to coat the moving parts inside the car's engine. Why is it important to make sure a car has clean oil? **S3P1a**

CRCT Practice

5. Which of the following uses electricity to produce heat?

  A the sun

  B a match

  C a refrigerator

  D a clothes dryer **S3P1a**

6. Which of these does **not** produce thermal energy?

  A the sun

  B an ice pack

  C a campfire

  D rubbing two objects together **S3P1a**

The **Big** Idea

 Writing ELA3W1k

Persuasive

Think about different sources of thermal energy. Write a **paragraph** explaining three ways that heat can be produced. Then decide which source of heat is most important in your life. Write a second paragraph explaining why you think it is important.

9÷3 **Math** M3A1a

Recognize a Pattern

A space heater produces 4 units of thermal energy in 2 hours and 12 units of thermal energy in 6 hours. How much thermal energy will it produce in 12 hours?

 Physical Education

Take a Hike

Take a hike with an adult. As you walk, touch different objects and see how warm or cold they are. Make a list and record whether the objects were in the sun or in the shade. Then put the objects in order from warmest to coldest. Did you notice any trends?

 For more links and activities, go to **www.hspscience.com**

Anders Celsius

▶ **ANDERS CELSIUS**

▶ Scientist from Sweden who lived from 1701–1744
▶ Developed a new scale for measuring temperature

When you look at a thermometer and you see a letter C, thank Anders Celsius. This Swedish scientist designed a scale of measuring temperatures more than 200 years ago. The Celsius scale is used in many countries today.

Celsius first stuck the bulb end of a thermometer into snow. Once the mercury stopped moving, he marked the level on the thermometer. He then stuck the thermometer into boiling water. Again, when the mercury stopped moving, he marked the thermometer.

Celsius divided the space between the two marks into 100 equal parts. On the Celsius scale, the freezing point of water is 0 degrees. The boiling point is 100 degrees.

 Think and Write

1 Is the work performed long ago by Anders Celsius still valuable today? S3CS7b

2 How did Anders Celsius use numbers in his investigations? S3CS5c

Hundreds of years ago, thermometers looked like this.

Marcia Bansley

What's the best way to escape the heat on a summer day? Forget air conditioning. Find a shady tree!

That's the advice Marcia Bansley gives. She is the director of Trees Atlanta. Bansley encourages Atlanta's citizens to plant trees in the city. Since 1985, volunteers have planted more than 14,000 large shade trees in downtown Atlanta alone.

Cities are usually hotter than rural areas. In fact, downtown Atlanta is often 3 to 5 degrees Celsius warmer than surrounding areas. That's because streets and buildings absorb the sun's heat. Shade trees and grassy fields don't absorb as much heat, so trees help keep Atlanta cool. They also help clean the air and water, and they help make the city beautiful.

▶ **MARCIA BANSLEY**
▶ Executive Director, Trees Atlanta
▶ Wants people to plant trees in cities

✍️ Think and Write

❶ How do trees benefit people who live in cities? S3P1c

❷ What technology helps scientists study temperatures in Atlanta? S3CS3b

These students are planting trees in Atlanta.

This special photograph taken from space shows temperatures in Atlanta. Red and orange areas are warmer than blue and green areas.

Visual Summary

Tell how each picture helps explain the **Big Idea**.

The Big Idea Many things can produce heat. Temperature can be measured by using a thermometer.

Lesson 1 S3P1d, S3P1c

Temperature and Thermometers

Thermal energy can be measured using a thermometer. Heat is the movement of thermal energy from warmer objects to cooler objects.

Lesson 2 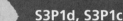 S3P1b

Slowing Down Thermal Energy

Thermal energy moves more quickly through some materials. These materials are good conductors. Good insulators slow the movement of thermal energy.

Lesson 3 S3P1a

Ways to Produce Heat

The sun produces the heat that warms Earth. Friction, mixing certain chemicals, and burning also produce heat.

Show What You Know

Chapter Writing Activity

Write About Heat Energy/Informational

Write a few paragraphs explaining some ways that heat energy can be produced. For each different way to produce heat energy, describe some ways that we use the heat that is produced.

ELA3W1c

Georgia Performance Task

Design and Test Solar Cookers

Design and build a solar cooker, a device that uses energy from the sun to cook food. Test your solar cooker to see how much it can raise the temperature of water in a beaker in 15 minutes.

S3P1c **S3P1d**

Vocabulary Review

Fill in each blank with a term from the list below. The page numbers after each word tell where to look in the chapter if you need help.

temperature p. 154   conductor p. 167

Celsius p. 155   insulator p. 168

thermal energy p. 156   insulation p. 169

heat p. 156   friction p. 178

1. An object that allows thermal energy to move easily through it is a _____. **S3P1b**

2. The metric scale for measuring temperature is _____. **S3P1d**

3. Energy that moves particles of matter is _____. **S3P1a**

4. A potholder is an example of an _____. **S3P1b**

5. The material inside a heavy winter coat is called _____. **S3P1b**

6. Rubbing your hands together is an example of _____. **S3P1a**

7. To find out how hot something is, measure its _____. **S3P1d**

8. The flow of thermal energy from a warmer to a cooler substance is _____. **S3P1c**

Check Understanding

Write the letter of the best choice.

9. Which particles are moving fastest? (p. 157) **S3P1c**
   A particles in ice
   B particles in boiling water
   C particles in water from the sink
   D particles in a glass with water and ice

10. Why does a diver wear a wet suit? (p. 168) **S3P1b**
    A to keep in thermal energy
    B to keep from getting cuts
    C to keep from sinking
    D to keep out cold

11. **COMPARE AND CONTRAST** Which beaker contains the most thermal energy? (p. 156) **S3P1d**
    A Beaker 1   C Beaker 3
    B Beaker 2   D Beaker 4

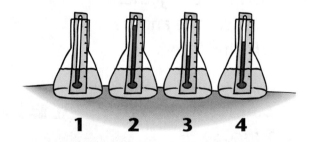

1   2   3   4

12. Water boils at _____. (p. 155) **S3P1d**
    A 100°F   C 0°C
    B 0°F   D 100°C

13. Which is a conductor? (p. 167)

S3P1b

A blanket   **C** metal spoon
B oven mitt   **D** sweater

14. MAIN IDEA AND DETAILS Which way of producing thermal energy is shown below? (p. 180) S3P1a

A burning
B rubbing
C using electricity
D mixing chemicals

15. What must your hands do to produce friction? (p. 177)

S3P1a

A rub together
B be close together
C touch one another
D be insulators

16. What causes a lake to warm in summertime? (p. 166) S3P1c

A friction   **C** snow
B the sun   **D** rain

Inquiry Skills

17. You leave a pan full of hot water on the counter overnight. Predict how the temperature of the pan, the water, and the countertop will compare the next morning. Explain your prediction. S3CS1b

18. From the pictures, infer which day the water in the pool will be warmer. Explain. S3CS4a

Monday   Tuesday

Critical Thinking

19. Two pots of water are put on a stove. The pots are the same size. The water in the pots is at the same temperature. Both burners are set at the same heat level. Five minutes later, the water in Pot 1 is boiling; the water in Pot 2 is not. What can you infer about Pot 2? S3P1b

20. Suggest three things that people could do to warm themselves on a cold winter day.

The **Big** Idea

S3P1b

Georgia Performance Standards in This Chapter

Content

S3P2 Students will investigate magnets and how they affect other magnets and common objects.

S3P2a **S3P2b**

This chapter also addresses these co-requisite standards:

Characteristics of Science

S3CS1 Students will be aware of the importance of curiosity, honesty, openness, and skepticism in science and will exhibit these traits in their own efforts to understand how the world works.

S3CS1a

S3CS4 Students will use ideas of system, model, change, and scale in exploring scientific and technological matters.

S3CS4b

S3CS5 Students will communicate scientific ideas and activities clearly.

S3CS5c

S3CS8 Students will understand important features of the process of scientific inquiry.

S3CS8a

What's the Big Idea?

Magnets are attracted to objects with iron. Opposite ends of two magnets attract each other.

Essential Questions

GO online for student eBook www.hspscience.com

Six Flags over Georgia

Dear Ryan,

I spent the week with my family at Six Flags over Georgia. I had fun on all of the rides. My dad explained how some of the rides work.

I think I'd like to design roller coasters when I'm older. Did you know that Goliath, one of the roller coasters, uses magnetic brakes to slow down the trains?

Your friend,
David

USA

What did David learn about magnets on his trip? How do you think that relates to the **Big Idea?**

Content

S3P2a Investigate to find common objects that are attracted to magnets.

S3P2b Investigate how magnets attract and repel each other.

Characteristics of Science

S3CS1a **S3CS8a**

LESSON 1

Essential Question

What Are Magnets?

Georgia Fast Fact

How Strong Is It?
Some magnets are strong enough to lift steel beams for buildings. Others can pick up only small objects, such as these fish. The magnet is picking up the paper clip that is attached to the paper fish. The magnet could not pick up the piece of paper alone.

This game uses a magnet.

magnet [MAG•nit]
An object that is attracted to iron (p. 196)

attract [uh•TRAKT]
To pull toward (p. 196)

repel [ree•PEL]
To push away (p. 197)

magnetic [mag•NET•ik]
Attracting objects that have iron in them (p. 198)

Simple Sorting

Start with Questions

Many people use magnets to hold papers to their refrigerator doors. You may have noticed that magnets stick to some things but not to others.

- What kinds of objects stick to a magnet?

- How can magnets be useful?

Investigate to find out. Then read to find out more.

Prepare to Investigate

Inquiry Skill Tip

Good observations are important when you infer information. Some of the most important things you learn from an investigation are not specifically found in the results. You have to think about what the results mean.

Materials
- steel paper clips
- bowl
- plastic beads
- magnet
- stopwatch

Make a Data Table

Sorting Objects	
Method	Time (seconds)
Without a magnet	
With a magnet	

Follow This Procedure

1 Put a handful of paper clips in the bowl. Add a handful of beads. Mix them up.

2 Remove the paper clips from the bowl by hand, making sure not to pick up any of the beads. Use a stopwatch to measure how long this takes.

3 Return the paper clips to the bowl of beads. Mix them up again.

4 Now use a magnet to remove the paper clips from the bowl. Use a stopwatch to measure how long this takes.

Step 2

Step 4

Draw Conclusions

1. How do the two times compare? Which is the quicker way to separate the steel paper clips from the plastic beads?

2. **Standards Link** How was the magnet helpful in sorting the objects? **S3P2a**

3. **Inquiry Skill** Scientists use what they know to infer, or conclude. Look at the picture on page 194. What are some things that you can infer about the picture? **S3CS0a**

Independent Inquiry

Mix various small metal objects together. **Predict** which objects you can separate by using a magnet. **Test your prediction.** **S3CS1a**

VOCABULARY
magnet p. 196
attract p. 196
repel p. 197
magnetic p. 198

SCIENCE CONCEPTS
▶ what a magnet is
▶ what magnets are attracted to
▶ how two magnets interact

Focus Skill **COMPARE AND CONTRAST**
Find out how magnets of different shapes work.

| alike | different |

Magnets

In the Investigate, you used magnets to pick up paper clips. A **magnet** is an object that attracts things that contain iron. To **attract** means to pull toward something.

Paper clips are made of steel, but steel has iron in it. That's why the magnets lift and hold steel paper clips. A magnet won't pick up plastic paper clips, because they don't contain iron.

This rock is magnetite. It's naturally magnetic.

How are magnets being used here?

How Magnets Interact

Magnets will attract only when the N and S poles match up.
Which magnets are attracting? Which are repelling?

For more links and animations,
go to **www.hspscience.com**

All magnets have two ends, called poles. One pole is
the north-seeking (N) pole and the other is the south-
seeking (S) pole. To see how a magnet works, use two bar
magnets. Hold the two N poles together. Can you push
them together? You probably can't. Poles that are alike
repel each other. **Repel** means "to push away." What do
you think will happen if you put the two S poles together?

Now hold opposite poles—an N pole and an S pole—
together. They pull toward each other. The opposite poles
of a magnet attract.

COMPARE AND CONTRAST

How are all magnets alike?

Magnetic Fields

If an object is **magnetic**, it attracts things that contain iron. *Magnetic* is a describing word that means something has the properties of a magnet. For example, the two poles of a magnet can be called magnetic poles.

Every magnet has a magnetic field. A magnetic field is the area around a magnet where the magnet attracts iron objects. Some magnets are stronger than others. Stronger magnets have larger magnetic fields.

> The black specks in these photos are iron filings, or small pieces of iron. They line up with a magnet's magnetic field.

> Putting opposite poles near each other causes the magnets to attract. The magnetic fields of these two magnets line up.

> Putting same poles near each other causes the magnets to repel. The magnetic fields do not line up.

You may know that Earth has a north pole and a south pole. That's because Earth is a giant magnet. The center of Earth is made of iron that is magnetic. Earth's magnetic field extends into space.

A compass is a tool that helps people find direction. Inside a compass is a bar magnet that can spin. Remember that opposite poles of two magnets attract. The small magnet in a compass spins so that its *N* pole points toward Earth's north pole.

 COMPARE AND CONTRAST

How is Earth like the magnets you have used?

People who go hiking use a compass and a map to know where they are in the woods.

A compass helps you tell which direction is north.

Are Horseshoe Magnets Like Bar Magnets?
Try to push two horseshoe magnets together. What happens? Turn one over and try again. What happens? Explain what you observe.

Essential Question

What are magnets?

Magnets are objects that attract things that contain iron. Opposite poles of two magnets attract each other, and like poles repel each other.

1. (Focus Skill) **COMPARE AND CONTRAST**

Draw and complete a graphic organizer that shows how all magnets are alike. Also tell how some magnets are different.

S3P2a

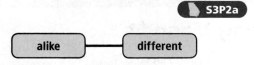

alike —— different

2. DRAW CONCLUSIONS Juan is using a bar magnet to pick up items in his room. Explain why the magnet he is using won't pick up a rubber ball. **S3P2a**

3. VOCABULARY Write two sentences about magnets. Use the words *attract* and *repel*. Then use the words in two sentences that are not about magnets. **S3P2b**

4. Critical Thinking You glue a small magnet to a box lid and another to the edge of the box. The lid pops back open every time you close it. What can you infer about the two magnets?

S3P2b

CRCT Practice

5. What must an object be made of to be attracted to a magnet?

A iron
B plastic
C rubber
D wood **S3P2a**

6. If you bring the *N* pole of one magnet toward the *S* pole of another, what will they do?

A repel
B attract
C spin
D create sparks **S3P2b**

The **Big** Idea

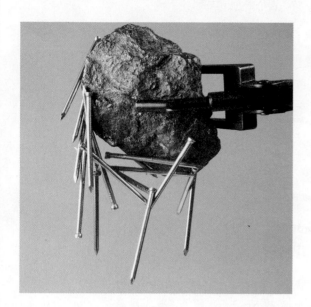

 Writing   ELA3W1c

Expository

Some objects are naturally magnetic. Research lodestone. Write a two-paragraph **description** of your findings.

9÷3 Math   M3M2b

Measuring Magnets

Use a ruler to measure the length of a bar magnet to the nearest millimeter. How long would 5 bar magnets in a row be?

 Social Studies

Magnets in History

Research the history of magnets. How did ancient civilizations use magnets? What scientists made discoveries about magnets? Share your findings in a report. Make a map that shows important places in your report.

For more links and activities, go to **www.hspscience.com**

Brunswick

MAGNETITE
in Georgia

The word *magnet* is related to the name of a mineral called *magnetite.* Magnetite is made of iron and oxygen. Magnetite is also magnetic—it acts like a magnet. People have known about its special properties since 800 B.C. Some scientists say the early Chinese may have used magnetite to make the first compass.

Magnetite is found in many counties in Georgia. Magnetite crystals are sold in rock shops. ▶

Using Earth's Resources

Magnetite is an important source of iron. In the 1800s, people dug magnetite from mines in northern Georgia. They broke up the rocks and separated the iron. The iron was used to make tools and nails. Some of it was used to make guns during the Civil War.

Finding Magnetite

In Chapter 2, you learned how rocks are weathered and broken down. Small pieces of magnetite have been carried to the coast by streams and rivers. For example, the Oconee and Altamaha Rivers carry magnetite from Georgia's mountains all the way to Brunswick on the coast. You can use a magnet to find small bits of magnetite mixed with sand and quartz on beaches.

Think And Write

1 How would you describe magnetite? S3E1b

2 Draw pictures that explain some uses of magnetite. S3P2a

Lodestone is a naturally magnetic rock.

Content

S3P2a Investigate to find common objects that are attracted to magnets.

Characteristics of Science

S3CS4b   **S3CS5c**

Essential Question

How Can We Make and Use Magnets?

Georgia Fast Fact

Recycling
Americans recycle more than 70 million tons of scrap metal each year. Powerful magnets are used to sort scrap metal. Metal that contains iron can easily be picked up by the magnets.

Powerful magnets are used to move scrap metal.

electromagnet
[ee•lek•troh•MAG•nit]
A magnet that can be turned on and off by using electricity (p. 208)

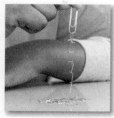

generator
[JEN•er•ayt•er]
A device that uses a magnet to produce electricity (p. 209)

temporary magnet
[TEM•puh•rair•ee MAG•nit]
A magnet made by passing an iron object near a magnet (p. 210)

Which Magnet Is Stronger?

Start with Questions

Magnets used to move scrap metal can lift very heavy objects.

- Are some magnets stronger than other magnets?

- Does a magnet have to touch an object to pull it?

Investigate to find out. Then read to find out more.

Prepare to Investigate

Inquiry Skill Tip
Graphs are a good way to communicate the data you collect in an investigation. Choose the graph style that best shows the type of data you collected. Bar graphs, line graphs, and circle graphs show data in different ways.

Materials
- bar magnet
- 10 to 20 steel paper clips
- horseshoe magnet

Make a Data Table

Magnet Data		
Kind of Magnet	Observations	Number of Paper Clips
Bar		
Horseshoe		

Follow This Procedure

1 Slowly slide the bar magnet toward a paper clip. Record what happens.

2 Slowly slide the horseshoe magnet toward a paper clip. Record what happens.

3 Pick up as many paper clips as one end of the bar magnet will hold. Count them. Record the data.

4 Pick up as many paper clips as one end of the horseshoe magnet will hold. Count them. Record the data.

Draw Conclusions

1. Which magnet is stronger? How can you tell?

2. Standards Link Why was it important to use paper clips made of steel for this investigation? **S3P2a**

3. Inquiry Skill Scientists can communicate data in graphs. Make a bar graph to show how many paper clips each magnet held. **S3CS4b**

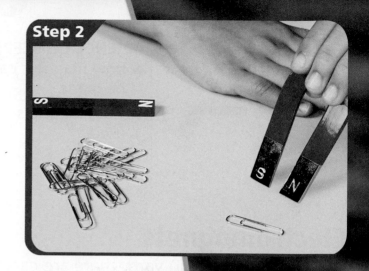

Step 2

Step 4

Independent Inquiry

If you hold two magnets together, can they lift as many paper clips as each one can separately? Plan an investigation to find out. **S3CS5c**

VOCABULARY
electromagnet p. 208
generator p. 209
temporary magnet
p. 210

SCIENCE CONCEPTS
▶ how magnets can be made
▶ ways magnets are used

Focus Skill MAIN IDEA AND DETAILS

Look for details about how magnets are used.

Main Idea

detail   detail   detail

Electromagnets

At a salvage (SAL•vij) yard, there are cars that no longer run. A very strong magnet is used to move the cars. There is one problem. After the car is on the magnet, how is it removed? A person cannot pull the car from the magnet. The magnet's pull is too strong.

Wouldn't it be handy if there were a magnet whose magnetism could be turned on and off? Well, there is—an electromagnet. An **electromagnet** is a device that uses electricity to make a magnet.

How does the boy know that the screw isn't magnetic?

It's easy to make an electromagnet. A plain screw isn't a magnet. However, the screw can be made into an electromagnet. First, wrap wire around the screw. Then, run electricity from a battery through the wire. The screw becomes a magnet that you can turn on and off. When the wires are taken off the battery, the screw is no longer a magnet.

If you wrap wire around a bar magnet, you can make a generator. A **generator** is a machine that uses a magnet to make electricity. The magnet spins inside a coil of wire and causes electricity to flow through the wire. Generators are used to make electricity when a storm knocks out power.

Focus Skill MAIN IDEA AND DETAILS

How does an electromagnet work?

What is the source of electricity for this electromagnet?

Making Magnets

An electromagnet is a kind of temporary magnet. A **temporary magnet** is a magnet that is not always a magnet. The bar magnets and horseshoe magnets you have used in Investigates are permanent magnets. They will be magnetic for a very long time.

Computers use magnetic metals to store data. The hard drive is a disk coated with iron or cobalt, a metal that acts like iron. An arm stores information on the disk by making very small sections of the disk magnetic. The arm can read the magnetic sections just as you read letters in a word.

Focus Skill MAIN IDEA AND DETAILS

How are magnets used in computers?

Insta-Lab

Make a Temporary Magnet

Hold the end of a steel needle near a steel paper clip and record what happens. Then pull the needle across the end of a bar magnet several times. Touch the needle to a steel paper clip again. What happened this time?

A computer hard drive uses magnets to store information.

Other Uses of Magnets

Magnets have many uses. They can keep cabinets closed or can hold papers on a refrigerator door. Some of your favorite games might use magnets.

Magnets can also be used to make electricity and to sort metals for recycling. Motors, computers, and compasses also use magnets.

 **MAIN IDEA AND DETAILS**

What are some ways that magnets are used?

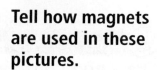

Tell how magnets are used in these pictures.

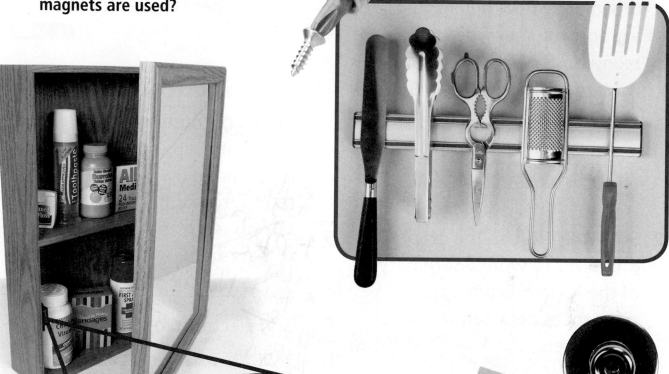

211

Essential Question

How can we make and use magnets?

Electromagnets use electricity to make a magnet. Magnets are used to move objects and to store data in computers. Generators use magnets to make electricity.

1. **(Focus Skill) MAIN IDEA AND DETAILS**
   Draw and complete a graphic organizer. Show details that support the main idea: *There are many kinds of magnets and many ways to use magnets.* **S3P2a**

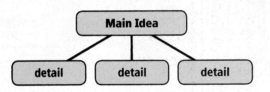

2. **SUMMARIZE** Use the graphic organizer to write a summary of the lesson. Explain the differences between the kinds of magnets. **S3P2a**

3. **VOCABULARY** Write a sentence that explains the difference between a temporary magnet and a permanent magnet. **S3P2a**

4. **Critical Thinking** Why is it important for a hospital to have an emergency generator? **S3P2a**

CRCT Practice

5. Which of these requires electricity?
   A generator
   B electromagnet
   C horseshoe magnet
   D bar magnet **S3P2a**

6. How are bar magnets and electromagnets similar?
   A They are both made of wire.
   B They both have an *N* pole and an *S* pole.
   C They are both strong, permanent magnets.
   D They both need electricity to work. **S3P2a**

The **Big** Idea

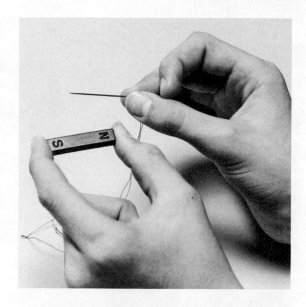

 Writing ELA3W1d

Magnetic Writing

In this lesson, you learned how to make a temporary magnet by using a needle and a bar magnet. Write an **explanation** for a friend who does not know how to do this. Make sure the steps in your explanation are clear.

9÷3 Math M3N5c

Use Fractions

There are 10 objects on a table. Only 4 of the objects contain iron. What fraction of the objects can be picked up by the magnet? Write the fraction as a decimal.

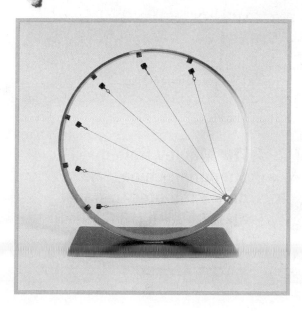

 Art

Uses for Magnets

List at least five ways that magnets are used in your home or classroom. Draw an illustration for each use.

 For more links and activities, go to **www.hspscience.com**

Using Magnets

You might not believe someone who tells you that he or she has ridden on a train that didn't have an engine. Thanks to magnets, such a train exists right now. Every day, thousands of people get to the airport in Shanghai, China, on a magnet-powered (Maglev) train. Magnetic forces in the train and in the track repel one another, so the train does not touch the track. Magnets are also used to move the train forward and keep it centered on the track. Maglev trains are only one of the many uses of magnets.

The Maglev train in Shanghai, China, takes only 8 minutes to travel about 30 km (18.6 miles). That's fast!

Magnets in Business

Magnets play an important role in business. Junkyards use big magnets to separate iron from other materials. Magnets are used in mining to separate metals from crushed rock. Credit cards have magnetic strips that contain information about the user.

Magnets at Home

You may know that magnets are used in some toys. But magnets do a lot of work around the house, too. Did you know that without magnets, some TVs would have no picture? Without magnets, many audio speakers could not vibrate to produce sound, and your music player's headphones wouldn't work. Magnets also store information on your computer's hard drive. They even hold your refrigerator door closed.

This toy uses magnets.

 Think and Write

1 Does the magnet in a refrigerator attract the door or repel the door? `S3P2a`

2 How is a Maglev train different from a typical train? `S3P2b`

 Find out more. Log on to
www.hspscience.com

Wrap-Up

▶ Visual Summary

Tell how each picture helps explain the **Big Idea**.

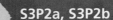 **The Big Idea** Magnets are attracted to objects with iron. Opposite ends of two magnets attract each other.

Lesson 1 S3P2a, S3P2b

The Pull of Magnets
Magnets are attracted to objects that contain iron. Every magnet has an *N* pole and an *S* pole. Similar poles on two magnets repel each other.

Lesson 2 S3P2a

Magnets All Around You
Magnets are used in many ways. Electromagnets use electricity and can be turned on and off. Generators use magnets to produce electricity.

Show What You Know

Write About Magnets/Narrative

Write a story about what would happen if your fingers or your toes were magnets. Explain how your everyday activities would be affected. What kinds of things would you not be able to do? What new things could you do?

ELA3W1g

Georgia Performance Task

Magnets in Magazines

Make a collage of pictures from old magazines showing several ways that magnets can be used. Include an explanation of how the magnets are used in each photo. Present your collage to your teacher or to the class.

S3P2a

Vocabulary Review

Match the terms to the definitions below. The page numbers tell where to look in the chapter if you need help.

magnet (p. 196)   **magnetic** (p. 198)

attract (p. 196)   **electromagnet** (p. 208)

repel (p. 197)   **generator** (p. 209)

1. To pull toward   `S3P2b`

2. A machine that uses a magnet to make electricity   `S3P2a`

3. A kind of magnet that can be turned on and off   `S3P2a`

4. To push away   `S3P2b`

5. Attracted to objects that contain iron   `S3P2a`

6. An object that attracts iron   `S3P2a`

Check Understanding

Write the letter of the best choice.

7. Which would help you know what direction is north? (p. 199)   `S3P2a`

   A electromagnet   **C** compass
   B generator   **D** magnetite

8. **COMPARE AND CONTRAST** What can electromagnets do that other magnets can't? (p. 208)   `S3P2a`
   A lift metal objects
   B coil around a wire
   C generate electricity
   D be turned on and off

9. What happens to two magnets when they are held like the magnets shown below? (p. 197)   `S3P2b`

   A They repel.
   B They attract.
   C They generate electricity.
   D They make an electromagnet.

10. **MAIN IDEA AND DETAILS** Which is **not** a use for magnets? (p. 211)   `S3P2a`
    A separating iron from other metals
    B keeping cabinet doors closed
    C heating an object
    D storing information in computers

11. Magnet A picks up six paper clips. Magnet B picks up eight paper clips. What conclusion can you draw? (p. 198) **S3P2a**

A Both magnets are strong.

B Magnet B is an electromagnet.

C Magnet B is a temporary magnet.

D Magnet A is weaker than Magnet B.

12. Which of these is **not** attracted to the *N* pole of a horseshoe magnet? (p. 197) **S3P2b**

A small pieces of iron

B the *S* pole of a bar magnet

C the *N* pole of a bar magnet

D the *S* pole of another horseshoe magnet

13. What does a generator make? (p. 209) **S3P2a**

A a magnet

B an electromagnet

C a temporary magnet

D electricity

14. A magnet attracts an object. What must the object contain? (p. 196) **S3P2a**

A iron   C rubber

B plastic   D wood

15. What are the ends of a magnet called? (p. 197) **S3P2b**

A circuits   C insulators

B conductors   D poles

16. What mineral can be identified by its magnetic properties? (p. 196) **S3P2a**

A magnetite

B quartz

C talc

D diamond

Inquiry Skills

17. Dana wants to separate steel paper clips from steel safety pins. She uses a magnet. Predict what will happen, and tell why.

S3P2a

18. As hard as Brooke tries, she can't push two horseshoe magnets together. Infer what she could do to get them to attract. **S3P2b**

Critical Thinking

19. Carson built an electromagnet. He used a battery, a nail, and some wire. His electromagnet doesn't work. Give one reason it might not work. **S3P2a**

20. Miguel held a magnet 8 cm above some steel safety pins. His magnet did not pick up any pins. Explain why.

The **Big** Idea

S3P2a

219

1. Which glass of water has the MOST heat energy?

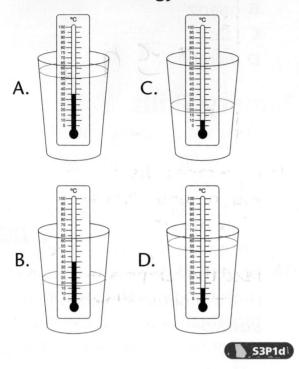

A.

C.

B.

D.

S3P1d

2. Which of these produces heat?

A. friction

B. magnetic attraction

C. recycling

D. a thermometer   S3P1a

3. Your neighbor wants to keep her home warm in winter. What could she do to help?

A. Keep the windows open.

B. Add insulation to the home.

C. Open her refrigerator door.

D. Turn on the air conditioner.

S3P1b

Use the diagram below to answer question 4.

Cup 1   Cup 2

4. Two foam cups each hold 100 mL of hot water. Brian adds 1 ice cube to Cup 1. He adds 4 ice cubes to Cup 2. What will he find when he measures the temperature of the water in both cups after one minute?

A. The temperature will be the same in both cups.

B. The temperature will be lower in Cup 2.

C. The temperature will increase in Cup 1.

D. The temperature in Cup 1 will rise. The temperature in Cup 2 will fall.   S3CS8a   S3P1d

5. What happens to hot soup when you put it into a refrigerator?

A. It changes to a gas.

B. It gets cold.

C. It freezes.

D. It bubbles.   S3P1d

6. Four roofing shingles made of different materials sit in the sun all day. The one that gets the HOTTEST is the one that

A. holds the sun's energy the most.

B. is the best insulator.

C. has the most friction.

D. is magnetic. **S3P1c**

7. Which of these releases heat?

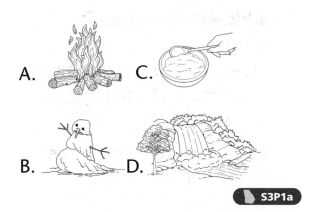

A. C.

B. D. **S3P1a**

8. Four students put hot soup in thermos bottles before they go to school. At lunchtime, they open the bottles. One student finds he has cold soup. What might be different about his bottle?

A. It conducts heat better.

B. It absorbs heat better.

C. It has better insulation.

D. It is bigger. **S3CS1b** **S3P1b**

Use the graph below to answer question 9.

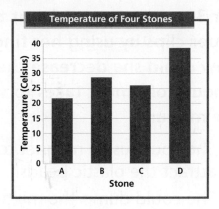

9. Uma taped thermometers to four different kinds of stones. After the stones had been in bright sunlight for 1 hour, she read the temperature on each thermometer. Which stone absorbed the sun's heat the MOST?

A. Stone A

B. Stone B

C. Stone C

D. Stone D **S3CS5c** **S3P1c**

10. Which would show the HIGHEST temperature reading on a thermometer?

A. hot tap water

B. cold tap water

C. an ice cube

D. hot tap water with an ice cube added **S3P1d**

11. Janeca mixed 20 plastic beads with 20 steel paper clips. It took her 30 seconds to pick out the paper clips by using her fingers. How could she decrease the amount of time it takes to sort the mixture?

A. She could use a magnet to attract the plastic beads.
B. She could dump the mixture into a larger bowl.
C. She could use forceps to pick out the plastic beads.
D. She could use a magnet to attract the paper clips.

S3P2b

12. Which of these will a magnet attract?

A. glass bottle
B. iron nail
C. pencil
D. basketball

S3P2a

13. Which of these magnets will attract each other?

A.

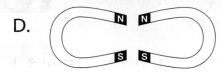
B.

C.

D.

S3P2b

Use the table below to answer question 14.

Picking Up Paper Clips	
Magnet	Number Picked Up
A	7
B	10
C	15
D	9

14. Marcia tested four magnets to see how many steel paper clips they would pick up. Which magnet is strongest?

A. Magnet A
B. Magnet B
C. Magnet C
D. Magnet D

S3P2a

15. A student finds a rock. A magnet sticks to the rock. What must the rock contain?

A. another magnet

B. carbon

C. thermal energy

D. iron

16. What do you need to make a magnet that you can turn on and off?

A. a magnet with an *N* pole and an *S* pole

B. a source of thermal energy

C. an object that is magnetic

D. an electric current

17. How can Carlos tell whether an object contains iron?

A. It will get hot when rubbed.

B. It will attract a magnet.

C. It will repel a magnet.

D. It feels cold to the touch.

Use the drawing below to answer question 18.

Magnet 1	Magnet 2

18. Which statement is true for these two magnets?

A. Their opposite poles are together.

B. Their like poles are together.

C. They are horseshoe magnets.

D. They don't have poles.

19. Georgia magnetite is

A. often recycled.

B. an electromagnet.

C. naturally magnetic.

D. loaded with copper.

20. Magnet 1 can pick up 8 steel paper clips. Magnet 2 is twice as strong. How many paper clips can Magnet 2 pick up?

A. 2

B. 8

C. 10

D. 16

UNIT C

LIFE SCIENCE

Luna moths

 GO online for student eBook www.hspscience.com

What do **you** wonder?

Luna moths are one of the largest moths in Georgia. Where can I go to see a luna moth? Why do luna moths have spots?

Unit Inquiry

Living Things and Change   Most plants and animals can only live in certain places. What happens to living things when the place that they live in changes? For example, how does a drought affect plants? Plan and conduct an experiment to find out.

Features of Georgia Plants and Animals

Georgia Performance Standards in This Chapter

Content

S3L1 Students will investigate the habitats of different organisms and the dependence of organisms on their habitat.

S3L1a   **S3L1b**

This chapter also addresses these co-requisite standards:

Characteristics of Science

S3CS1 Students will be aware of the importance of curiosity, honesty, openness, and skepticism in science and will exhibit these traits in their own efforts to understand how the world works.

S3CS1b

S3CS2 Students will have the computation and estimation skills necessary for analyzing data and following scientific explanations.

S3CS2a

S3CS7 Students will be familiar with the character of scientific knowledge and how it is achieved.

S3CS7a

S3CS8 Students will understand important features of the process of scientific inquiry.

S3CS8b

What's the Big Idea?

Certain body parts and behaviors can help plants and animals live in different places.

Essential Questions

GO online for student eBook www.hspscience.com

Seminole State Park

Dear Travis,

I learned all about woodpeckers on our trip to Seminole State Park. They have strong, sharp beaks for drilling holes in trees. Then they use their long tongues to reach insects in the holes.

Woodpeckers even have special feet for climbing up and down trees. Two toes point forward and two toes point backward to help them grasp the bark.

Talk to you soon,
Crystal

USA

What features of animals did Crystal see on her field trip? How do the features relate to the **Big Idea?**

Content

S3L1a Differentiate between habitats of Georgia (mountains, marsh/swamp, coast, Piedmont, Atlantic Ocean) and the organisms that live there.

S3L1b Identify features of green plants that allow them to live and thrive in different regions of Georgia.

Characteristics of Science

S3CS1b   **S3CS7a**

LESSON 1

Essential Question

How Do Plant Features Help Plants?

Georgia Fast Fact

Stuck on You
Sundews make two kinds of liquids. One is a sweet-smelling, sticky nectar that attracts insects into a trap. The other is a juice that digests the trapped insects. Sundews grow in swamps throughout Georgia.

Insect trapped on a sundew

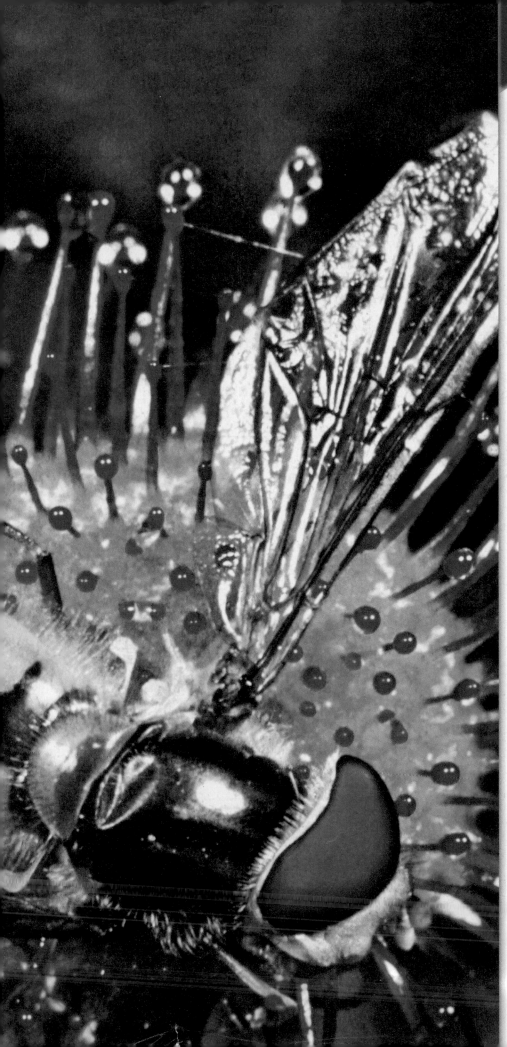

trait [TRAYT]
A characteristic, or feature, of a plant or animal (p. 232)

survive [ser•VYV]
To stay alive (p. 232)

adaptation
[ad•uhp•TAY•shuhn]
A trait that helps a living thing survive (p. 233)

reproduce
[ree•pruh•DOOS]
To produce new living things (p. 236)

Saving Water

Guided Inquiry

Start with Questions

Plants need water to live and grow. Plants have parts and features that help them save water and grow where there is not much water.

- In what ways do some plants save water?

- Are some leaf shapes better at saving water?

Investigate to find out. Then read to find out more.

Prepare to Investigate

Inquiry Skill Tip
It's a good idea to do an investigation more than once. Then you can compare the results you got every time you did the investigation. If you get different results, you must find out why.

Materials
- water
- 3 paper towels
- large, flat baking pan
- wax paper
- paper clips

Make an Observation Chart

Leaf Models	
Type of Leaf	My Observations
Flat	
Rolled	
Rolled, with waxy coating	

Follow This Procedure

1. Wet each paper towel. The paper towels will be models of leaves.

2. Place one towel flat on the pan. Roll up the second towel. Place it next to the flat towel.

3. Roll up the third towel. Fasten wax paper around it with paper clips. Place it on the pan.

4. Put the pan in a sunny place.

5. Wait about two hours. Feel the towels and record your observations.

Draw Conclusions

1. Which towel felt the dampest? Which one was the driest?

2. **Standards Link** Why do you think some plants have a waxy coating on their leaves?
   S3L1b

3. **Inquiry Skill** Compare your observations with the observations from other groups in the class. Did all groups have the same results? What could have caused any differences in the results between groups?
   S3CS7a

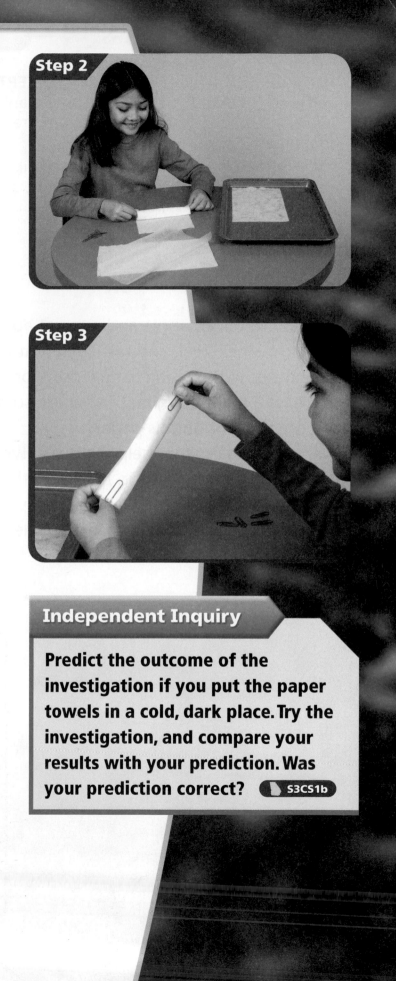

Step 2

Step 3

Independent Inquiry

Predict the outcome of the investigation if you put the paper towels in a cold, dark place. Try the investigation, and compare your results with your prediction. Was your prediction correct? **S3CS1b**

VOCABULARY
trait p. 232
survive p. 232
adaptation p. 233
reproduce p. 236

SCIENCE CONCEPTS
▶ what some plant adaptations are
▶ how a plant's features help it survive, grow, and reproduce

Focus Skill MAIN IDEA AND DETAILS
Look for examples of different kinds of adaptations.

Main Idea

detail   detail   detail

Plant Parts

It's easy to tell an apple and a carrot apart. They look, smell, feel, and taste different from one another. A **trait** is a characteristic, or feature, of a plant or animal. What are some traits of the plant on this page?

Plants have parts that help them **survive**, or stay alive. Their roots take in the water they need from the soil. Some plants also have thorns that keep animals from eating them.

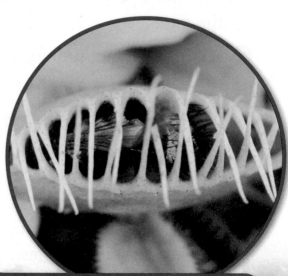

The Venus' flytrap has leaves that close when insects land on them. The plant gets nutrients from the insects because the soil is missing some nutrients the plant needs.

▲ This corn plant has roots called prop roots. They are adaptations that help some plants stand up.

The thorns on this rosebush are an adaptation. They protect it from some animals that would eat it.

A feature that helps a living thing survive is called an **adaptation**. Sharp spines are one kind of adaptation. They protect plants such as cacti from being eaten by animals. Not many animals try to eat plants that have spines!

Some adaptations are not parts. They are ways plants or animals act that help them survive. Sunflowers turn slowly during the day to keep facing the sun. This helps them get as much sunlight as they can.

Focus Skill MAIN IDEA AND DETAILS

What is an example of an adaptation that helps a plant survive?

233

Adaptations Help Plants Grow

Plants need nutrients, water, sunlight, and air. Many plants have adaptations that help them get these things so that they can grow.

Wood is an adaptation that helps trees grow tall. In a forest, the tallest plants get the most sunlight. Tree trunks are made of wood, which is very strong. It can support the tree as it grows upward. Without wood, a tree would bend or fall over.

Vines have an adaptation for growth, too. Their stems can wrap around other plants. This helps them grow toward the sunlight.

The stem of this vine has parts that hold on to other plants. This adaptation helps the vine climb upward.

The roots of carrot and radish plants store food. The plants use this food to grow.

Roots are used for getting water and nutrients. Some plants have fat roots, in which they store food. They use this food for growth.

Without water, a plant can't grow. Some desert plants have roots that grow deep into the soil. They reach water that is far under the ground. Other desert plants have roots that spread out just under the surface. This lets them take in water quickly when it rains.

 MAIN IDEA AND DETAILS

What is an example of an adaptation that helps a plant grow?

The leaves of this plant form a cup that collects rainwater. This adaptation helps the plant get the water it needs to grow. ▼

Adaptations That Help Plants Reproduce

Have you ever planted a seed and watched a new plant grow? Some plants use seeds to **reproduce**, or produce new living things. All living things reproduce.

The flowers of plants need pollen from other flowers to make seeds. They have adaptations that help them get that pollen. Their smell, color, and shape may attract insects and other animals. The animals get pollen on them and carry it from flower to flower.

Smell can be an adaptation. This flower that grows in Indonesia smells like rotten meat. The smell attracts flies, which carry the pollen to other carrion flowers.

Flowers make a sweet liquid called nectar. This adaptation attracts bees, which carry pollen from one flower to another.

The coconut palm grows on tropical beaches. A coconut is a giant seed. It travels from one island to another by floating on the water.

When seeds fall from a maple tree, they spin like helicopter blades. This adaptation helps the seeds "fly" to new places.

Soft fluff covers thistle seeds. These seeds can be blown by the wind to new places.

Sometimes seeds need to spread to new places to grow. Some plants have seeds that stick to animals. The animals spread the seeds as they move about. Other plants have tiny seeds that the wind can carry. Some seeds can float on water. They may be carried far from the parent plant.

MAIN IDEA AND DETAILS

What is one adaptation that helps plants reproduce?

Hide and Seek

Put 10 peas and 10 kernels of corn on yellow paper. Close your eyes for a minute. Then open them and pick up the first 5 seeds you see. Which ones did you pick up? How can the color of a seed protect it?

Essential Question

How do plant features help plants?

In this lesson, you read about many examples of plant adaptations. Plants have adaptations that help them survive, grow, and reproduce.

1. **Focus Skill** MAIN IDEA AND DETAILS

Draw and complete a graphic organizer. Show the supporting details of the main idea: *Plants have adaptations.*   **S3L1b**

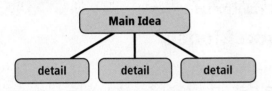

Main Idea

detail   detail   detail

2. DRAW CONCLUSIONS What might happen to a cactus if it did not have spines?   **S3L1b**

3. VOCABULARY Write a sentence for each of the four vocabulary words. Show that you know what the words mean.   **S3L1b**

4. Critical Thinking Explain why a plant that lives under water can't survive in a desert.   **S3L1a**

CRCT Practice

5. Which feature would be **most** helpful to a plant in a desert?

A waxy leaves

B large seeds

C small roots

D smelly flowers   **S3L1a**

6. Which feature of a rose helps it grow without being eaten by large animals?

A flowers with bright colors

B sharp thorns

C small seeds

D deep roots   **S3L1b**

The **Big** Idea

Writing ELA3W1j

Write a Description

Choose a plant with an adaptation that interests you. Write a description of what the adaptation looks like. Tell how it helps the plant survive, grow, or reproduce.

Math M3N5g

Use Fraction Models

The mesquite tree grows long roots that reach water in the desert. In one area, water is 4 meters underground. One mesquite tree's roots are now 3 meters long. Make a drawing of the tree, its roots, and the water. Have the roots grown more or less than half the distance to the water?

Social Studies M&G 8

Georgia Plants

Find out more about a plant that grows in Georgia, such as the prickly pear cactus. Draw a map showing where the plant grows in Georgia. Tell what adaptations the plant has that help it survive, grow, and reproduce.

For more links and activities, go to www.hspscience.com

Mistletoe State Park

Northwest of Augusta, Georgia, is Mistletoe State Park. The park was named for the American mistletoe, a plant that grows in all parts of Georgia. You won't find mistletoe growing out of the ground. That's because mistletoe lives by attaching itself to the branches of trees. Mistletoe is a parasite. This means it takes energy or nutrients from other plants.

Visitors to the park enjoy fishing and camping. People hike the nature trails through the pine and hardwood forests. Sweet gum, tulip poplar, red maple, and white oak trees also grow in the park.

How Mistletoe Lives

Most plants use their roots to get water and nutrients from the soil. However, mistletoe takes water and nutrients from the tree it lives on. It has rootlike structures that grow through the tree's bark and into the tree. Mistletoe stays green all year. A few mistletoe plants will not kill a healthy tree, but a lot of them can. They weaken the tree, so wind and cold injure it more easily.

Mistletoe Provides Food

Mistletoe berries have sticky seeds inside. The berries are poisonous for people to eat, but birds can eat them. The seeds stick to their beaks. When the birds wipe their beaks off on tree branches, the seeds stick. That's how mistletoe seeds end up high in trees.

Mistletoe attaches to the branches of trees.

Think And Write

1. It's easier to see mistletoe in winter than in summer. Suggest a reason why. **S3L1a**

2. What are some adaptations that help mistletoe grow? **S3L1b**

Content

 S3L1a Differentiate between habitats of Georgia (mountains, marsh/swamp, coast, Piedmont, Atlantic Ocean) and the organisms that live there.

 **S3L1c** Identify features of animals that allow them to live and thrive in different regions of Georgia.

Characteristics of Science

S3CS2a **S3CS8b**

LESSON 2

Essential Question

How Do Animal Features Help Animals?

Georgia Fast Fact

Snappy Adaptations
The tip of an alligator snapping turtle's tongue looks like a worm. They wait under water for a fish to swim by and approach the "worm." Then, they snap their mouths shut and capture the fish. Alligator snapping turtles live in southwestern Georgia.

hibernate [HY•ber•nayt]
To spend the winter in a kind of deep sleep (p. 248)

migrate [MY•grayt]
To travel from one place to another and back again (p. 249)

Alligator snapping turtle

Keeping Warm

Start with Questions

On a cold day, you might wear a jacket and a hat to keep warm.

● How do animals that live in cold places stay warm?

Investigate to find out. Then read to find out more.

Prepare to Investigate

Inquiry Skill Tip
How do seals stay warm in the cold ocean? To answer that question, scientists would plan an experiment. An experiment should test a hypothesis, or possible answer to a question.

Materials

● large plastic bowl
● water
● ice
● spoon
● plastic bag
● solid vegetable shortening
● pair of plastic gloves

Make an Observation Chart

Description of Hand	Observations of Hand
With shortening	
Without shortening	

Follow This Procedure

1 Fill the bowl with water and ice. Half-fill the bag with shortening.

2 Put on the plastic gloves. Put one hand into the bag. Mold the shortening so that it evenly covers your hand.

3 Now put both hands into the ice water. Compare the ways your hands feel. Record your observations.

Step 2

Step 3

Draw Conclusions

1. Which hand felt warmer in the ice water?

2. Standards Link How do you think the layer of blubber, or fat, under a seal's skin is like the shortening? **S3L1c**

3. Inquiry Skill Scientists plan experiments to answer questions. What question did this experiment answer?

S3CS8b

Independent Inquiry

You could improve your data by using a thermometer. Make three balls of shortening that are different thicknesses. Place a thermometer in each ball. Then put the balls of shortening into ice water and record the changes in temperature. **S3CS2a**

VOCABULARY
hibernate p. 248
migrate p. 249

SCIENCE CONCEPTS
▶ what adaptations animals have
▶ how adaptations help animals survive, grow, and reproduce

Focus Skill **CAUSE AND EFFECT**
Look for ways that adaptations affect the lives of animals.

cause ⟶ effect

Adaptations for Survival

In Lesson 1, you read about some plant adaptations. Animals also have adaptations to help them survive.

For example, eagles have adaptations for flying and for catching food. An eagle's eyes can spot prey from a mile away! The birds' strong wings help them fly fast. Eagles have sharp claws they can use to grab and hold their prey. They also have sharp beaks for eating their food.

▲ Eagles have sharp claws and strong wings.

The large mouth of a largemouth bass is an adaptation for catching and eating food.

Black bears have short, curved claws for climbing. These claws help them reach fruit and leaves in trees.

◀ A crab's shell and claws protect it from other animals that would eat it. Its claws also help it catch food.

Eagles would not be able to live in the water. They do not have features for surviving there. Fish have gills that can take oxygen out of the water. Fish use their tail and fins to swim through the water, just like an eagle uses its wings to fly through the air.

CAUSE AND EFFECT What is one effect of an eagle's sharp claws?

Insta-Lab

Thumbs Down
Tuck your thumb into the palm of your hand. Without moving your thumb, try to pick up an object. Now try to write your name. Share your observations with a classmate. How is the thumb a useful adaptation for humans?

Behaviors

Animals have behaviors, or ways of acting, that help them survive. You do, too. You eat when you are hungry. In winter, you wear a coat to stay warm.

Winter is hard for some animals. There is little food. In fall, some animals eat more and build up fat. Then they **hibernate**, or spend the winter in a kind of deep sleep. They do not use much energy. They live off their fat. Hibernating is an adaptation.

▲ A hibernating animal's body gets cold. The lower body temperature helps it use less energy.

This chipmunk spends the winter months hibernating. It curls into a ball and moves very little.

Math in Science
Interpret Data

When an animal hibernates, its heart beats more slowly. Use this graph to find each animal's active heartbeat rate and hibernating heartbeat rate. Find the differences between them.

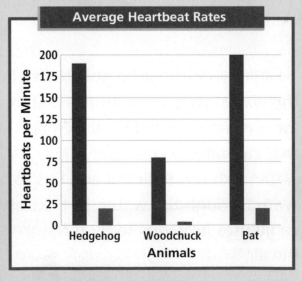

Average Heartbeat Rates

KEY ■ = Active ■ = Hibernation

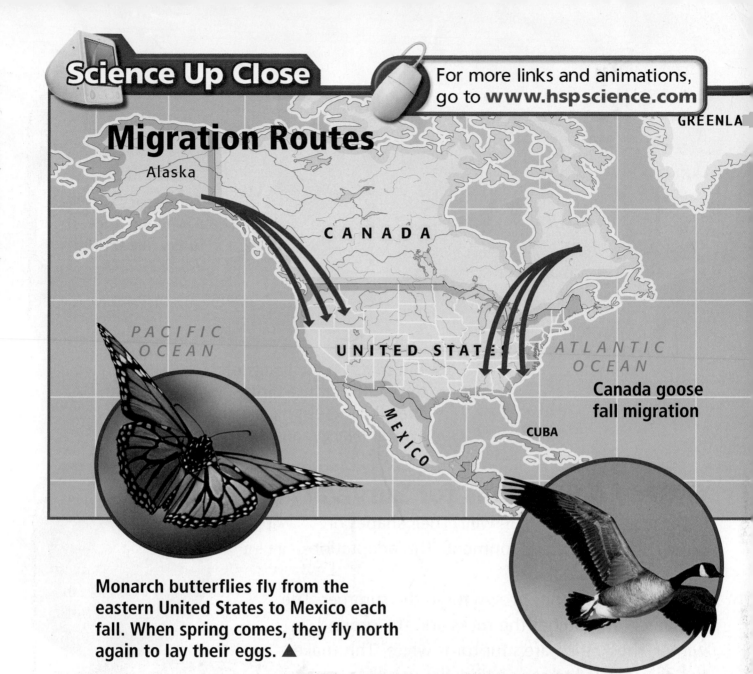

Migration Routes

Alaska

GREENLA

C A N A D A

PACIFIC
OCEAN

UNITED STATE

ATLANTIC
OCEAN

MEXICO

CUBA

Canada goose
fall migration

**Monarch butterflies fly from the
eastern United States to Mexico each
fall. When spring comes, they fly north
again to lay their eggs.** ▲

▲ **In fall, Canada
geese fly south.**

Other animals **migrate** to survive. To migrate is to
travel from one place to another and back again. In
summer, gray whales live near Alaska. In fall, when the
ocean becomes colder, they swim south. They migrate to
warmer waters off the coast of California. In spring, they
swim north.

Animals do not need to learn how and when to
hibernate and migrate. They know these behaviors
without being taught. These behaviors are adaptations.

 **CAUSE AND EFFECT**   What causes animals to hibernate?

This insect is called a walking stick. It looks like a twig.

◀ The spots on the wings of this moth confuse birds. They think the spots are the eyes of a larger animal.

Other Adaptations for Survival

Some animals can hide well. Their shapes or colors match their environment. This adaptation helps them hide.

The Arctic hare has brown fur in the summer. The brown color matches the rocks and the ground. In winter, the Arctic hare's fur turns white. This makes the animal hard to see against the snow. Animals that eat hares may not see them.

▲ A green anole can change colors to match its background so other animals do not see it.

◀ These stonefish look like rocks. Smaller fish swim close by and get eaten!

Some animals survive by looking like other animals. The milk snake is not deadly. The coral snake is. These snakes look very much alike. People can tell them apart. Animals that eat snakes cannot, so they leave both alone. Looking like the deadly coral snake keeps the milk snake safe.

Focus Skill CAUSE AND EFFECT

What is the effect of looking like a dangerous animal?

Many animals do not take care of their eggs or young. Some frogs lay hundreds of eggs, as you see here. Laying large numbers of eggs is an adaptation that makes sure some eggs survive.

Some animals have only a few young, but they take care of them. Most of these young survive. ▼

Brown thrashers

Essential Question

How do animal features help animals?

In this lesson, you learned that animals have adaptations. Adaptations help animals grow, survive, and reproduce. Adaptations help living things meet their needs in the environment in which they live.

1. (Focus Skill) **CAUSE AND EFFECT** Choose three animal features. Complete a graphic organizer for each feature to show how the feature affects the animal's life. **S3L1c**

2. SUMMARIZE Write a summary of this lesson. Begin with the sentence *Animals have features that help them survive.* **S3L1c**

3. VOCABULARY Write a paragraph that explains how the terms *adaptation, hibernate,* and *migrate* are related. **S3L1c**

4. Critical Thinking Some small animals in the ocean migrate to the surface at night and back to deep water during the day. Why might they do this? **S3L1a**

CRCT Practice

5. In which month would a bat in Georgia have the slowest heartbeat rate?

A April   **C** October

B July   **D** January

S3L1c

6. Which feature helps an animal hide from other animals?

The **Big** Idea

A looking like a dangerous animal

B being the same color as the place it lives

C having sharp claws or a strong shell

D having only a few young and caring for them **S3L1c**

Writing
ELA3W1g

Write a Narrative
Choose an animal that hibernates, such as a bat, a chipmunk, a hedgehog, a woodchuck, or a ground squirrel. Write a **story** about how that animal gets ready for hibernation. Develop the characters in your story by telling what they say or do.

Math
M3N4f

Use Division
A gray whale comes to the surface every three minutes to take a breath. How many times will a gray whale come to the surface in 15 minutes? In one hour?

Art

Make-Believe Adaptations
Make up an animal with an adaptation that helps it survive. Then make a model of that animal out of clay, or draw it on a sheet of paper. Explain its adaptations to a small group or to the class.

For more links and activities, go to **www.hspscience.com**

▶ **AKIRA OKUBO**

▶ Oceanographer

▶ Learned why fish swim in large groups

Akira Okubo

When he was a boy, Akira Okubo watched schools of fish, or large groups of fish swimming together. He learned that fish form schools for protection. A school of tiny fish can look like one large fish, too big for other hungry fish to eat.

Okubo became an oceanographer, a scientist who studies oceans. He studied schools that had several million fish. All of the fish in a school are about the same size. Adult fish and young fish swim in different schools.

Tiny fish can't fight bigger fish, but they can fool them! Schooling is an adaptation that helps fish survive in their ocean environment.

 Think and Write

❶ How is schooling an adaptation? **S3L1c**

❷ Think about animals that live on land. Give two examples of land animals that live together to survive. **S3L1a**

Some fish swim together their whole lives!

Rebecca Champion

At a bend of the Chattahoochee River near Columbus lies Oxbow Meadows Environmental Learning Center. For many years, Dr. Rebecca Champion directed the center. Visitors can see many kinds of Georgia plants and animals.

The center's "treetop trail" is a walkway through the forest canopy. Many animals have adaptations for living in treetops. However, to see the treetops, people needed to build a bridge. From nearly 11 meters (35 feet) above the ground, visitors can see snakes, birds, insects, and frogs. Students learn about adaptations that enable animals to live in treetops.

Dr. Champion invited many people to visit the center and "touch a turtle, measure a tree, visit a beaver's home, or soar with a butterfly." She feels that people who learn about nature will want to help protect it.

▶ **DR. REBECCA CHAMPION**

▶ Associate Professor of Biology, Columbus State University
▶ Former Director, Oxbow Meadows Environmental Learning Center

Think and Write

❶ What features of birds help them live in treetops?　S3L1c

❷ Is protecting some forests important? Explain why or why not.　S3L1d

> By using a special bridge, students learn about plants and animals that live in treetops.

Wrap-Up

▶ Visual Summary

Tell how each picture helps explain the **Big Idea**.

The Big Idea Certain body parts and behaviors can help plants and animals live in different places.

Lesson 1 S3L1a, S3L1b

Features of Plants

Plants have adaptations, or features that help them survive, grow, and reproduce. The features of a plant depend on the place the plant lives. Different places require different features.

Lesson 2 S3L1a, S3L1c

Features of Animals

Animals also have adaptations. Adaptations can be body parts or behaviors. Like a plant's adaptations, an animal's adaptations help it survive, grow, and reproduce where it lives.

Show What You Know

Write About Animal Features/Informational

Write two paragraphs explaining the differences between a fish and a bird. Explain how the features of the two animals help them live in different places. Also describe features that both fish and birds have in common.

ELA3W1d

Georgia Performance Task

Make a Plant or Animal Diorama

Make a diorama that shows the features of one kind of plant or animal. Add labels that explain how the features help the plant or animal survive where it lives. For example, you could show how the features of a cactus help it survive in the desert.

S3L1b   **S3L1c**

Vocabulary Review

Match the terms to the definitions below. The page numbers tell you where to look in the chapter if you need help.

trait p. 232   **reproduce** p. 236

survive p. 232   **hibernate** p. 248

adaptation p. 233   **migrate** p. 249

1. To travel from one place to another and back again **S3L1c**

2. A trait that helps a living thing survive and reproduce **S3L1b**

3. A feature, or characteristic, of a plant or animal **S3L1b**

4. To spend the winter in a kind of deep sleep **S3L1c**

5. To stay alive **S3L1b**

6. To produce more of a living thing **S3L1b**

Check Understanding

Choose the best answer.

7. Which is **not** a feature of an eagle? (p. 246) **S3L1c**
   A strong claws
   B good eyesight
   C sharp beak
   D webbed feet

8. What happens to an animal when it hibernates? (p. 248) **S3L1c**
   A Its heart beats faster.
   B Its heart beats slower.
   C Its breathing speeds up.
   D It moves from one habitat to another.

9. **CAUSE AND EFFECT** Which animal has an adaptation that causes other animals to fear it? (p. 251) **S3L1c**
   A a white arctic hare in the snow
   B a fly with stripes like a bee's
   C a frog burrowing deep into the ground for winter
   D ducks traveling in a group in search of food

10. A bird flies south each fall and north each spring. What is it doing? (p. 249) **S3L1c**
    A adapting   C migrating
    B hibernating   D reproducing

11. Which kind of adaptation does the animal in the picture below have? (p. 250) **S3L1c**
    A It blends in with its environment.
    B It eats brown leaves.
    C It hibernates.
    D It migrates.

12. Why do plants produce a sugary, sweet-smelling liquid called nectar? (p. 236) **S3L1b**

  A to attract insects

  B to feed their young

  C to keep from being eaten

  D to survive cold winters

13. Why do magnolia trees have wax on their leaves? (p. 231) **S3L1b**

  A to make the leaves taste bad

  B to cause insects to slide off

  C to help the leaves stay cool

  D to keep water inside

14. **MAIN IDEA AND DETAILS**

How do seeds from maple trees travel far from their parent plant? (p. 237) **S3L1b**

  A They are covered with soft fluff that is blown by the wind.

  B They float on water and are moved by waves.

  C They spin like helicopter blades.

  D They stick to the fur of animals.

15. Where would you expect to find plants with special stems that can wrap around other plants? (p. 234) **S3L1a**

  A in a pond

  B in a forest

  C in a desert

  D in a field of grasses

16. Which plant can grow in soil that is missing some of the nutrients the plant needs to survive? (p. 232) **S3L1b**

  A sunflower   **C** radish

  B venus flytrap   **D** corn

Inquiry Skills

17. You are working on a science fair project. You do an experiment, and you get interesting results. Why would you want to repeat the experiment? **S3CS7a**

18. Marco made a model of a seal by spreading shortening on his hand. How is Marco's model like a seal? How is the model different? **S3CS4c**

Critical Thinking

19. While on vacation in Georgia's mountains, Gina finds a flower that she thinks is beautiful. She collects some seeds from the plant. Do you think the plant will grow well at Gina's house near the beach? Explain why or why not. **S3L1a**

20. Choose a living thing and describe an adaptation it has. How does the adaptation help the living thing survive?

The Big Idea

S3L1c

Georgia Performance Standards in This Chapter

Content

S3L1 Students will investigate the habitats of different organisms and the dependence of organisms on their habitat.

S3L1a **S3L1b**
S3L1c **S3L1d**

This chapter also addresses these co-requisite standards:

Characteristics of Science

S3CS1 Students will be aware of the importance of curiosity, honesty, openness, and skepticism in science and will exhibit these traits. . . .

S3CS1b

S3CS4 Students will use ideas of system, model, change, and scale in exploring scientific and technological matters.

S3CS4b

S3CS5 Students will communicate scientific ideas and activities clearly.

S3CS5b

S3CS8 Students will understand important features of the process of scientific inquiry.

S3CS8a **S3CS8b**

What's the Big Idea?

Georgia has many habitats. Each habitat contains different living things.

Essential Questions

Go online ▸ for student eBook
www.hspscience.com

Piedmont National Wildlife Refuge

USA

Dear Todd,

Today our class visited the Piedmont National Wildlife Refuge. The refuge is about 20 miles north of Macon. We had to drive several hours to get there.

We saw a lot of interesting plants and animals that don't live near my house on the coast. My favorite thing that we saw was a mother deer and her young fawn.

I'll send you pictures!
Kendra

What did Kendra notice about the plants and animals at the refuge? How do you think that relates to the **Big Idea?**

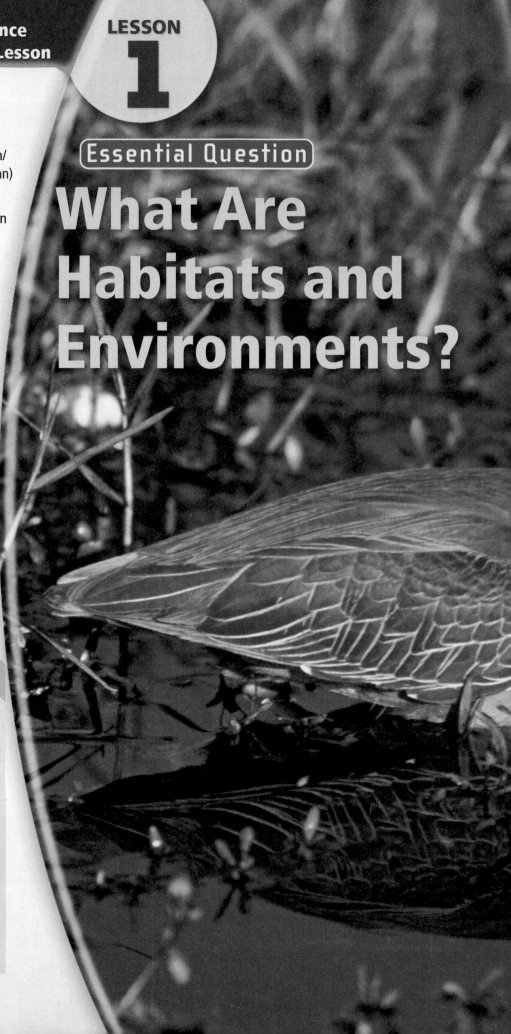

Content

 S3L1a Differentiate between habitats of Georgia (mountains, marsh/swamp, coast, Piedmont, Atlantic Ocean) and the organisms that live there.

S3L1d Explain what will happen to an organism if the habitat is changed.

Characteristics of Science

S3CS1b **S3CS8a**

LESSON

1

Essential Question

What Are Habitats and Environments?

Georgia Fast Fact

Stuck in the Muck
Try to walk through a swamp, and you may get stuck in the mud. Some birds, such as this green heron, have adaptations for living in swamps. In fact, green herons can't live in places where there are no swamps, lakes, or ponds.

Green heron at Banks Lake
National Wildlife Refuge

environment
[en•vy•ruhn•muhnt]
Everything that is around
a living thing (p. 267)

ecosystem
[EE•koh•sis•tuhm] All the
living and nonliving
things that interact in
a place (p. 268)

habitat [HAB•ih•tat]
The place where a plant
or an animal lives (p. 269)

263

Observe an Environment

Start with Questions

Every day, you see the same things all around you. The people, cars, and buildings around you don't change much.

- Do you see more things when you look closely at a place?

- What are some things that are all around other animals?

Investigate to find out. Then read to find out more.

Prepare to Investigate

Inquiry Skill Tip
Before you infer, define any important terms. In this Investigate, for example, you must understand what *living* and *nonliving* mean before you can infer which things fit in each category.

Materials
- safety goggles
- wire coat hanger

Make a Data Table

Things in My Environment			
Living Things	Number	Nonliving Things	Number

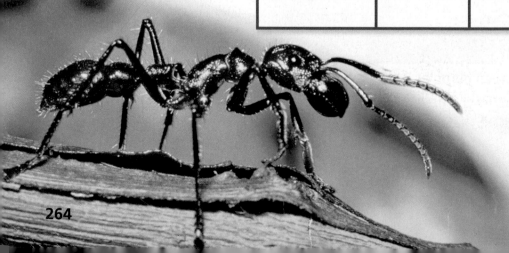

Follow This Procedure

CAUTION: Put on safety goggles to bend the wire hanger.

1. Bend the coat hanger into a square. Ask your teacher for help if necessary.

2. Go outside. Place the square on the ground. Closely observe the ground inside the square.

3. Record all the living things you observe and how many there are of each. Then record all the nonliving things and how many there are of each.

4. Share your table with a classmate. Compare the environments you observed.

Step 2

Step 3

Draw Conclusions

1. Compare the things you found in your environment with the things a classmate found. Why do you think you found different things?

2. **Standards Link** Choose one living thing you observed. Describe the things that are important in its environment.

   🔖 S3L1a

3. **Inquiry Skill** How did you Infer which things were nonliving and which things were living?

   🔖 S3CS1b

Independent Inquiry

With an adult, observe an environment at or near your home. Compare the environment you observed at school with the environment you observed at or near your home.   🔖 S3CS8a

265

VOCABULARY
environment p. 267
ecosystem p. 268
habitat p. 269

SCIENCE CONCEPTS
▶ what an environment is
▶ what an ecosystem is

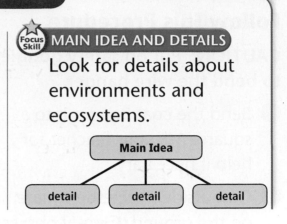

Focus Skill MAIN IDEA AND DETAILS
Look for details about environments and ecosystems.

Where Things Live

Living things need a place to live and grow. Fish live in water. Many birds live in trees and fly through the air. Most plants grow where there is soil, water, and sun.

Living things can be found almost everywhere on Earth. Some fish can live in the deepest parts of the oceans. Some plants can live on the tops of high mountains. Scorpions can survive in dry deserts. Cattails can grow in wetlands.

Some plants live in between the cracks of pavement to get the sunlight they need.

Everything that surrounds a living thing makes up its **environment**. Plants and animals use things from their environments to meet their needs. What is your environment like?

Many living things may share an environment and its resources—food, water, oxygen, and space. If the environment has too little of any of these things, the living things compete with one another to get what they need.

▲ **Koalas in Australia live in eucalyptus trees, whose leaves are their only food.**

 MAIN IDEA AND DETAILS

What do living things get from their environments?

These prairie dogs can survive and grow in a grassy environment. ▼

This bird makes its nest on a chimney high above the city. ▼

267

Parts of an Ecosystem

The living things in and around a pond interact with one another. Fish eat insects. Frogs sit on lily pads. Birds hide and build nests in grasses and reeds.

Living things also interact with nonliving things in their environment. Turtles rest on the mud and warm themselves in the sun. Deer and raccoons drink water from the pond. Plants need nutrients in the soil.

An **ecosystem** is made up of all the living and nonliving things that interact in one place. Georgia has many different ecosystems. The Okefenokee swamp ecosystem is different than a forest ecosystem in north Georgia.

Science Up Close

Pond Ecosystem

Many plants and animals live in a pond ecosystem. The ecosystem includes all the living and nonliving things that interact with one another.

Fish live in the water. They may reach up to eat insects just above the surface.

Turtles are faster in water than on land. They eat frogs, small fish, worms, and plants.

For more links and animations, go to **www.hspscience.com**

There are many kinds of living things in an ecosystem. However, they don't all live in the same part of the ecosystem. Fish swim in water, but ducks live on top of the water. The place in an ecosystem where a plant or animal lives is its **habitat**. A habitat includes both living and nonliving things.

Focus Skill MAIN IDEA AND DETAILS

Which is larger—a turtle's habitat or a pond ecosystem?

Insta-Lab

Ecosystems Around You
Find out about an ecosystem that is close to where you live. Research what types of plants and animals live there. Draw and color the ecosystem. Label the animals and plants.

Birds such as this kingfisher hunt for fish and frogs near the pond's edge.

Waterlilies float on the surface of the pond. Frogs often rest on their leaves.

Snails crawl on plants that live in shallow water near the pond's edge.

269

Living Things and Their Habitats

Most living things can survive only in certain habitats. A polar bear, for example, could not find the water it needs in a desert. A rain forest would be too wet for a desert owl.

A living thing's habitat gives it everything it needs to survive. For example, a pond has the water, food, and oxygen that a fish needs. The fish could not survive without these things. What does your habitat provide for you?

MAIN IDEA AND DETAILS

What does a living thing's habitat provide for it?

▲ **The scarlet macaw lives high in the trees of the rain forest. It feeds on the fruits and large nuts that grow there.**

◀ **Mountain goats live on rocky cliffs, where they feed on plants growing among the rocks.**

Changes to Ecosystems

You learned that all the living and nonliving things in an ecosystem interact. When one part of an ecosystem changes, it can affect all the other parts.

For example, beavers cut down trees to build a dam on a stream. Birds and insects that live in the trees lose their homes. The dam blocks the flow of water and causes a pond to form. Animals that can live only in streams must move or they may die.

People also change ecosystems. When we cut down trees or drain wetlands, we destroy the habitats of many living things. These living things must find new places to live.

 **MAIN IDEA AND DETAILS**

What happens when an ecosystem changes?

This forest is being cut down. Many living things are affected by the changes to this ecosystem. ▼

Essential Question

What are habitats and environments?

Different living things are found in different places. Although many kinds of plants and animals can be found in one ecosystem, each kind has a different habitat.

1. **(Focus Skill) MAIN IDEA AND DETAILS**
Draw and complete a graphic organizer. Show details that support this main idea: *A pond ecosystem has living and nonliving parts.* **S3L1a**

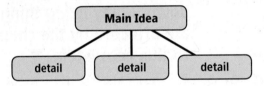

Main Idea

detail detail detail

2. **DRAW CONCLUSIONS** What happens to plants and animals when an environment changes? **S3L1d**

3. **VOCABULARY** Write two sentences that explain how an environment and an ecosystem are different. **S3L1a**

4. **Critical Thinking** Explain why a plant that lives under water can't survive in a forest. **S3L1a**

CRCT Practice

5. Which of these is a good description of the habitat of an alligator?
   A Alligators live in swamps.
   B Alligators live on the bottom of a pond and come on land when it is sunny and warm.
   C Alligators eat fish, birds, and other small animals.
   D Alligators have scales on their skin for protection. **S3L1a**

6. Which animal is **not** affected when a pond dries up?
   A frog
   B turtle
   C fish
   D whale **S3L1d**

The Big Idea

 Writing ELA3W1m

Describe a Habitat

Identify plants and animals that live near your home. Make a list. Choose one of the plants or animals. Make a word web describing its habitat. Then write a **description** of the plant or animal's habitat, including some of the terms in your word web.

 Math M3N2a

Counting Birds

Doug lives in the mountains of Georgia. He counts 32 different kinds of birds living there. On a vacation to the coast, he counts 19 different kinds of birds. How many more kinds of birds did Doug count in the mountains? Show your work. Then write a sentence explaining how you can check your answer.

 Art

Label a Drawing

Choose an animal and draw a picture showing the animal's habitat. Then label the parts of the habitat. Use one color label for the parts of the habitat that are living, and use a different color for nonliving parts.

 For more links and activities, go to **www.hspscience.com**

Content

 S3L1a Differentiate between habitats of Georgia (mountains, marsh/swamp, coast, Piedmont, Atlantic Ocean) and the organisms that live there.

 S3L1b Identify features of green plants that allow them to live and thrive in different regions of Georgia.

 S3L1c Identify features of animals that allow them to live and thrive in different regions of Georgia.

Characteristics of Science

 S3CS4b   **S3CS5b**

Georgia Fast Fact

Where Ocean Meets Land
Georgia's coastline is more than 160 kilometers (100 miles) long. The Atlantic coast of Georgia stretches from the Savannah River, in the north, to the Cumberland Island National Seashore, in the south. There are many small islands just off Georgia's coast. Sandy beaches make up much of Georgia's coastline.

LESSON 2

Essential Question

What Are Some Habitats in Georgia?

Cumberland Island
National Seashore

mountain [MOWNT•uhn]
A high, raised part of
Earth's surface (p. 278)

piedmont [PEED•mahnt]
An area, with many
hills, located between
the mountains and the
coastal plain (p. 280)

coastal plain
[KOH•stuhl PLAYN] An area
of low, flat land near an
ocean (p. 282)

wetland [WET•lund]
Land that is covered with
water most of the time
(p. 285)

Plant and Animal Homes

Guided Inquiry

Start with Questions

Think about the land around you. What plants and animals live in Georgia?

- Name a plant or an animal you have seen or heard about.

- What habitat does the plant or animal use as its home?

Investigate to find out. Then read to find out more.

Prepare to Investigate

Inquiry Skill Tip

To draw a conclusion, use the data you have collected and what you already know. Then decide what makes sense.

You Need

- this book and other reference books
- index cards
- crayons or markers

Make an Observation Chart

Plant and Animal Homes	
Plant or Animal	Habitat

Follow This Procedure

1. Look through the book to find a picture of a plant or an animal that lives in Georgia. Read about it.

2. Record the name of each plant and animal in your data table. Record a description of each habitat.

3. On an index card, draw a picture of the plant or animal. Write the name of the plant or animal below the picture.

4. On another index card, draw a picture of where the plant or animal lives, and write a sentence to describe the place.

5. Play a game in which you trade cards with a partner and match each plant or animal picture with its habitat. Tell your partner what you learned about your plants and animals.

Step 3

Step 5

Draw Conclusions

1. Compare two animals that live in the same habitat. How are their body structures alike and different?

2. **Standards Link** Choose two Georgia animals or plants that you discussed. How are their habitats different? **S3L1a**

3. **Inquiry Skill** What conclusions can you draw about animals' homes? **S3CS5b**

Independent Inquiry

When you classify, you group things that are alike and separate things that are different. Classify the plants and animals on the cards. You might group them by color, size, habitat, or other characteristics. What groups can you form? **S3CS4b**

277

VOCABULARY
mountain p. 278
piedmont p. 280
coastal plain p. 282
wetland p. 285

SCIENCE CONCEPTS
▶ what the regions in Georgia are
▶ what plants and animals live in each region

 COMPARE AND CONTRAST
Look for ways in which Georgia's regions are alike and different.

[alike]————[different]

Mountains

A **mountain** is land that rises to a high peak. Northern Georgia has many mountains. The mountains get more rain and snow than any other part of the state. The mountains can be warm in summer, but temperatures often drop below freezing in winter. The mountain region provides habitats for many plants and animals.

Mountains

In Georgia, red squirrels are found only in pine forests in the mountains. They feed on pine seeds and buds.

278

Animals that live in the mountains must be able to survive cold winters. Bobcats and skunks grow more fur in winter to help them stay warm. Bats hibernate in mountain caves. Many animals, like snakes and turtles, are less active during winter. In autumn, squirrels hide food and store it until winter. Birds that cannot survive the cold, such as orioles and warblers, migrate south every winter.

Mountain soils are usually very rocky and shallow. Where the soil is only a few inches deep, grasses, wildflowers, and small shrubs grow. Where the soil is deeper, forests of oaks, maples, poplars, and beeches cover the land. Evergreen trees such as the eastern hemlock grow near the tops of the mountains. Farther down the slopes, azaleas and mountain laurel grow close to the ground.

(Focus Skill) COMPARE AND CONTRAST

How are mountain animals different in winter than they are in summer?

The eastern hemlock grows on mountaintops and stays green all year.

Smoky shrews live in burrows in the Blue Ridge Mountains.

The Piedmont

In Georgia, the **piedmont** is the region just south of the mountains. The piedmont has many rolling hills. A thick layer of red clay soil covers much of the piedmont. Many streams and small rivers run through the region.

Before people settled in Georgia, the piedmont had mostly oak and hickory trees. Settlers cut down the trees and cleared the land for farms. The forests that grew back had mostly pine trees. Sweet gums, beeches, maples, elms, and birches still grow near the rivers.

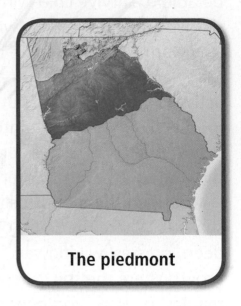

The piedmont

Oak and hickory forest

The relict trillium lives on the forest floor. It is hard to find today. People have built homes, cities, and farms where trilliums once grew.

Pine forest

Birds, chipmunks, deer, fox squirrels, and white-footed mice are a few of the animals that live in the piedmont. Spotted salamanders survive in the forests by eating worms, insects, and snails. They hunt at night and live under logs during the day.

Shoal bass, sunfish, and catfish live in piedmont rivers. Beavers build dams and lodges on the smaller streams. In fields and pastures, you can find butterflies, birds, foxes, and coyotes.

 COMPARE AND CONTRAST

How is the piedmont of today different from the piedmont before settlers came?

Spotted salamanders have rows of spots down their backs.

Math in Science
Interpret Data

Study the data table below. It shows data about the weather in two towns. Which town is more likely to be in the mountains than in the piedmont? Explain your answer.

Georgia Weather Data		
Town	Average Temperature in January (°C)	Average Yearly Snowfall (in cm)
1	3	10.0
2	10	2.5

The Coastal Plain

Millions of years ago, most of southern Georgia was covered by the ocean. Today, this region is called the **coastal plain**. In the coastal plain, the land is flat and the soils are sandy. Compared with other regions in Georgia, the coastal plain has mild winters and hot summers.

Sweet gum, magnolia, bay, and hickory trees grow along the streams. In the flatwoods of the coastal plain grow pine, live oak, saw palmetto, wax myrtle, and wiregrasses. Deer, bobcats, eastern diamondback rattlesnakes, skunks, opossums, raccoons, quail, and many songbirds live there.

The coastal plain

Gopher tortoises eat low-growing plants.

Long ago, the red-cockaded woodpecker was common in the flatwoods of the coastal plain. It lived in pine forests where wildfires were frequent. Today, the woodpecker is rare. Gopher tortoises also live in the coastal plain. Their front legs are shaped like shovels. They use them to dig burrows in the sandy soil. Many other animals, such as gopher frogs, use tortoise burrows as homes.

The coast is the region where the coastal plain meets the ocean. Salty spray from the ocean covers the beaches and sand dunes. Only a few plants, such as sea oats and beach grass, can survive in the salty sand.

Laws help protect the red-cockaded woodpecker from becoming extinct.

Focus Skill COMPARE AND CONTRAST

How is the coastal plain different from the mountains and the piedmont?

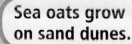

Sea oats grow on sand dunes.

Insta-Lab

Model Georgia's Habitats

Make a model of the ocean, coastal plain, piedmont, and mountains by using a shallow pan, modeling clay, and water. Compare your model to those of your classmates.

Atlantic Ocean and Wetlands

On the east coast of the United States is the Atlantic Ocean, a very large body of salt water. Many animals live in or near the ocean. Bottlenose dolphins live in shallow bays and inlets. They eat fish, shrimp, and crabs. The slender shape of dolphins' bodies helps them glide easily through the water.

Dolphins must come to the surface to breathe. Fish, on the other hand, use gills to take oxygen directly from the water. Brown pelicans dive into the water to catch fish in their large bills. They build nests in low shrubs and small trees on islands near the ocean.

The Atlantic Ocean and wetlands

A brown pelican uses its pouch to scoop up fish.

Bottlenose dolphins are found in all oceans except the Arctic and Antarctic Oceans.

Leopard frog

Waterlilies are familiar wetland plants.

A **wetland** is an area of land that is wet all or most of the time. In Georgia, mountain bogs, piedmont marshes, and swamps in the coastal plain are all types of wetlands. The soil is usually wet and spongy. Many wetlands plants, such as waterlilies, have long stems that grow under water.

Many animals have adaptations for living in wetlands. Some ducks dive under water to get food. Alligators can stay under water for a long time without breathing.

Wetlands include bogs, marshes, and swamps.

 **COMPARE AND CONTRAST**

Where in Georgia are wetlands found?

285

Essential Question

What are some habitats in Georgia?

In this lesson, you learned about habitats in the mountains, piedmont, coastal plain, ocean, and wetlands. Different living things are found in each region of Georgia.

1. (Focus Skill) **COMPARE AND CONTRAST**

Draw a graphic organizer that compares the habitats of a dolphin and a beaver. **S3L1a**

2. SUMMARIZE Fill in the blanks.

Georgia's regions have different characteristics. Rolling hills are found in the _____. Flat land and sandy soils make up the _____. The _____ get more snow than any other part of the state. The _____ is a large body of salt water. Swamps and marshes are both types of _____. **S3L1a**

3. VOCABULARY Choose a term from this lesson. Make a word web with the word you chose in the center. **S3L1a**

4. Critical Thinking Why are there only a few plants and animals that are found everywhere in Georgia? **S3L1a**

CRCT Practice

5. In which region would you find fish that live in the fastest flowing streams?

A coastal plain

B piedmont

C mountains

D wetlands **S3L1a**

6. What feature best describes Georgia's coast?

A rolling hills

B sandy beaches

C large rocks

D red clay soils **S3L1a**

 Writing ELA3W1f

Write a Description

Write a **travel brochure** for one of the regions in this lesson. Describe things visitors will enjoy about that region. Include a description of the plants and animals that can be found there.

 Math M3G1d

Measure a Circle

Draw pictures to show how you could use a long rope and a measuring tape to find the radius, the diameter, and the circumference of this pond.

 Social Studies M&G4

Georgia's Regions

Color a blank map of Georgia to show the different regions in the state. Include a key to explain the colors you use. Use a map of Georgia to find your town, and label it on your map.

 For more links and activities, go to **www.hspscience.com**

287

Okefenokee
National Wildlife
Refuge

The Okefenokee Swamp

The Okefenokee Swamp is one of Georgia's best-known wetlands. It got its name from Choctaw Indian words meaning "land of the trembling earth." The muddy soil in the swamp is called peat. If you tried to walk through the swamp, your legs would sink deeper and deeper into the ground with every step.

The swamp is a vast region of lakes, islands, marshes, and forests. More than 600 kinds of plants grow in the swamp. Saw palmettos, cypresses, black gums, and red maples are common. There are also large areas called prairies that are always covered with several inches of water. On these prairies grow water lilies, golden club, sedges, and grasses.

A wet prairie in the Okefenokee Swamp

Okefenokee Animals

Many different animals live in the Okefenokee. Sandhill cranes build nests in the spring. Alligators sun themselves along the trails. Ducks, white ibises, egrets, and herons feed in shallow lakes and prairies. Many different songbirds stop by to feed during their migrations. Hawks and wild turkeys stay year-round. Black bears feed on nuts and berries. More than a dozen kinds of frogs sing on summer evenings.

Hungry Plants

Some of the plants of the Okefenokee have an unusual adaptation—they capture insects. Pitcher plants, sundews, and bladderworts are some of these "meat-eating" plants. Each kind of plant captures insects in a different way. The plants get nutrients from the insects.

Insects get trapped inside pitcher plants.

✍ Think and Write

1 What adaptation helps pitcher plants and sundews survive in the swamp? **S3L1b**

2 Suggest a reason why many different kinds of plants and animals live in the Okefenokee. **S3L1a**

Content

S3L1d Explain what will happen to an organism if the habitat is changed.

Characteristics of Science

S3CS1b   **S3CS8b**

LESSON 3

Essential Question

How Do Changes to Habitats Affect Living Things?

Georgia Fast Fact

Big Changes
People cause many changes to the land. When land is cleared for development, many plants and animals lose the habitats they need to survive. Thousands of acres of land in Georgia are developed for use by homes and businesses every year.

drought [DROWT] A long period of time with very little rain (p. 294)

balance [BAL•uhns] Not too many and not too few of a kind of living thing (p. 298)

Clearing land in north Georgia

291

Changing the Environment

Start with Questions

You have learned that plants have adaptations to help them survive in their environments. Some environments are very dry. Others are very wet.

- What happens if an environment changes and a plant doesn't get enough water?

- Can a plant get too much water?

Investigate to find out. Then read to find out more.

Prepare to Investigate

Inquiry Skill Tip

There are many ways you can communicate the results of an investigation. When you have an idea you want to share, decide whether writing, speaking, or using pictures or diagrams will work best.

Materials
- 3 medium pots
- potting soil
- grass seeds
- watering can filled with water
- paper and pencil
- ruler

Make a Data Table

Plant Growth Data					
	Day				
	1	2	3	4	5
No Water					
Normal Water					
Extra Water					

Follow This Procedure

1. Half-fill the pots with potting soil.

2. Sprinkle grass seeds on top of the soil. Add a little soil to cover the seeds. Water each day just enough to keep the soil moist.

3. When the seeds begin to grow, label the pots. One pot will continue to get the same amount of water. One pot will not get any water, and one pot will get twice as much water.

4. Each day, measure how tall the grass is in each pot. Record your observations.

Step 2

Step 3

Draw Conclusions

1. Compare the plants in the three pots. What differences did you notice?

2. **Standards Link** How might a long period without rain affect a plant? How might a flood affect a plant? **S3L1d**

3. **Inquiry Skill** Scientists can communicate their results by displaying their data. Use the data from your data table to make a graph. Display your data table and graph. **S3CS8b**

Independent Inquiry

Your partner concludes that all plants will die after a flood. What observations could you make that would prove your partner wrong? Design an investigation that could help you draw a different conclusion. Try it! **S3CS1b**

VOCABULARY
drought p. 294
balance p. 298

SCIENCE CONCEPTS
▶ how climate and fire affect living things
▶ what living things do when their environment changes

Focus Skill **CAUSE AND EFFECT**
Look for changes to the environment caused by climate and fire.

cause ──▶ effect

Climate Affects Living Things

Environments have different climates. Plants and animals have adaptations that help them survive in their environments. What is the climate like where you live?

If the climate in a place changes, it affects all of the things that live there. A **drought** is a long period of time with very little rain. Plants that live in a place where it usually rains may not survive a drought.

▲ Many plants die during a drought.

These students are staying cool on a hot summer day.

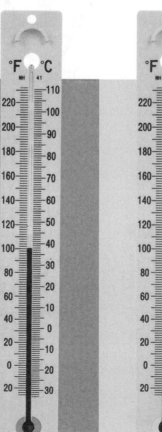

On cold days, people wear heavy clothing to stay warm.

During a flood, a river flows onto the land around the river. Plants and animals may die. After the flood, the river goes back to its usual size. It leaves behind the soil it was carrying. Crops will grow well on this land.

A desert has a hot, dry climate. Few kinds of plants can grow in a desert because there is very little water. As a result, few animals live there. Those that do live there have adaptations that help them survive.

When it does rain in the desert, many plants begin to grow. After a rain, the desert may be covered with colorful wildflowers. These wildflowers grow quickly to make seeds before they die in the dry climate.

CAUSE AND EFFECT What effect does a drought have on living things?

Fire Affects Living Things

A fire can cause a lot of changes to an environment. It can kill living things. Sometimes a fire can help an environment. If a tree burns, it is likely to fall. It leaves an open space in the forest. New plants can get more sunlight and have room to grow.

Fires can also be harmful. They can destroy animals' habitats. Those animals may not be able to survive in a new habitat.

Fire is helpful to some plants and animals. It is harmful to others.

This fire is causing many changes to the forest environment.

A firefighter sets a small fire carefully to help plants and animals that need fires to survive.

◀ The cones of the longleaf pine open and drop their seeds only when fire heats them. Without fire, these pine trees can't reproduce.

Some plants have adaptations that help them live in places that have fires. There are many fires in grassland environments. Grasses have many roots and can grow back quickly after a fire. Other plants cannot.

Ashes from burned plants add nutrients to the soil. The nutrients help new plants grow.

▲ This sign warns people that the forest is dry and a fire could spread easily.

 **CAUSE AND EFFECT** What is one helpful and one harmful effect of fire?

Balance Between Living Things

An environment is in **balance** when there are not too many and not too few of any kind of living thing. An environment needs the right amount of the right plants. Without the plants, animals will have no food. The animals will have to find new places to live, or they will die.

The environment on the next page is in balance. More animals would upset this balance. More bison would eat too many plants. Other animals would not have enough food.

Focus Skill **CAUSE AND EFFECT** How does having too few plants affect an environment?

This environment is not in balance. The plant you see growing is called kudzu. Kudzu was brought to the United States from Asia. It grows quickly and covers large parts of fields and forests. The plants below the kudzu do not get sunlight and die.

This grassland is in balance. If one kind of plant or animal was taken out of the environment, it would upset the balance of living things in the grassland.

◄ If there were more bison, they would eat all the plants.

If there were not as many mice, this snake would have nothing to eat. ▶

How do changes to habitats affect living things?

In this lesson you learned about changes to the environment, such as fires and droughts. When these changes happen, living things may survive, may die, or may move to a new place.

1. **(Focus Skill) CAUSE AND EFFECT** Draw and complete a graphic organizer to show the effects of a forest fire.

   S3L1d

   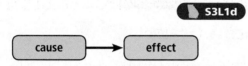

2. **DRAW CONCLUSIONS** Do living things cause all the harmful changes in the environment? Explain your answer. **S3L1d**

3. **VOCABULARY** Explain how *climate* can affect the *balance* in an environment. Use both words in your answer. **S3L1d**

4. **Critical Thinking**
   Why should you use evidence to draw a conclusion instead of using your opinion? **S3CS6a**

CRCT Practice

5. Which is **not** a natural change?
   A Plants wilt during a drought.
   B Lightning starts a forest fire.
   C Trees are cut to build new homes.
   D A flood erodes the banks of a river. **S3L1d**

6. Which change will **most likely** have the greatest effect on an environment?
   A A tree is cut down.
   B A piece of trash is thrown into a pond.
   C A fire burns down a forest.
   D There is no rain for a week in a desert. **S3L1d**

 Writing ELA3W1h

Write a Narrative

Choose an animal, and write a story about what happens to it when its environment changes. Explain the cause of the change, such as climate, fire, or an upset in the balance of living things. Underline important words that describe things in your story.

 Math M3D1a

Construct a Graph

Choose an animal that is disappearing from Georgia, and find out why it is in trouble. Then make a bar graph. On it, show how many of these animals are alive now in Georgia. Show how many were alive 10 years ago and 20 years ago.

 Drama

Lights, Camera . . .

With a group, act out how living things change when their environment changes. One member can hold up a sign explaining the environmental change. The other members can wear labels telling which living thing they are.

 For more links and activities, go to **www.hspscience.com**

Where the Wild Things Are

Don't bother looking for the yellow-billed cuckoo at the beach. You won't find the bird there. But you might spot a creature like it in a city near you.

Recently, scientists spotted a yellow-billed cuckoo in a city park in Connecticut. The scientists were at the park to take part in BioBlitz, a 24-hour race to count every type of plant and animal in sight. By the end of the long day, they had found nearly 2,000 different kinds of living things.

A Range of Life

BioBlitz is held in cities across the country. The program teaches people about the biodiversity of wildlife at their doorsteps. Biodiversity refers to the number and variety of life forms in a certain area.

Seek and Identify

BioBlitz combines education with round-the-clock fun. The participants compete to collect the most—and the most unusual—species. Hundreds of people come to watch.

Teams use insect nets and special lights in their search. One volunteer brought a recording of an owl. The noise attracted other owls for the team to count. Teams use microscopes and wildlife guides help people identify the species they find. Cameras help document rare finds.

In many cases, computers play an important role in keeping track of the information gathered by scientists and students. In New York City, the BioBlitz data was input into a special software program created just for the event.

Divers search a lake in New York City during a recent BioBlitz.

Perhaps the best part of BioBlitz is that everyone who participates sees something new. "We hope this event helps people pay closer attention to the world around them," another program organizer said.

 ### Think and Write

1 Why don't scientists find the same living things in every environment?

> S3L1a

2 In what ways are computers and cameras being used to help the environment?

> S3CS3b

Health Check

One of the goals of BioBlitz is to measure the health of city parks. Healthy parks should have a variety of mammals, insects, fish, and reptiles. BioBlitz volunteers record every kind of plant and animal that they find. Over time, scientists can compare the current number of plants and animals with the number from previous years. That way they can see whether some park creatures are in danger of dying out.

Find out more. Log on to
www.hspscience.com

Visual Summary

Tell how each picture helps explain the **Big Idea**.

The Big Idea Georgia has many habitats. Each habitat contains different living things.

Lesson 1 S3L1a, S3L1d

Habitats and Environments

Living things have adaptations that help them live in certain places. Everything that surrounds a living thing is part of its environment. A plant or an animal's habitat is the specific place where it lives.

Lesson 2 S3L1a, S3L1b, S3L1c

Regions of Georgia

Georgia's different regions include the mountains, the piedmont, the coastal plain, the Atlantic Ocean, and wetlands. Each region has different habitats and contains different living things.

Lesson 3 S3L1d

Changes to Habitats

When a habitat changes, some plants and animals may no longer be able to get the things they need to survive. They must move to a new habitat or they may die.

Show What You Know

Chapter Writing Activity

Write About Plants and Animals/Informational

Make a list of plants and animals in your region. Write letters or e-mails to students who live in other regions of Georgia. Trade lists. Keep track of the plants and animals that live in other regions of Georgia on large sheets of paper.

ELA3W1j

Georgia Performance Task

Make a Field Guide Entry

Use the lists you made in the Writing activity to make a class field guide to Georgia's plants and animals. Choose one plant or animal, draw a picture of it, write a description, and draw a map showing where it can be found. Combine your entry with the entries of other students in the class to make the field guide.

S3L1a

Georgia Performance Standards

Vocabulary Review

Use the terms below to complete the sentences. The page numbers tell you where to look in the chapter if you need help.

environment p. 267   coastal plain p. 282

habitat p. 269   wetland p. 285

mountain p. 278   drought p. 294

piedmont p. 280   balance p. 298

1. The region of Georgia with flat land and sandy soils is the _____.
   S3L1a

2. The place where a plant or animal lives is its _____. **S3L1b**

3. An ecosystem with just the right number and kinds of living things is in _____. **S3L1d**

4. The region of Georgia with rolling hills is the _____. **S3L1a**

5. Everything that surrounds a living thing is its _____. **S3L1c**

6. A long period of time with very little rain is a _____. **S3L1d**

7. A high, raised part of Earth's surface is a _____. **S3L1a**

8. An area that is covered with water for most of the year is a _____.
   S3L1a

Check Understanding

Choose the best answer.

9. Which animal would you expect to find in the same ecosystem as a dolphin? (p. 268) **S3L1c**
   A bat
   B lizard
   C whale
   D rabbit

10. **CAUSE AND EFFECT** What causes a flood? (p. 295) **S3L1d**
    A too much rain
    B not enough rain
    C too much sunlight
    D not enough sunlight

11. Which animal will be **most** affected by the change shown in the drawing below? (p. 290) **S3L1d**

    A dog
    B deer
    C duck
    D dolphin

12. What is **not** part of the habitat of the red squirrel? (p. 278) **S3L1a**

A salt water

B tall pine trees

C rocks and mountains

D acorns and other nuts

13. MAIN IDEA AND DETAILS Which of the following is **not** a good way to describe the coastal plain? (p. 282) **S3L1a**

A flat

B wide rivers

C sandy soils

D very few animals

14. Which statement describes how a change to an ecosystem affects living things? (p. 296) **S3L1d**

A Changes are helpful to all living things.

B Changes are harmful to all living things.

C Changes help some living things and harm others.

D Changes do not affect living things.

15. In which region do gopher tortoises dig burrows into the sandy soil? (p. 282) **S3L1a**

A coastal plain

B mountains

C piedmont

D ocean

16. What feature helps a longleaf pine grow on the coastal plain? (p. 297) **S3L1b**

A They can survive most fires.

B They do not need nutrients.

C They can grow in windy places.

D Their roots grow in wet mud.

Inquiry Skills

17. Explain how you could make a model of Georgia's mountains. In what ways is your model similar to the mountains? What is one way your model differs from Georgia's mountains? **S3CS4c**

18. What do you predict will happen to a mountain plant that is moved to the coast? **S3CS4a**

Critical Thinking

19. Houses are built near an area where raccoons live. How might this change be helpful and harmful to raccoons? **S3L1d**

20. Are Georgia's habitats all the same? Write a sentence to explain your answer. Write another sentence to give an example. **S3L1a**

The Big Idea

Georgia Performance Standards in This Chapter

Content

S3L2 Students will recognize the effects of pollution and humans on the environment.

S3L2a **S3L2b**

This chapter also addresses these co-requisite standards:

Characteristics of Science

S3CS1 Students will be aware of the importance of curiosity, honesty, openness, and skepticism in science. . . .

S3CS1a

S3CS2 Students will have the computation and estimation skills necessary for analyzing data. . . .

S3CS2c

S3CS4 Students will use ideas of system, model, change, and scale in exploring scientific and technological matters.

S3CS4a

S3CS5 Students will communicate scientific ideas and activities clearly.

S3CS5a **S3CS5c**

S3CS8 Students will understand . . . scientific inquiry.

S3CS8a

What's the Big Idea?

There are many ways to conserve resources and to protect the environment from harmful materials.

Essential Questions

GO online for student eBook www.hspscience.com

Rome

Dear Linda,

Our class celebrated Earth Day yesterday. We planted trees in a park near Rome. When they are grown, the trees will provide habitats for many animals.

The other classes celebrated Earth Day in different ways. Some students cleaned up trash from a stream. Another group handed out information about recycling.

Write back soon!
Cory

USA

What did Cory's class do to help the environment? How do you think that relates to the **Big Idea?**

Content

 S3L2b Identify ways to protect the environment.

1. Conservation of resources
2. Recycling of materials

Characteristics of Science

S3CS4a **S3CS5b**

Georgia Fast Fact

Gone Fishin'
Georgia Veterans Memorial State Park, near Cordele, Georgia, is a great place for fishing. The cypress trees on the lake's shore are a great place for young fish to grow larger. To make sure there are plenty of fish for everyone, the Georgia Department of Natural Resources issues fishing licenses and sets rules about the kinds and number of fish people can catch.

LESSON

1

Essential Question

What Are Some Natural Resources?

Georgia Veterans
Memorial State Park

natural resource
[NACH•er•uhl REE•sawrs] A material that is found in nature and that is used by living things (p. 314)

renewable resource
[rih•NOO•uh•buhl REE•sawrs] A resource that can be replaced quickly (p. 316)

nonrenewable resource
[nahn•rih•NOOuh•buhl RFF•sawrs] A resource that, when it is used up, will not exist again during a human lifetime (p. 318)

Mining Resources

Start with Questions

Some of the resources we use are found underground. To reach valuable rocks and minerals, people dig mines.

- How do mines affect the environment?

- Are some ways of mining less harmful to the environment than other ways?

Investigate to find out. Then read to find out more.

Prepare to Investigate

Inquiry Skill Tip

To help you infer, start by making a list of all your observations. Then draw a conclusion based on your observations. Check to see if your inferences agree with your observations and data.

Materials
- oatmeal-raisin cookie
- paper plate
- dropper
- water
- toothpick

Make an Observation Chart

Mining a Cookie	
Step	Observations
Before mining	
After mining	

Follow This Procedure

1. Observe your cookie. Record the number of raisins you see.

2. Put a few drops of water around each raisin. The cookie should become moist but not wet.

3. Use the toothpick to "mine" all the raisins from the cookie. If they are hard to get out, put a few more drops of water around them. Put the raisins you remove on the plate. Record the number you removed.

Draw Conclusions

1. Were there any raisins that you didn't see in the cookie the first time? If so, why didn't you see them?

2. **Standards Link** How is mining raisins from a cookie like mining resources from Earth?
   S3L2b

3. **Inquiry Skill** Scientists use their observations to infer how similar things work. Use your observations to infer how mining could affect the land around the mine.
   S3CS4a

Step 2

Step 3

Independent Inquiry

Can the cookie be completely "mined" without tearing it up? Hypothesize how this might be done. Test your hypothesis.
S3CS5a

VOCABULARY
natural resource p. 314
renewable resource
    p. 316
nonrenewable
resource p. 318

SCIENCE CONCEPTS
▶ what natural
   resources are
▶ which resources
   will not run out and
   which may run out

Focus Skill **MAIN IDEA AND DETAILS**
Look for details about
resources.

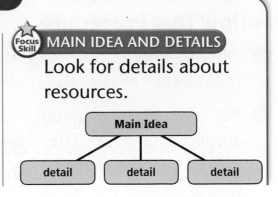

Resources

What materials have you used so far today? You
ate food for breakfast. Then you used water to
brush your teeth. Now you are using this book. The
food, the water, and even this book all came from
resources. A **natural resource** is a material found in
nature that is used by living things.

▼ **People use
fish as a
resource.**

People use many kinds of
animals as resources. For
example, cows are used for
both meat and milk. ▼

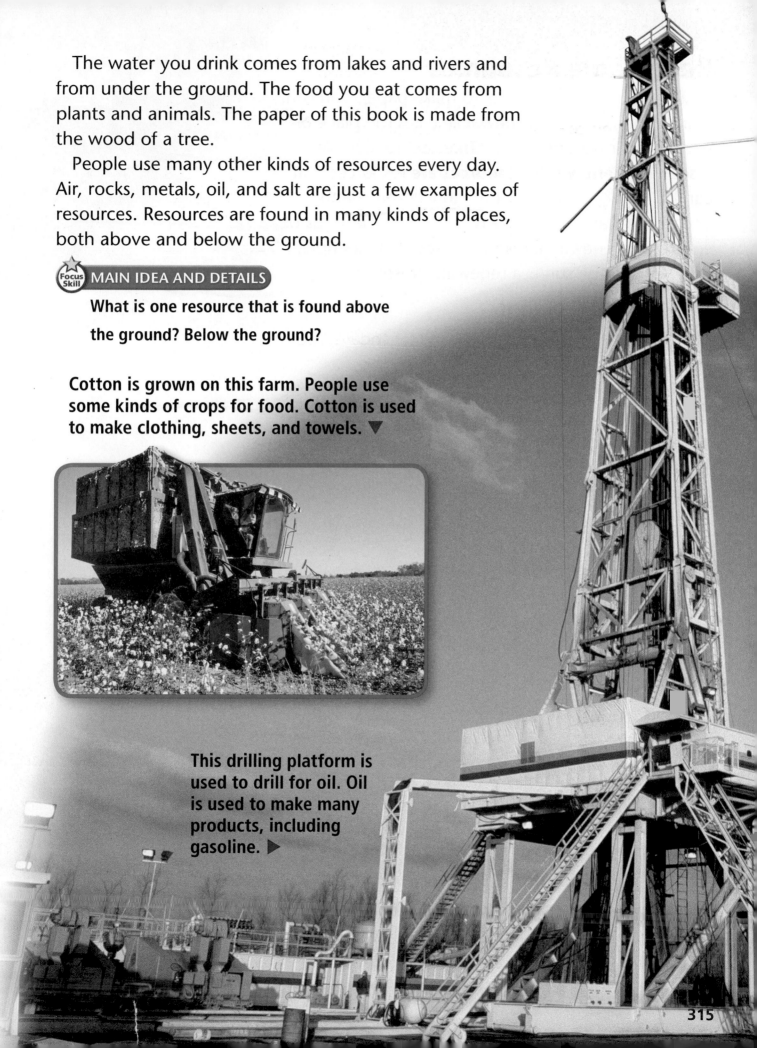

The water you drink comes from lakes and rivers and from under the ground. The food you eat comes from plants and animals. The paper of this book is made from the wood of a tree.

People use many other kinds of resources every day. Air, rocks, metals, oil, and salt are just a few examples of resources. Resources are found in many kinds of places, both above and below the ground.

Focus Skill **MAIN IDEA AND DETAILS**

What is one resource that is found above the ground? Below the ground?

Cotton is grown on this farm. People use some kinds of crops for food. Cotton is used to make clothing, sheets, and towels. ▼

This drilling platform is used to drill for oil. Oil is used to make many products, including gasoline. ▶

315

Renewable Resources

After you cut down a tree to make paper, you can plant another tree. The new tree takes the place of the tree that was cut down. Trees are renewable resources. **Renewable resources** are resources that can be replaced during a human lifetime. Plants and animals are renewable resources. Some kinds of energy are renewable resources, too. For example, energy from the sun is a renewable resource.

Trees and water are renewable resources. Trees in a forest can be used to make houses, furniture, pencils, and paper. New trees can be planted to take the place of the ones that are cut down. ▼

Chattahoochee National Forest

▲ **Air is a kind of renewable resource that can be reused again and again.**

Some renewable resources can be used again and again. These kinds of resources are called reusable resources. Air and water are two kinds of reusable resources.

After you take a bath, the water is dirty. When you drain the tub, the water goes to a water treatment plant. There the water is cleaned so it can be reused.

Air is a resource you need to breathe. Cars and factories make the air dirty. Plants, wind, and rain help clean the air to make it safe to breathe again.

 MAIN IDEA AND DETAILS

What are some examples of renewable resources?

Nonrenewable Resources

You probably have watched someone fill up a car's tank with gasoline. Cars burn gasoline for energy. When the gasoline is used up, the tank needs to be filled again.

The oil that is used to make gasoline is not renewable or reusable. One day, it will all be gone. Oil is a nonrenewable resource. **Nonrenewable resources** are resources that cannot be replaced in a human lifetime. When these resources are used up, there will be no more. Some other nonrenewable resources are natural gas, soil, and metals.

At this mine, a kind of clay called kaolin is dug up. Georgia produces more kaolin than any other state. Most of it is used in making paper. ▼

Coal is an important nonrenewable resource. ▼

Some coal mines are deep underground.

Coal is another nonrenewable resource. It takes thousands of years for coal to form. There is only a certain amount of coal on Earth. Once we have used it all, there will be no more left.

We burn coal to generate electricity. Electricity from power plants that use coal is not very expensive. However, burning coal produces gases that are not good for the environment. Scientists and engineers are finding less harmful ways to make electricity. Wind, a renewable resource, is being used in some places to generate "clean" electricity.

 **MAIN IDEA AND DETAILS**

What are some nonrenewable resources?

Hunting for Resources
Go outside or look out a window. Make a list of the resources you see. Which of those resources are renewable? Which are reusable?

Essential Question

What are some natural resources?

Natural resources are materials from nature that are used by living things. There are limited supplies of some natural resources.

1. **Focus Skill** MAIN IDEA AND DETAILS

   Draw and complete a graphic organizer. Show details about the kinds of natural resources. **S3L2b**

   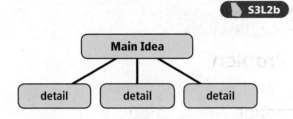

2. **DRAW CONCLUSIONS** Is the sun a renewable or a nonrenewable resource? Explain. **S3L2b**

3. **VOCABULARY** Write a short paragraph that describes the differences between renewable resources and nonrenewable resources. **S3L2b**

4. **Critical Thinking** Why is it important for scientists and engineers to develop new ways for cars to run? **S3L2b**

CRCT Practice

5. Which of the following resources is nonrenewable?

   A air   **C** coal

   B animals   **D** water

   S3L2b

6. Which statement about natural resources is true?

   The **Big Idea**

   A We will never run out of oil.

   B Burning coal is good for the environment.

   C Trees, sunlight, water, and air are nonrenewable.

   D Some resources can be reused more than one time. **S3L2b**

 Writing ELA3W1i

Write a Narrative

Choose a nonrenewable resource that you have used today. Write a **story** that describes how your life would be different without that resource.

 Math M3P1b

Solve a Problem

Suppose your town uses 5 tons of coal a year and has enough coal to produce energy for 20 years. If your town used only 4 tons each year, how long would the coal last?

 Social Studies SS3E1

Find Productive Resources

Make a chart with three columns, labeled *Natural Resources, Human Resources,* and *Capital Goods.* Flip through the textbook and find photos that show productive resources. Classify the resources by listing them on your chart.

 For more links and activities, go to **www.hspscience.com**

Content

S3L2a Explain the effects of pollution (such as littering) to the habitats of plants and animals.

Characteristics of Science

S3CS1a **S3CS8a**

LESSON 2

Essential Question

How Do People Affect the Environment?

Georgia Fast Fact

Slowing the Flow
When a dam is built on a river, it slows the river's flow and forms a large lake behind the dam. Animals that lived behind the dam must find new places to live. Fish that migrate up the river cannot make it past the dam. Many dams have special fish ladders to allow migrating fish to get from one side of the dam to the other.

pollution
[puh•LOO•shuhn]
Harmful material
that is added to the
environment (p. 328)

Russell Dam

323

Pollution and Plants

Guided Inquiry

Start with Questions

Trash thrown on the ground is a kind of pollution. Trash is not a natural part of a plant's environment.

- What are some other kinds of pollution?
- How do different kinds of pollution affect plants?

Investigate to find out. Then read to find out more.

Prepare to Investigate

Inquiry Skill Tip

When you compare things, think about the characteristics that are important for the investigation. Sometimes you need to consider the way things look. Other times you only need to consider the behavior of things.

Materials
- 3 clear plastic cups
- grass seeds
- clean water
- salt water
- oily water
- potting soil
- measuring cup

Make a Data Table

Plant Growth Data			
Day	Clean Water	Salty Water	Oily Water
1			
2			
3			
4			
5			

Follow This Procedure

1. Put soil in the cups. Plant a few seeds in each cup.

2. Label the cups Clean, Salty, and Oily. Water each cup with the kind of water on its label. Predict which seeds will grow best.

3. Place the cups near a sunny window. Each day for 10 days, water each cup with the kind of water on its label.

4. When the seeds sprout, measure the growth of the plants. Record your observations.

Draw Conclusions

1. What did you observe? In which cup did the seeds grow best?

2. **Standards Link** Did it matter if the water you used was polluted? How can you tell?

   🏴 S3L2a

3. **Inquiry Skill** Compare your results to your prediction. Which seeds did you predict would grow best? Were you correct?

   🏴 S3CS8a

Step 2

Step 3

Independent Inquiry

Would watering plants with water containing vinegar or dish detergent affect their growth? Predict what would happen. Then try it! Make sure to wear goggles.

🏴 S3CS1a

VOCABULARY
pollution p. 328

SCIENCE CONCEPTS
▶ how land is used
▶ what the different types of pollution are

Focus Skill **CAUSE AND EFFECT**
Look for ways people affect the environment.

cause ⟶ effect

Uses of the Land

The land people live on is a very important resource. People use land in many different ways. People build on land. They use resources from the land to make buildings. Rocks and wood are building materials that come from the land.

Many other resources that are useful to people also come from the land. Metals, gemstones, and coal are dug up, or mined, from the land. Land is also used for farming. Farmers use the soil to grow plants that are used for food, medicine, cloth, and more.

Big cities like Atlanta spread out for many miles. There are many uses of land in this picture.

Whenever people use land, they change it in some way. Building, mining, and farming all change the land. Sometimes the effects are good. For example, planting trees helps keep the soil in place. But sometimes the effects are bad. For example, mining can tear up the land. This harms the plants and animals that live in the area.

 **CAUSE AND EFFECT**

What effects can people's actions have on land?

It is important for city planners to include open spaces such as parks for people to enjoy. ▶

Land Pollution

People can also change land by polluting it. **Pollution** is any harmful material in the environment. There are many types of harmful materials, or pollutants. Solid waste, chemicals, noise, and even light can be pollutants.

One kind of pollution is land pollution. Land pollution can happen when people throw trash away in the wrong places. The trash can harm plants and animals. It can also pollute the water under the ground.

 **CAUSE AND EFFECT** What are some effects of land pollution?

Every year in the United States, more than 150 million tons of trash are put into landfills. ▼

**Math in Science
Interpret Data**

A T-shirt can take 6 months to break down. A rope can take a year. How many years does it take for a tin can to break down? A glass bottle?

**How Long It Takes for
Materials to Break Down**

Material	Months
Newspaper	1
Cotton T-shirt	6
Rope	12
Tin can	1,200
Glass bottle	6,000

▲ After a windy or rainy day, the pollution over the city is cleared away.

▲ If the air over the city does not move, the pollution will stay in place. This makes the air unhealthful to breathe.

Air Pollution

Pollution affects more than just the land. Air can be polluted, too. Smoke, mostly from trucks, cars, and factories, is one cause of air pollution.

Air pollution can make it hard for people to breathe. Air pollution can also change the weather. For example, air polluted by car and factory gases traps heat from sunlight. This makes Earth warmer. Scientists call this *global warming*.

Focus Skill **CAUSE AND EFFECT**

What can air pollution do to people?

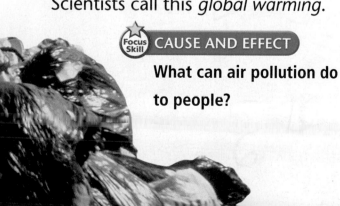

Insta-Lab

Seeing Air Pollution

Smear a circle of petroleum jelly in the center of a white paper plate. Leave the plate outdoors for a day or two. Observe the plate. How has it changed? What caused the change?

329

Water Pollution

Pollution in the air and on the land can get into water when there is rain. Rain washes pollutants from the air and land into the water. People who dump trash, oil, and other pollutants into the water also cause water pollution.

Drinking polluted water can make people sick. Animals that live in polluted water can also get sick. Some kinds of water pollution can be cleaned up. Water treatment plants can take pollutants out of water to make it clean again.

 CAUSE AND EFFECT

What can cause water to become polluted?

Sometimes, oil enters the oceans as a result of an accident. It takes many people to clean up an oil spill.

Oil is being cleaned from this bird's feathers. Without this help, the bird would probably die. ▼

Helping the Environment

There are many ways that you can help protect the environment. You could join a group that teaches people about environmental problems. You could raise money to donate to an important environmental cause.

Some people help the environment by organizing a group of people to clean up a park. Litter can be harmful to plants and animals. Animals may eat trash and get sick. Litter can contain chemicals that harm plants.

Writing letters or e-mails to people in the government can help persuade them to protect the environment.

Focus Skill CAUSE AND EFFECT What effect does litter have on plants and animals?

This sign warns people not to dump chemicals and litter into this drain. ▼

These students are throwing away garbage so litter does not get into the habitats of plants and animals.

331

Essential Question

How do people affect the environment?

One way people harm the environment is by polluting land, water, and air. People also can help the environment by cleaning up pollution.

1. 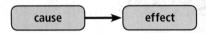 **CAUSE AND EFFECT**
Draw and complete a graphic organizer. Show the effects of pollution and mining on the environment. **S3L2a**

2. SUMMARIZE Write a summary of this lesson by describing the different kinds of pollution.
S3L2a

3. VOCABULARY Describe what pollution is, and list three examples. **S3L2a**

4. Critical Thinking Can things other than people cause pollution? Explain. **S3L2a**

CRCT Practice

5. Which is a way that people help the environment?
A cleaning up litter
B building new cities
C turning a forest into a farm
D building a dam **S3L2a**

6. What kind of pollution is most harmful to fish?
A air
B light
C water
D land **S3L2a**

The **Big** Idea

Writing   ELA3W1I

Persuasive

Write a **letter** to the editor of your community's newspaper. Ask people to protect the environment in some way. Explain why this action is important. For example, you could ask people not to litter and explain why littering is bad.

9÷3   **Math**   M3P1c

Pollution in the Food Chain

In one day, a large fish eats 3 smaller fish. Each small fish eats 10 shrimp. Every shrimp has 1 milligram of mercury, a kind of pollution. How much mercury does the large fish eat in one day?

Health

Breathe Deeply

Find out how air pollution can affect your health. Then make a poster to share what you learned. Include tips on how to avoid polluted air to stay healthy.

For more links and activities, go to **www.hspscience.com**

333

LESSON

3

Content

S3L2b Identify ways to protect the environment.
1. Conservation of resources.
2. Recycling of materials.

Characteristics of Science

 S3CS2c **S3CS5c**

▶ **DR. JU**

▶ Teache
Institu
▶ Studie
in the

Essential Question

How Can Resources Be Used Wisely?

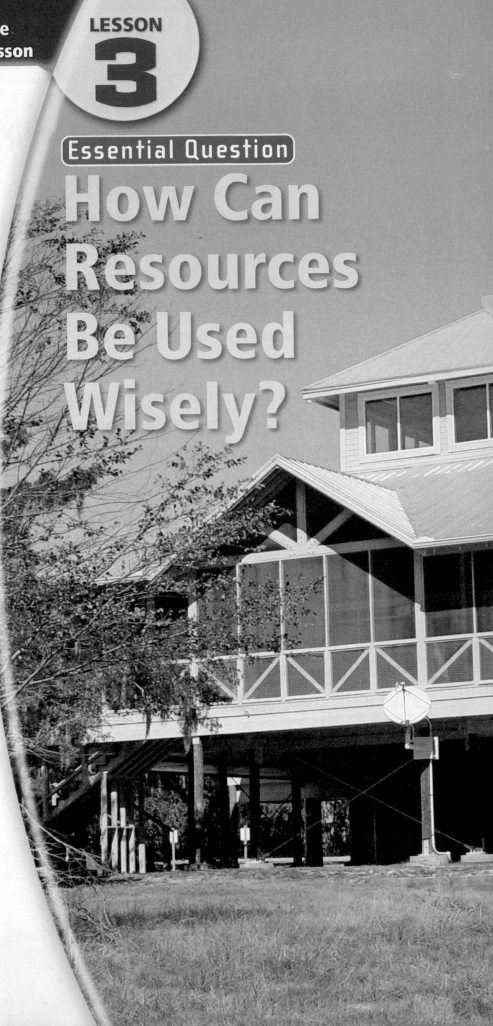

Georgia Fast Fact

A Friendly Building
The Suwannee River Visitor's Center was built with the environment in mind. One-third of the materials used to make the building were made from recycled materials. The deck, for example, is made of recycled plastic bottles. The insulation in the building was made from recycled newspaper.

Suwannee River Visitor's
Center in Fargo, Georgia

Vocabulary Preview

conservation
[kahn•ser•VAY•shuhn]
The saving of resources
by using them wisely
(p. 340)

reduce [ree•DOOS]
To use less of a resource
(p. 342)

reuse [ree•YOOZ]
To use a resource again
and again (p. 343)

recycle [ree•SY•kuhl]
To reuse a resource by
breaking it down and
making a new product
(p. 344)

337

Taking a Look at Trash

Start with Questions

Most garbage that is thrown away is taken to a landfill.

- How much do we throw away each week?

- How much of what we throw away can be recycled?

Investigate to find out. Then read to find out more.

Prepare to Investigate

Inquiry Skill Tip

When you communicate with numbers, measure carefully. In this Investigate, you will multiply your measurements. A small mistake would be multiplied and become a large mistake. The numbers you communicate would be wrong.

Materials
- large plastic trash bags
- bathroom scale
- calculator

Make a Data Table

Paper Recycling Data	
Day	Weight of Trash (kg)
1	
2	
3	
4	
5	
Total Weight:	

Follow This Procedure

1. With the rest of your class, save all the paper you would normally throw away for one week.

2. At the end of each day, weigh the paper. Record the weight.

3. Use your data to make a line graph showing the weight of each day's collection.

4. Add up all the weights in your data table. The sum tells how many pounds of paper the class collected in one week.

Draw Conclusions

1. Suppose that 1 pound of paper takes up 2 cubic feet of space. How much landfill space would your class save by recycling the paper you saved this week? **S3CS2a**

2. **Standards Link** How does recycling paper help the environment? **S3L2b**

3. **Inquiry Skill** There are many ways you can communicate an idea. In this investigation, you used numbers to describe the weight of the paper collected. How does using numbers help you tell people what you found out? **S3CS5c**

Step 2

Step 3

Independent Inquiry

Predict **how much paper your class could save by using both sides of each sheet. Plan and conduct an investigation to find out.** **S3CS2c**

VOCABULARY
conservation p. 340
reduce p. 342
reuse p. 343
recycle p. 344

SCIENCE CONCEPTS
▶ how conservation saves resources
▶ how to reduce, reuse, and recycle

Focus Skill **MAIN IDEA AND DETAILS**
Look for details about how to protect the environment.

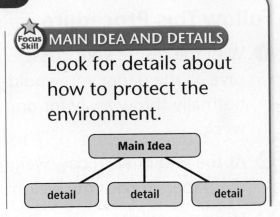

Main Idea

detail · detail · detail

Ways to Protect the Environment

People use a lot of resources. You have read that many resources are nonrenewable. This means that if we use up those resources, we will have none of them left. To protect Earth's resources, it is important to practice conservation. **Conservation** (kahn•ser•VAY•shuhn) is saving resources by using them wisely. Making sure resources do not get used up is one way to protect the environment.

Using certain resources can cause the environment to become polluted. You have read that pollution can harm people, animals, and plants. Because of this, it is important to keep pollution from getting into the environment. It is also important to clean up any pollution that has already gotten into it. In this lesson, you will learn how to conserve resources and cut down on pollution.

 **MAIN IDEA AND DETAILS**

What are two ways to protect the environment?

When people protect the environment, they make it safer and more enjoyable.

Reduce

One of the ways you can protect the environment is to reduce the amount of resources you use. To **reduce** your use of resources means to use less of them. For example, you can use less water by taking showers instead of baths. You can use less electricity if you turn the TV off when you are not watching it. If people use fewer resources, there will be more resources to use in the future.

 **MAIN IDEA AND DETAILS**

What are two ways you can reduce your use of resources?

Science Up Close

Reduce Your Use

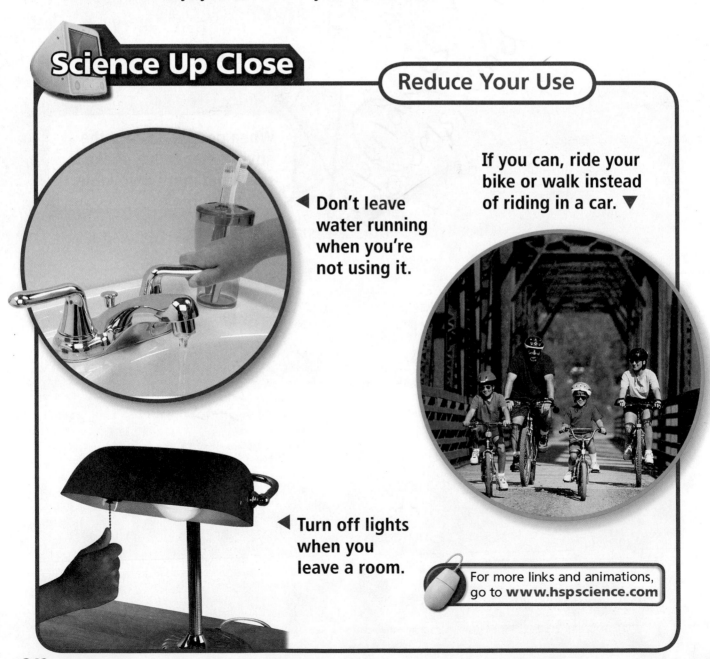

◀ **Don't leave water running when you're not using it.**

If you can, ride your bike or walk instead of riding in a car. ▼

◀ **Turn off lights when you leave a room.**

For more links and animations, go to **www.hspscience.com**

342

▲ These students are reusing paper bags to make gift wrap.

Reuse

Do you wear clothes that no longer fit your older brother or sister? Do you fix toys when they break, instead of buying new ones? If so, you are reusing resources. When you **reuse** a resource, you use it again and again. Reusing helps reduce the amount of resources that would be needed to make new things. Reusing resources also saves people money.

 **MAIN IDEA AND DETAILS** Why is it important to reuse resources?

What Can Be Reused?
Take a look at some of the things around you. Which of these things can be reused? How can they be reused? Make a table that lists some of your ideas.

Recycle

Another way to save resources is to recycle them. To **recycle** means to break a product down or change it in some way and then use the material to make something new. Many materials, such as paper, glass, the aluminum from cans, and some plastics, can be recycled.

When you place an aluminum can in a recycling bin, it is taken to a recycling plant. It is melted down with other cans and poured into a block. The blocks are sent to manufacturing plants where they are made into new cans.

▲ This symbol means that a product can be recycled.

When you recycle, you help conserve resources by reusing the same resource. ▼

When you recycle, it helps save space in landfills. It also conserves resources. When cans are recycled, we do not have to mine aluminum from rocks in the ground. Usually, recycling materials is cheaper and uses less energy than making new materials from raw materials.

Recycled materials can be used to make many new products. Paper that is recycled can be used to make cards, paper towels, and newspaper. Plastic that is recycled can be used to make park benches, doormats, and much more.

Focus Skill MAIN IDEA AND DETAILS

What are some materials that can be recycled?

This volunteer is collecting old tires to be recycled. ▼

This playground is made from recycled materials. ▼

Essential Question

How can resources be used wisely?

When you conserve resources, you are using them wisely. You can conserve resources by recycling materials, by reducing your use of resources, and by reusing resources more than once.

1. **(Focus Skill) MAIN IDEA AND DETAILS**
Draw and complete a graphic organizer. Show details to support this main idea: *There are three ways to protect the environment and conserve resources.* **S3L2b**

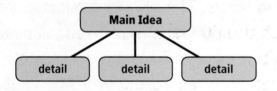

2. **DRAW CONCLUSIONS** List all the resources that you save when you reuse a cotton T-shirt instead of buying a new one. **S3L2b**

3. **VOCABULARY** Write a paragraph that correctly uses the terms *reduce, reuse,* and *recycle.* **S3L2b**

4. **Critical Thinking** Angie reads the newspaper every day. What resource would she conserve if she recycled the newspapers? **S3L2b**

CRCT Practice

5. Which is **not** a way to conserve resources?
   A recycle
   B throw away
   C reuse
   D reduce **S3L2b**

6. Which student is reducing his use of resources?
   A Dan picks up litter.
   B Mike uses a paper bag instead of a plastic bag.
   C Scott turns off the water while he brushes his teeth.
   D Jake puts a can in the recycling bin. **S3L2b**

The Big Idea

346

Writing

ELA3W1I

Form and Defend an Opinion

Suppose your leaders want to pass a law that says everyone must recycle. If you don't recycle, you could be fined. Decide how you feel about the law. Then write a **letter** to the governor explaining how you feel. Support your opinion with facts.

Math

M3P1b

A Bright Idea

The amount of electricity a light bulb uses is measured in watts. The old light bulbs in your school each use 60 watts every hour. A new kind of bulb uses only 20 watts every hour. Your teacher changed 15 old bulbs to new bulbs. Every day, the lights are on for 8 hours. How much electricity is being conserved each

Music

Recycling Rhyme

Write the words to a song that tells people why it's good to recycle. Use a tune you already know. Sing your song in class.

For more links and activities, go to **www.hspscience.com**

Trash Man

Chad Pregracke grew up on the banks of the Mississippi River. He spent summers fishing, sailing, water-skiing, and canoeing. When Pregracke was 15, he started working with his brother, a commercial shell diver.

During their travels, Pregracke noticed that the riverbanks were lined with trash. "We're talking refrigerators, barrels, tires. There was this one pile of 50 or 60 barrels that had been there for [more than] 20 years. … I saw there was a problem, basically in my backyard. And I wanted to do something about it," explained Pregracke.

Taking Action

Pregracke started picking up garbage. He also wrote letters to local companies requesting donations to launch a river cleanup. When he started in 1997, Pregracke single-handedly cleaned 160 kilometers (100 miles) of the Mississippi River shoreline with money he raised in the community.

Since then, Pregracke's project has grown. He now has a ten-person crew, a fleet of barges and boats, and thousands of volunteers to help keep the Mississippi and other rivers in the United States clean. "There's been a lot of accomplishments, and I've had a lot of help," said Pregracke. "But I feel like I'm just getting started."

Did You Know?

- The majority of Americans live within 10 miles of a polluted body of water.
- Water pollution has caused fishing and swimming to be prohibited in 40 percent of the nation's rivers, lakes, and coastal waters.
- Your own daily habits can help reduce water pollution. For more information, visit the U.S. Environmental Protection Agency's website for kids.

Phantom Garbage

Although Pregracke has hauled tons of garbage from the Mississippi, the river is still polluted by a type of waste that can't be picked up with a forklift: runoff.

When it rains, the water either soaks into the ground or flows over Earth's surface as runoff. Runoff carries pollution to rivers, oceans, lakes, and wetlands. Many of the pollutants in runoff come from oil and gasoline leaked by automobiles; pesticides sprayed on lawns; and fertilizers spread on fields. Other water pollutants include heavy metals, such as iron, copper, zinc, tin, and lead; oil from spills; and sewage. Water pollution can cause human health problems and harm wetlands.

✍ Think and Write

❶ How might runoff affect your drinking water? **S3L2a**

❷ What can you do to help keep rivers clean? **S3L2a**

Find out more. Log on to
www.hspscience.com

Wrap-Up

Visual Summary

Tell how each picture helps explain the **Big Idea**.

The Big Idea There are many ways to conserve resources and to protect the environment from harmful materials.

Lesson 1  S3L2b

Resources in Nature

Materials in nature that living things use are natural resources. Some resources will run out if we do not use them wisely.

Lesson 2 S3L2a

Addressing Pollution

Pollution harms plants and animals when it is added to the environment. People have polluted the land, air, and water.

Lesson 3 S3L2b

Conservation Is Key

Resources are conserved when they are used wisely. Reducing how much of a resource is used is a way to conserve the resource. Recycling and reusing materials are also examples of conservation.

Show What You Know

Chapter Writing Activity

Write About Conservation/Informational

Research and write a report about a conservation issue in your community. Use reference sources to write your report. For example, you might find out how pollution is affecting a stream or river near your home. Another activity would be to visit a local park and learn about an issue that is important to the park manager. **ELA3W1j**

Georgia Performance Task

Tell Others About Conservation

Plan activities to raise awareness of conservation issues in your town or city. Make posters to hang up at school, write announcements for radio stations, or make handouts describing the issues. Help people understand what they can do to fix the problems. **S3L2a** **S3L2b**

Georgia Performance Standards

Vocabulary Review

Use the terms below to complete the sentences. The page numbers tell you where to look in the chapter if you need help.

natural resource p. 314

renewable resource p. 316

nonrenewable resource p. 318

pollution p. 328

conservation p. 340

reduce p. 342

reuse p. 343

recycle p. 344

1. To make a new product from an old product is to _____. **S3L2b**

2. A resource that may be used up one day is a _____. **S3L2b**

3. To use resources wisely is to practice _____. **S3L2b**

4. To use less of a resource is to _____ your use of it. **S3L2b**

5. A harmful material in the environment is _____. **S3L2a**

6. A resource that can be replaced in a human lifetime is a _____. **S3L2b**

7. To use something again is to _____ it. **S3L2b**

8. Something found in nature that is used by living things is a _____. **S3L2b**

Check Understanding

Write the letter of the best choice.

9. Which kind of pollution is **most** harmful to fish? (p. 330) **S3L2a**
   A air   **C** light
   B land   **D** water

10. Which type of resource is the oil that gasoline is made from? (p. 318) **S3L2b**
    A nonrenewable resource
    B refundable resource
    C renewable resource
    D reusable resource

11. Instead of using her boat's motor, Jenny uses the sail. What is she conserving? (p. 340) **S3L2b**
    A wind
    B water
    C plastic
    D gasoline

12. COMPARE AND CONTRAST
How is a polluted lake different from a lake without any pollution? (p. 328) **S3L2a**

A A polluted lake has more fish.

B A polluted lake is healthier.

C A polluted lake has materials that harm living things.

D A polluted lake has salt water instead of fresh water.

13. MAIN IDEA AND DETAILS
Which technology can you use to help decrease air pollution? (p. 329) **S3L2a**

A a bicycle **C** a cell phone

B a car **D** a camera

14. Which technology is used to clean polluted water? (p. 330) **S3L2a**

A a car engine

B an oil tanker

C a tire-recycling plant

D a water treatment plant

15. Which of these resources can you conserve by recycling paper? (p. 344) **S3L2b**

A aluminum **C** gasoline

B coal **D** trees

16. Look at the symbol below. What does it represent? (p. 344) **S3L2b**

A conservation

B recycling

C renewing

D soil formation

Inquiry Skills

17. List the resources you observe on your way to school. Be sure to list at least one of each kind of resource—renewable, reusable, and nonrenewable. **S3L2b**

18. Compare recycling resources with reducing the use of resources. **S3L2b**

Critical Thinking

19. Suppose you want to start a recycling program at your school. Explain why recycling is important and what materials you could recycle. **S3L2b**

20. Would you prefer to live in a place with a lot of pollution or in a place with very little pollution? Explain. **S3L2a**

The Big Idea

Look at the picture below to answer question 1.

1. What feature of this plant stops large animals from eating it?

A. the flower's sweet smell

B. the flower's bright colors

C. the plant's sharp thorns

D. the plant's waxy leaves

S3L1b

2. A black bear's heartbeat rate slows down during winter. This happens because the bear is

A. migrating.   C. developing.

B. hibernating.   D. growing up.

S3L1c

3. How do a plant's roots help the plant?

A. Roots absorb water and nutrients from the soil.

B. Roots provide support for flowers and leaves.

C. Roots make food for the rest of the plant.

D. Roots make seeds so more plants can grow.

S3L1b

4. In which Georgia habitat are you most likely to find cattails, waterlilies, and leopard frogs?

A. a river valley in the mountains

B. a pond in the coastal plain

C. where the Atlantic Ocean meets the shoreline

D. on top of a hill in the piedmont

S3L1a

Use the map below to answer question 5.

☐ Summer
■ Winter

5. Study the map that shows where a kind of bird lives. What feature helps it survive cold winters?

A. It migrates.

B. It hibernates.

C. It looks like another animal.

D. It blends in with its surroundings.

S3CS4b   **S3L1c**

Use the drawing below to answer question 6.

6. In what way is the animal shown above adapted to its environment?

A. It has sharp claws for grabbing prey.

B. It has many layers of fat to keep it warm.

C. It has fur to keep its body warm.

D. It has a large beak for scooping up prey.

7. Which adaptation do pine trees have for staying green year-round?

A. They have thin needles with a waxy coating.

B. They have very shallow roots.

C. They have large, colorful flowers.

D. They have prop roots to hold them up. **S3L1b**

8. Which is the BEST example of an adaptation used for protection from predators?

A. a beaver's wide tail

B. a snake's leathery skin

C. a skunk's strong-smelling spray

D. a woodpecker's strong beak

9. In which region of Georgia would you find rolling hills, hickory and oak forests, and river valleys?

A. mountains

B. piedmont

C. coastal plain

D. wetlands **S3L1a**

Use the map below to answer question 10.

10. Which location will probably have the coldest temperatures?

A. Location 1

B. Location 2

C. Location 3

D. Location 4 **S3L1a**

11. Some oil from a lawn mower leaked into a pond in Maggie's yard. What probably happened to the plants in the pond?

A. The plants in the pond grew bigger.

B. The plants in the pond reproduced more quickly.

C. The plants in the pond died.

D. The number of plants in the pond increased.

S3CS4a   S3L2a

12. How are grasses adapted to living in places that have fires?

A. Their stems have a waxy coating.

B. Their seeds are fireproof.

C. They do not need a lot of water.

D. Their roots can grow back quickly.

S3CS4a   S3L1d

13. Which of the following is NOT a renewable resource?

A. sunlight

B. trees

C. air

D. gasoline

S3L2b

Use the table below to answer question 14.

Rainfall Amounts		
Location	Normal Rainfall in August	Rainfall this August
Houston	5 inches	$\frac{1}{2}$ inch
Los Angeles	$\frac{1}{2}$ inch	$\frac{1}{2}$ inch
New York	6 inches	5 inches
Atlanta	4 inches	6 inches

14. Which location in the table is going through a drought?

A. Houston

B. Los Angeles

C. New York

D. Atlanta   S3CS2a   S3L1d

15. Brendan is starting a club at his school to help conserve natural resources. Which of these ideas would NOT conserve resources?

A. recycling aluminum soda cans

B. reusing cloth lunch bags

C. using plastic forks instead of metal ones

D. turning off lights when no one is in a room   S3L2b

16. Rodney did a report on frogs. He read about frogs that have extra or missing legs. What type of pollution is most likely causing this to happen?

A. noise pollution
B. air pollution
C. water pollution
D. land pollution **S3L2a**

17. Which plants most likely have features for removing extra salt from their leaves and stems?

A. plants near a mountain stream
B. plants on a piedmont hill
C. plants in the Blue Ridge mountains
D. plants in a marsh near the ocean **S3L1b**

18. Which of these activities is a direct cause of water pollution?

A. using plastic bags instead of paper
B. spraying chemical fertilizer on your lawn
C. not recycling your bottles and cans
D. driving a car that uses a lot of gasoline **S3L2a**

Use the drawings below to answer question 19.

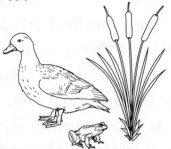

19. In which ecosystem would you expect to find all of these living things?

A. the Okefenokee swamp
B. the Atlantic Ocean
C. the top of a mountain
D. a cave in the piedmont **S3L1a**

20. Which is the BEST way for a class to gather the information they need to make a map of the habitats near their school?

A. They could look at an online encyclopedia about habitats and write a report.
B. They could explore different locations around the school and take pictures.
C. They could all explore one area and make guesses about what the other areas are like.
D. They could each write a report about a different habitat and then compare one another's reports. **S3CS8a** **S3L1a**

1. Lillian wants to find out how light affects the growth of algae in fish tanks. She has two fish tanks. One tank is in the sun near the window. The other tank is away from the window. Every day she looks at the tanks. What else should she do?

   A. Add more fish to each tank.

   B. Try to guess which tank will have the most algae.

   C. Add more water to the tanks.

   D. Record her observations each day. **S3CS8a** **S3L1d**

2. Which is NOT a characteristic of a mineral?

   A. found in nature

   B. is made of rocks

   C. has never been alive

   D. made of units that repeat in a pattern **S3E1a**

3. Which of the following is a way to reduce your use of resources?

   A. Take shorter showers.

   B. Eat only natural foods.

   C. Throw out as much garbage as possible.

   D. Leave radios and televisions on all day. **S3L2b**

4. A fire is burning in a fireplace. Which of the following is the best way to increase the amount of heat from the fire?

   A. Cover the fire with a metal screen.

   B. Add more logs.

   C. Put water on the fire.

   D. Stand closer to the fire. **S3P1a**

Use the drawing below to answer question 5.

5. What other living thing would you expect to see in this environment?

   A. an oak tree

   B. a blue crab

   C. a sunflower

   D. a striped skunk **S3CS4b** **S3L1a**

6. Tanya has four identical pots. They all contain the same amount of water. The temperature in each is 10°C. Tanya heats the four pots of water until they reach the following temperatures: 20°C, 25°C, 30°C, and 40°C. Which shows the greatest change in heat?

A. the 20°C pot

B. the 25°C pot

C. the 30°C pot

D. the 40°C pot

S3CS5c   S3P1d

7. Which property of a diamond makes it useful?

A. its shape

B. its strength

C. its hardness

D. its shine

S3E1b

8. Which Georgia habitat has dry, sandy land and the fewest types of plants?

A. a mountain bog

B. a piedmont forest

C. a swamp in the coastal plain

D. dunes at the beach

S3L1a

9. Parker pulled a muscle in gym class. The school nurse puts an instant hot pack on his leg. Categorize the way in which heat energy is produced in the hot pack.

A. burning

B. rubbing

C. friction

D. mixing two things together

S3P1a

10. Sandstone forms when layers of tiny grains of sediment harden. Why is sandstone a rock and not a mineral?

A. Sandstone is formed by nature.

B. It is made of several minerals.

C. It is used in buildings.

D. It erodes easily.

S3E1a

11. Manatees depend on sea grass for food. What happens when sea grass is ripped away by boat motors?

A. Fewer manatees are trapped by sea grass.

B. Boats attract more manatees to an area by making noise.

C. Sea grass populations increase.

D. Manatees have no food and may die.

S3L1d   S3L2a

Use the diagram below to answer question 12.

Talc

1 2 3 4 5 6 7 8 9 10

12. What does this scale tell you about talc?

A. Talc shines more than most other minerals.

B. Talc can be scratched by most other minerals.

C. Talc is more valuable than most other minerals.

D. Talc is heavier than most other minerals. **S3CS4b** **S3E1b**

13. Which of the following will repel the *N* pole of a bar magnet?

A. the *S* pole of a bar magnet

B. the *S* pole of a horseshoe magnet

C. the *N* pole of a horseshoe magnet

D. a steel paper clip **S3P2b**

14. Which is one way fire can be helpful to a forest ecosystem?

A. Heat from fire makes some trees release their seeds.

B. Animal habitats are destroyed.

C. Humans can build houses on the newly cleared land.

D. Smoke is given off, causing air pollution. **S3L1b** **S3L1d**

15. Why do you wear a coat on a cold day?

A. to reduce the amount of cold that gets to your body

B. to keep the transfer of thermal energy constant between your body and the air

C. to reduce the amount of heat energy that leaves your body

D. to increase the conduction of heat energy in your body **S3P1b**

16. Joyce wants her juice to stay cold as long as possible. She has four different mugs. Which one should she use?

A. the tin mug

B. the glass mug

C. the plastic foam mug

D. the copper mug **S3P1b**

17. Marshall wants to find out how water pollution affects plants. He sets up an experiment to study this. In his experiment, Marshall uses two plants, water, soil, and a chemical found in polluted water. What safety step should Marshall follow?

A. Read all the directions for the experiment.

B. Boil the water before using it.

C. Trim some leaves off the plants before using them.

D. Wear safety goggles when using chemicals.

S3CS3c S3L2a

18. Which property is NOT always a good way to identify a mineral?

A. the color of the mineral

B. the color of the mineral's streak

C. how hard the mineral is

D. how much the mineral shines

S3CS7a S3E1b

19. Which adaptation helps a fox squirrel escape from predators?

A. hibernation

B. ability to climb trees

C. has babies in the spring

D. migration

S3L1c

Use this graph to answer question 20.

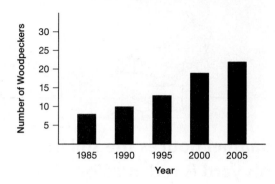

Woodpeckers living in my town

20. The graph above shows the number of woodpeckers living in a town for 21 years. Which of the following actions most likely caused the change in the number of woodpeckers?

A. The amount of air and water pollution decreased.

B. More homes for people were built in the town.

C. More trees were planted in the town's parks.

D. More cans and bottles were recycled in the town.

S3CS4b S3L1d

21. Which of the following is true of ALL soils in Georgia?

A. They are all the same color.

B. They all have the same texture.

C. They are all made of humus, water, and tiny bits of rock.

D. They are all good for growing fruits and vegetables.

S3E1c

Use the drawing below to answer question 22.

22. Samuel notices the soil in his yard is red in color. The soil feels slippery between his fingers. Which sentence tells about the type of soil in Samuel's yard?

A. It contains a lot of humus.
B. The grains of rock in it are so small that you need a microscope to see them.
C. You can clearly see the grains of rock in it.
D. Water runs through this soil quickly.
S3E1c

23. Which is a way people can conserve nonrenewable resources?

A. by recycling
B. by mining metals
C. by reducing pollution
D. by cutting down forests
S3L2b

24. Which experiment measures the transfer of heat energy from the sun to different materials?

A. Measure the temperature of two materials left in sunlight for the same length of time.
B. Measure the temperature of two materials left in sunlight for different periods of time.
C. Measure the temperature of one material in sunlight and one material in shade.
D. Measure the temperature of one material on a cold day and one material on a hot day.
S3CS5a **S3P1c**

25. Which kind of soil contains the most humus?

A. clay
B. sand
C. silt
D. loam
S3E1c

26. Which garden plant has roots adapted for storing food?

A. corn
B. lettuce
C. carrots
D. peas
S3L1b

Use the graph below to answer question 27.

Testing Materials for a Cooler

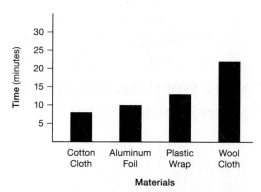

27. **Marcy wrapped each of four cups with a different material. She placed an ice cube in each cup and measured how long it took the ice cube to melt. Which material was the best insulator?**

A. cotton cloth

B. aluminum foil

C. plastic wrap

D. wool cloth **S3CS6a** **S3P1b**

28. **You find the fossil of a plant. Which conclusion can you draw?**

A. This plant lived long ago.

B. This plant is now extinct.

C. This plant could not live in today's environment.

D. This plant was an important source of food for ancient animals. **S3CS1b** **S3E2a**

Use the diagram below to answer questions 29 and 30.

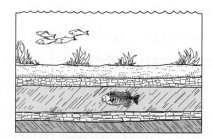

29. **Study this diagram. Which of the following steps happened first?**

A. The remains were covered with sediment.

B. Pressure turned the sediment to rock over time.

C. A living thing died long ago.

D. A fossil was found in a rock. **S3CS4b** **S3E2b**

30. **Look at the diagram again. What kind of rock is this?**

A. There is no way to tell.

B. metamorphic

C. sedimentary

D. igneous **S3E1b**

31. **The large claws and beak on an eagle help the animal to**

A. catch and eat food.

B. get rid of excess body heat.

C. hold in body heat.

D. hide from predators. **S3L1c**

32. Jamal has a cup of boiling water. He sets the cup on his desk and measures the temperature of the water. After ten minutes and after twenty minutes, he measures the temperature again. Which drawing BEST shows his results?

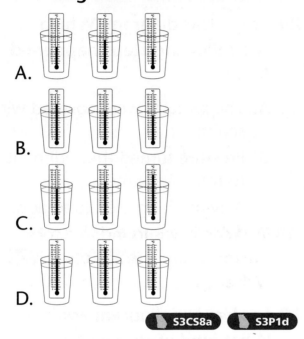

A.

B.

C.

D.

33. A student has a cup of water. The temperature of the water is 10°C. The air temperature in the room is 25°C. What will be the temperature of the water in the cup after it sits in the room for a day?

A. 10°C
B. 20°C
C. 25°C
D. 30°C

Use the drawing below to answer question 34.

34. How do you think this seed pod ends up in other places?

A. It is carried by the wind.
B. It is carried by water.
C. Animals eat it.
D. It attaches to an animal's fur.

35. Which of these magnets will repel each other?

A. S N S N

B. N S N S

C. S N N S

D. N S / S N

36. How can water make the cracks in a sidewalk get bigger?

A. When water freezes, it takes up more room.

B. Water can soften a rock.

C. Water can wear away the edges of the rock.

D. When water freezes, it takes up less room.

S3E1d

Use the graph to answer question 37.

Body Temperature of a Bat

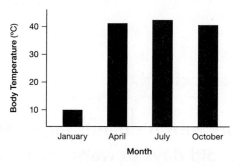

37. Which adaptation does the graph show the effect of?

A. extinction

B. migration

C. hibernation

D. thick fur

S3L1c

38. Which does NOT cause weathering or erosion?

A. wind blowing

B. water flowing

C. ice forming in cracks

D. volcanoes erupting

S3E1d

39. In which investigation would a student be MOST likely to use a thermometer?

A. to compare the thickness of insulating materials

B. to determine how long water takes to evaporate

C. to find out how quickly water heats up on a gas burner

D. to see which materials will burn

S3CS8c   S3P1d

Use this drawing to answer question 40.

40. A delta is an area of land that forms at the mouth of a river. What causes a delta to form?

A. weathering by water

B. weathering by wind

C. erosion by water

D. erosion by wind

S3E1d

41. Ann took a trip to Georgia. She saw red squirrels and hemlock trees while hiking up a steep slope. Ann visited the

A. mountains.

B. Atlantic coast.

C. wetlands.

D. piedmont.

S3L1a

42. Maureen has three magnets. She puts them on a chalkboard, a refrigerator door, and a corkboard to see if they will stick. Which question is Maureen investigating?

A. To which surfaces will magnets stick?

B. How can I make magnets stick to different surfaces?

C. How do magnets change the surface they stick to?

D. Why do magnets stick to surfaces that contain iron?

 S3P2a

Use this drawing to answer question 43.

43. What can these fossils show about the dinosaur that made them?

A. what the dinosaur ate

B. what color the dinosaur was

C. what animals ate the dinosaur

D. where the dinosaur lived

 S3E2a

44. What will probably happen to a population of ducks if the pond they live near is filled in by soil?

A. The ducks will have to learn to live without the plants they normally eat.

B. The ducks will stop migrating.

C. The ducks will have to move to another pond, or they will die.

D. The ducks will grow stronger.

 S3CS4a S3L1d

Use the drawing below to answer question 45.

45. Mark rubs his hands together on cold days to warm them up. How does rubbing his hands together produce heat?

A. Heat is produced by friction.

B. Heat is produced by small sparks between his hands.

C. Heat moves from the sun into his hands.

D. Heat is produced by a chemical reaction. S3P1a

46. Why are more animal fossils found than plant fossils?

A. Animal fossils formed on Earth's surface, but plant fossils were buried.

B. Plants have softer parts, so very few left fossils.

C. Long ago, there were more animals than plants.

D. Plants did not leave behind any imprints. **S3E2a**

47. Water is called a renewable resource because

A. it can be cleaned and used again and will not run out.

B. pollution does not affect water.

C. more water is being made in clouds all the time.

D. there is always plenty of water available. **S3L2b**

48. Suppose a magnet suddenly drops an object. What is the BEST conclusion you can draw?

A. It is an electromagnet, and the current was turned off.

B. It is an electromagnet, and the current was turned on.

C. It is a permanent magnet, and the poles switched.

D. It is a permanent magnet without a magnetic field. **S3P2a**

Use the table to answer question 49.

Paper Clip Investigation	
Magnet	Number of Paper Clips Picked Up
A	
B	
C	
D	

49. A student makes the data table shown. What is she investigating?

A. the strengths of four magnets

B. whether magnets repel paper clips

C. whether paper clips contain iron

D. the location of the magnets' north and south poles **S3CS8a** **S3P2a**

50. How is a cast fossil formed?

A. A dead animal is buried and decays, leaving behind an opening in the shape of its body.

B. An animal steps in mud, which hardens into rock.

C. Bits of minerals slowly replace a dead plant.

D. Mud or minerals fill an opening left after an animal decays. **S3E2b**

References

Contents

Health Handbook

Reading in Science Handbook

Math in Science Handbook

Your Skin

Your skin is your body's largest organ. It provides your body with a tough protective covering. It protects you from disease. It provides your sense of touch, which allows you to feel pressure, textures, temperature, and pain. Your skin also produces sweat to help control your body temperature. When you play hard or exercise, your body produces sweat, which cools you as it evaporates. The sweat from your skin also helps your body get rid of extra salt and other wastes.

▼ The skin is the body's largest organ.

Epidermis
Many layers of dead skin cells form the top of the epidermis. Cells in the lower part of the epidermis are always making new cells.

Pore
These tiny holes on the surface of your skin lead to your dermis.

Oil Gland
Oil glands produce oil that keeps your skin soft and smooth.

Dermis
The dermis is much thicker than the epidermis. It is made up of tough, flexible fibers.

Hair Follicle
Each hair follicle has a muscle that can contract and make the hair "stand on end."

Fatty Tissue
This tissue layer beneath the dermis stores food, provides warmth, and attaches your skin to the bone and muscle below.

Caring for Your Skin

- To protect your skin and to keep it healthy, you should wash your body, including your hair and your nails, every day. This helps remove germs, excess oils and sweat, and dead cells from the epidermis, the outer layer of your skin. Because you touch many things during the day, you should wash your hands with soap and water frequently.

- If you get a cut or scratch, you should wash it right away and cover it with a sterile bandage to prevent infection.

- Protect your skin from cuts and scrapes by wearing proper safety equipment.

- Always protect your skin from sunburn by wearing protective clothing and sunscreen when you are outdoors.

Your Digestive System

Your digestive system is made up of many organs that are connected. It breaks down the food you eat and disposes of the leftover wastes your body does not need.

Mouth to Stomach

Digestion begins when you chew your food. Chewing your food breaks it up and mixes it with saliva. When you swallow, the softened food travels down your esophagus to your stomach. In your stomach, the food is mixed with digestive juices. These are strong acids that continue the process of breaking your food down into the nutrients your body needs to stay healthy. Your stomach squeezes your food and turns it into a thick liquid.

Small Intestine and Liver

Your food leaves your stomach and goes into your small intestine. This organ is a long tube just below your stomach. Your liver is an organ that sends bile into your small intestine to continue the process of digesting fats in the food.

The walls of the small intestine are lined with millions of small, finger-shaped bumps called villi. Tiny blood vessels in these bumps absorb nutrients from the food as it moves through the small intestine.

Large Intestine

When the food has traveled all the way through your small intestine, it passes into your large intestine. This is the last organ of your digestive system. The large intestine absorbs water from the food. The remaining wastes are held there until you go to the bathroom.

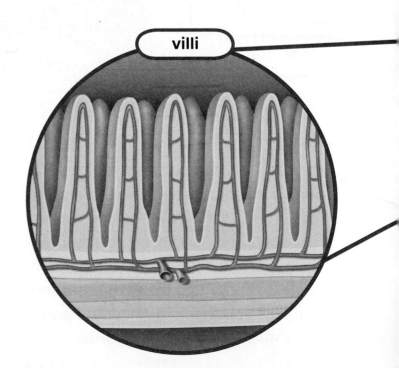

villi

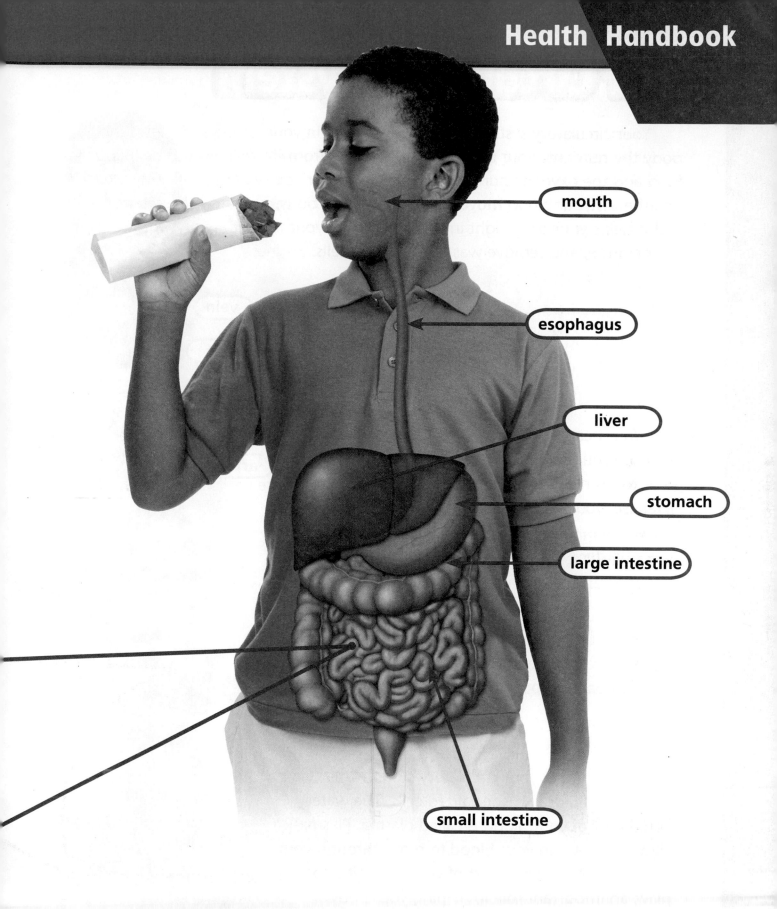

mouth

esophagus

liver

stomach

large intestine

small intestine

Your Circulatory System

Your circulatory system carries to every cell in your body the nutrients your digestive system takes from food and the oxygen your lungs take from the air you breathe. As your blood moves throughout your body, it also helps your body fight infections, control your temperature, and remove wastes from your cells.

vein

heart

artery

Your Heart and Blood Vessels

Your heart is the organ that pumps your blood through your circulatory system. Your heart is a strong muscle that beats continuously. As you exercise, your heart adjusts itself to beat faster to deliver the energy and oxygen your muscles need to work harder.

Blood from your heart is pumped through veins into your lungs, where it releases carbon dioxide and picks up oxygen. Your blood then travels back to your heart to be pumped through your arteries to every part of your body.

Your Blood

The blood in your circulatory system is a mixture of fluids and specialized cells. The watery liquid part of your blood is called plasma. Plasma allows the cells in your blood to move through your blood vessels to every part of your body. It also plays an important role in helping your body control your temperature.

Blood Cells

blood cells

There are three main types of cells in your blood. Each type of cell in your circulatory system plays a special part in keeping your body healthy and fit.

Red Blood Cells are the most numerous cells in your blood. They carry oxygen from your lungs throughout your body. They also carry carbon dioxide back to your lungs from your cells, so you can breathe it out.

White Blood Cells help your body fight infections when you become ill.

Platelets help your body stop bleeding when you get a cut or other wound. Platelets clump together as soon as you start to bleed. The sticky clump of platelets traps red blood cells and forms a blood clot. The blood clot hardens to make a scab that seals the cut and lets your body begin healing the wound.

Caring for Your Circulatory System

- Eat foods that are low in fat and high in fiber. Fiber helps take away substances that can lead to fatty buildup in your blood vessels.

- Eat foods high in iron to help your red blood cells carry oxygen.

- Drink plenty of water to help your body replenish your blood.

- Avoid contact with another person's blood.

- Exercise regularly to keep your heart strong.

- Never smoke or use tobacco.

Your Skeletal System

Your skeletal system includes all of the bones in your body. These strong, hard parts of your body protect your internal organs, help you move, and allow you to sit and to stand up straight.

Your skeletal system works with your muscular system to hold your body up and to give it shape.

Your skeletal system includes more than 200 bones. These bones come in many different shapes and sizes.

Your Skull

The wide flat bones of your skull fit tightly together to protect your brain. The bones in the front of your skull give your face its shape and allow the muscles in your face to express your thoughts and feelings.

Your Spine

Your spine, or backbone, is made up of nearly two dozen small, round bones. These bones fit together and connect your head to your pelvis.
Each of these bones, or vertebrae, is shaped like a doughnut, with a small round hole in the center. Your spinal cord is a bundle of nerves that carries information to and from your brain and the rest of your body. Your spinal cord runs from your brain down your back to your hips through the holes in your vertebrae. There are soft, flexible disks of cartilage between your vertebrae. This allows you to bend and twist your spine. Your spine, pelvis, and leg bones work together to allow you to stand, sit, or move.

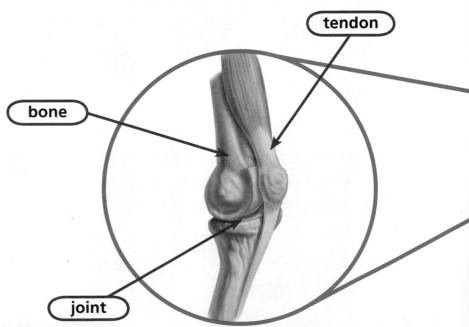

tendon

bone

joint

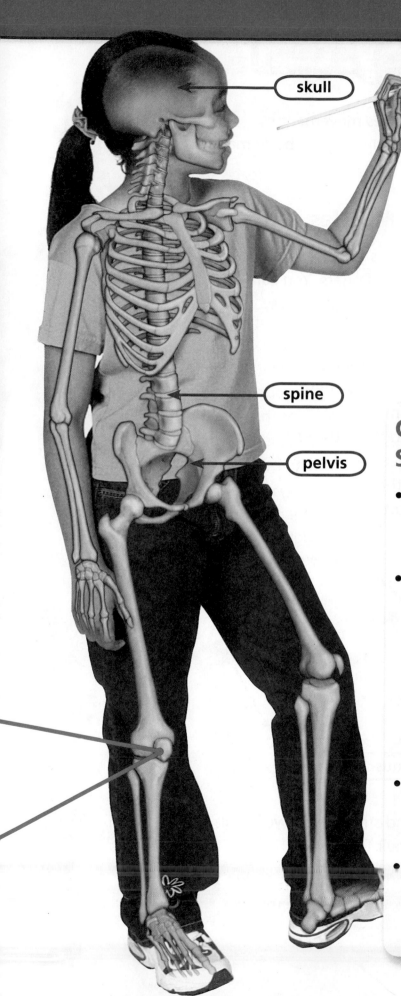

skull

spine

pelvis

Caring for Your Skeletal System

- Always wear a helmet and proper safety gear when you play sports, skate, or ride a bike or a scooter.

- Your bones are made mostly of calcium and other minerals. To keep your skeletal system strong and to help it grow, you should eat foods, like milk, cheese, and yogurt, that are high in calcium. Dark green, leafy vegetables like broccoli, spinach, and collard greens are also good sources of calcium.

- Exercise to help your bones stay strong and healthy. Get plenty of rest to help your bones grow.

- Stand and sit with good posture. Sitting slumped over puts strain on your muscles and on your bones.

Your Muscular System

A muscle is a body part that produces movement by contracting and relaxing. All of the muscles in your body make up the muscular system.

Voluntary and Involuntary Muscles

Voluntary Muscles are the muscles you use to move your arms and legs, your face, head, and fingers. You can make these muscles contract or relax to control the way your body moves.

Involuntary Muscles are responsible for movements you usually don't see or control. These muscles make up your heart, your stomach and digestive system, your diaphragm, and the muscles that control your eyelids. Your heart beats and your diaphragm powers your breathing without your thinking about them. You cannot stop the action of these muscles.

How Muscles Help You Move

All muscles pull when they contract. Moving your body in more than one direction takes more than one muscle. To reach out with your arm or to pull it back, you use a pair of muscles. As one muscle contracts to extend your arm, the other relaxes and stretches. As you pull your arm back, the muscles reverse their functions.

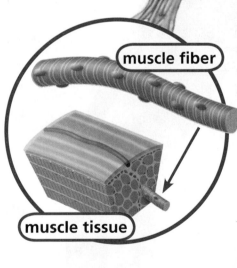

muscle fiber

muscle tissue

Your muscles let you do many kinds of things. The large muscles in your legs allow you to walk and run. Tiny muscles in your face allow you to smile.

arm muscle

Your Muscles and Your Bones

The muscles that allow you to move your body work with your skeletal system. Muscles in your legs that allow you to kick a ball or ride a bicycle pull on the bones and joints of your legs and lower body. Your muscles are connected to your skeletal system by strong, cordlike tissues called tendons.

Your Achilles tendon, just above your heel, connects your calf muscles to your heel bone. When you contract those muscles, the tendon pulls on the heel bone and allows you to stand on your toes, jump, or push hard on your bicycle's pedals.

Caring for Your Muscular System

- Always stretch and warm up your muscles before exercising or playing sports. Do this by jogging or walking for at least ten minutes. This brings fresh blood and oxygen into your muscles and helps prevent injury or pain.

- Eat a balanced diet of foods to be sure your muscles have the nutrients they need to grow and remain strong.

- Stop exercising if you feel pain in your muscles.

- Drink plenty of water when you exercise or play sports. This helps your blood remove wastes from your muscles and helps you build endurance.

- Always cool down after you exercise. Walk or jog slowly for five or ten minutes to let your heartbeat slow and your breathing return to normal. This helps you avoid pain and stiffness after your muscles work hard.

- Get plenty of rest before and after you work your muscles hard. They need time to repair themselves and recover from working hard.

Your Eyes and Vision

Your eyes allow you to see light reflected by the things around you. This diagram shows how an eye works. Light enters through the clear outer surface called the cornea. It passes through the pupil. The lens bends the incoming light to focus it on the retina. The retina sends nerve signals along the optic nerve. Your brain uses the signals to form an image. This is what you "see."

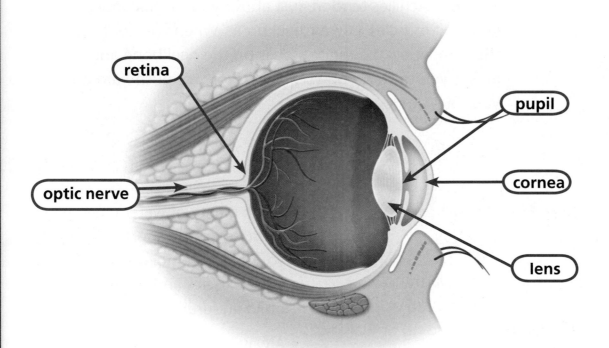

Caring for Your Eyes

- Never touch or rub your eyes.

- Protect your eyes by wearing safety goggles when you use tools or play sports.

- Wear swim goggles to protect your eyes from chlorine or other substances in the water.

- You should have a doctor check your eyesight every year. Tell your parents or your doctor if your vision becomes blurry or if you are having headaches or pain in your eyes.

- Wear sunglasses to protect your eyes from very bright light. Looking directly at bright light or at the sun can damage your eyes permanently.

Your Ears and Hearing

Sounds travel through the air in waves. When some of those waves enter your ear, you hear a sound. This diagram shows the inside of your ear.

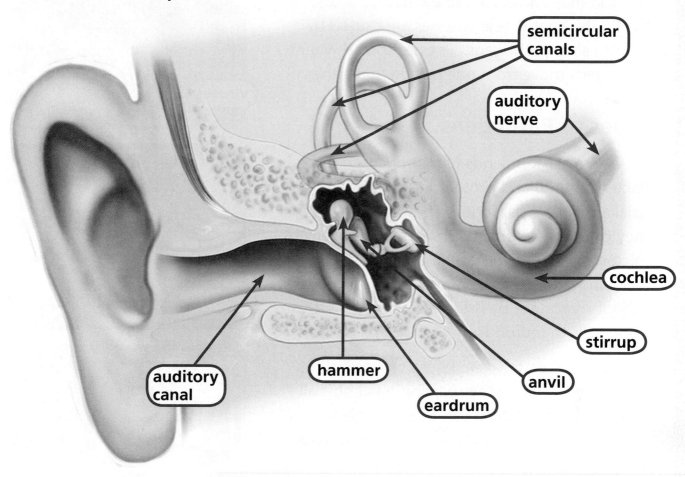

- semicircular canals
- auditory nerve
- cochlea
- stirrup
- anvil
- eardrum
- hammer
- auditory canal

Caring for Your Ears

- Never put anything in your ears.

- Wear a helmet that covers your ears when you play sports.

- Keep your ears warm in winter.

- Avoid loud sounds and listening to loud music.

- Have your ears checked by a doctor if they hurt or leak fluid or if you have any loss of hearing.

- Wear earplugs when you swim. Water in your ears can lead to infection.

Your Immune System

Pathogens and Illness

You may know someone who had a cold or the flu this year. These illnesses are caused by germs called pathogens. Illnesses spread when pathogens move from one person to another.

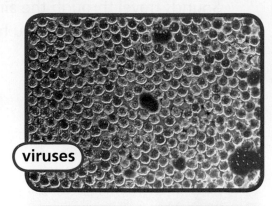
viruses

Types of Pathogens

There are four kinds of pathogens—viruses, bacteria, fungi, and protozoans. Viruses are the smallest kind of pathogen. They are so small that they can be seen only with very powerful electron microscopes. Viruses cause many types of illness, including colds, the flu, and chicken pox. Viruses cannot reproduce by themselves. They must use living cells to reproduce.

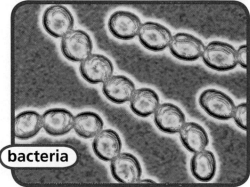
bacteria

Bacteria are tiny, single-cell organisms that live in water, in the soil, and on almost all surfaces. Most bacteria can be seen only with a microscope. Not all bacteria cause illness. Your body needs some types of bacteria to work well.

The most common type of fungus infection is athlete's foot. This is a burning, itchy infection of the skin between your toes. Ringworm is another skin infection caused by a fungus. It causes itchy round patches to develop on the skin.

fungi

Protozoans are the fourth type of pathogen. They are single-cell organisms that are slightly larger than bacteria. They can cause disease when they grow in food or drinking water.

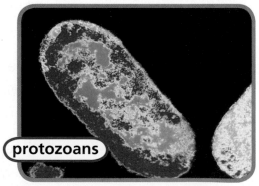
protozoans

Fighting Illness

Pathogens that can make you ill are everywhere. When you become ill, a doctor may be able to treat you. You also can practice healthful habits to protect yourself and others from the spread of pathogens and the illnesses they can cause.

The best way to avoid spreading pathogens is to wash your hands with warm water and soap. This floats germs off of your skin. You should wash your hands often. Always wash them before and after eating, after handling animals, and after using the bathroom. Avoid touching your mouth, eyes, and nose. Never share hats, combs, cups, or drinking straws. If you get a cut or scrape, pathogens can enter your body. It is important to wash cuts and scrapes carefully with soap and water. Then cover the injury with a sterile bandage.

When you are ill, you should avoid spreading pathogens to others. Cover your nose and mouth when you sneeze or cough.

Don't share anything that has touched your mouth or nose. Stay home from school until an adult or your doctor tells you that you are well enough to go back.

Even though pathogens are all around, most people become ill only once in a while because the body has systems that protect it from pathogens. These defenses keep pathogens from entering your body.

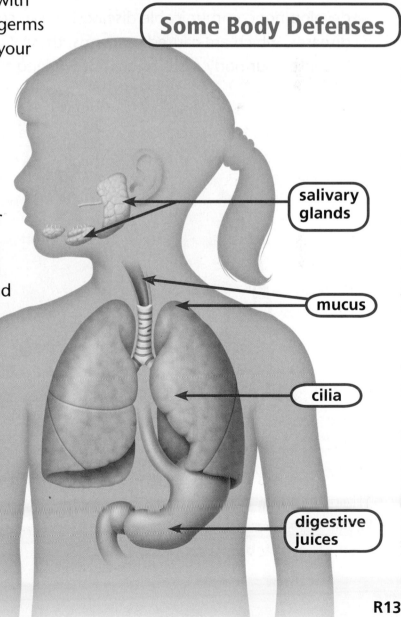

Some Body Defenses

salivary glands

mucus

cilia

digestive juices

Eat a Balanced Diet

Eating the foods that your body needs to grow and fight illness is the most important thing you can do to stay healthy. A balanced diet of healthful foods gives your body energy. Your body's systems need nutrients to function properly and work together.

Choosing unhealthful foods can cause you to gain excess weight and to lack energy. Inactivity and poor food choices can lead to you becoming ill more frequently. Unhealthful foods can also cause you to develop noncommunicable diseases. Unlike communicable diseases, which are caused by germs, these illnesses occur because your body systems are not working right.

Exercise Regularly

Exercise keeps your body healthy. Regular exercise helps your heart, lungs, and muscles stay strong. It helps your body digest food. It also helps your body fight disease. Exercising to keep your body strong also helps prevent injury when you play sports.

Exercise allows your body to rest more effectively. Getting enough sleep prepares your body for the next day. It allows your muscles and bones to grow and recover from exercise. Resting also helps keep your mind alert so you can learn and play well.

Identify the Main Idea and Details

This Reading in Science Handbook provides tips for using the ⊕ Reading Focus Skills you see throughout this book. Many of the lessons in this science book are written so you can understand main ideas and the details that support them. You can use a graphic organizer like this one to show a main idea and details.

Main Idea: The most important idea of a selection

| **Detail:** Information that tells more about the main idea | **Detail:** Information that tells more about the main idea | **Detail:** Information that tells more about the main idea |

Tips for Identifying the Main Idea and Details

• To find the main idea, ask *What is this mostly about?*

• Remember that the main idea is not always stated in the first sentence.

• Look for details that answer questions such as *Who, What, Where, When, Why,* and *How.* Use pictures as clues to help you figure out the main idea.

Here is an example.

Main Idea

Soil is an important resource. The plants you eat are grown in soil. Animals such as cows and chickens eat plants that grow in soil, too. The plants we use for lumber also grow in soil.

Detail

Main Idea: Soil is an important resource.

| **Detail:** Plants you eat grow in soil. | **Detail:** Animals eat plants that grow in soil. | **Detail:** Plants used for lumber grow in soil. |

More About Main Idea and Details

Sometimes the main idea of a paragraph is at the end instead of the beginning. If the main idea is not given at all, look at the details to figure it out. Look at the graphic organizer. What do you think the main idea is?

Main Idea:

Detail:
Topsoil is the top layer of soil. It is made up of humus.

Detail:
Subsoil is the next layer of soil. It is made up of small rocks.

Detail:
The bottom layer is bedrock. It is mostly solid rock.

Sometimes a paragraph's main idea might contain details of different types. In this paragraph, identify whether the details give reasons, examples, facts, steps, or descriptions.

Farmers and scientists have found a type of soil that is best for growing plants. It is soil that contains an equal mixture of sand, clay, and humus. Soil with this mixture can hold the right amount of water. It also has enough nutrients.

Skill Practice

Read the following paragraph. Use the Tips for Identifying the Main Idea and Details to answer the questions.

Soil helps all living things meet their needs. It provides a home for some animals and plants. Soil is used to grow plants for food. It is also used to grow resources such as trees for lumber and paper.

1. What is the main idea of the paragraph?

2. What supporting details give more information?

3. What details answer any of the questions *Who, What, Where, When, Why,* and *How?*

Compare and Contrast

Some lessons are written to help you see how things are alike or different. You can use a graphic organizer like this one to compare and contrast.

> **Topic:** Name the topic—the two things you are comparing and contrasting.

> **Alike**
> List ways the things are alike.

> **Different**
> List ways the things are different.

Tips for Comparing and Contrasting

- To compare, ask *How are things alike?*

- To contrast, ask *How are things different?*

- When you compare, look for signal words and phrases such as *similar, alike, both, the same as, too,* and *also.*

- When you contrast, look for signal words and phrases such as *unlike, different, however, yet,* and *but.*

Here is an example.

Compare

> Both dogs and cats have been kept by people for thousands of years. These four-legged companions have lived in our homes and shared our food. They are different in many ways. Cats help keep small animals like mice and rats out of the house. Dogs warn us of danger. Cats like to nap, but dogs like to play.

Contrast

Here is what you could record in the graphic organizer.

> **Topic: Dogs and Cats**

> **Alike**
> They live with humans, have four legs, and share our foods.

> **Different**
> Cats chase mice, dogs bark at danger. Cats nap, dogs play.

More About Compare and Contrast

You can better understand new information about things when you know how they are alike and how they are different. Use the graphic organizer from page R18 to sort the following new information about cats and dogs.

Cats	Like fish	Afraid of dogs	Climb trees	Very independent

Dogs	Like meats	Bark at strange dogs	Run very fast	Will come when called

Sometimes a paragraph compares and contrasts more than one topic. In the following paragraph, the sentence that compares things is underlined. Find the sentences that contrast things.

> The first boats and the first airplanes were both powered by using wooden parts. People pulled wooden oars to move the first boats through water. Early airplanes were pulled through the air by wooden propellers. Wood is a strong, flexible material that is easy to shape into tools. A single oar can move a boat over water with each stroke, but a propeller must turn continuously to keep an airplane flying.

Skill Practice

Read the following paragraph. Use the Tips for Comparing and Contrasting to answer the questions.

> Both boats and airplanes seem to float easily. But water is much denser than air. Boats float on top of water because their weight is spread over the bottom of the boat. Airplanes are held up by the air under their wings. Boats can float when they are not moving. However, airplanes must move forward all the time. This creates the lifting force under their wings.

1. What is one likeness that boats and airplanes share?

2. What is one difference between boats and airplanes?

3. What are two signal words that helped you identify likenesses and differences?

Cause and Effect

Focus Skill

Some of the lessons in this science book are written to help you understand why things happen. You can use a graphic organizer like this one to show cause and effect.

Cause	Effect
A cause is the reason, or why, something happens.	An effect is what happens.

Tips for Identifying Cause and Effect

- To find an effect, ask *What happened?*
- To find a cause, ask *Why did this happen?*
- Remember that events can have more than one cause or effect.
- Look for signal words such as *because, as a result, so,* and *therefore.*

Here is an example.

Effect

A gecko is a small lizard. It can climb up walls and walk upside down without falling. Scientist have found out how geckos stick on things so well. They have millions of tiny hairs on their feet. The hairs have flat ends that stick to almost anything. So, the gecko can walk on a ceiling without falling down.

Cause

Here is what you could record in the graphic organizer.

Cause	Effect
Geckos have tiny hairs on their feet with flat ends that stick to almost anything.	Geckos can climb walls and walk upside down.

More About Cause and Effect

Events can have more than one cause or effect. For example, suppose the paragraph on page R20 included a sentence that said *This helps the gecko escape from predators.* You could then identify two effects of geckos and their sticky feet.

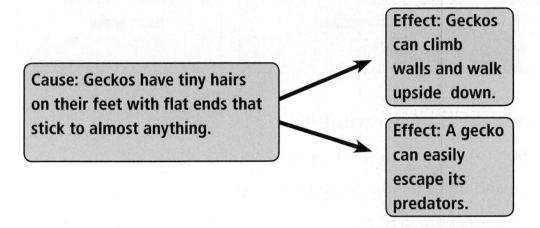

Cause: Geckos have tiny hairs on their feet with flat ends that stick to almost anything.

Effect: Geckos can climb walls and walk upside down.

Effect: A gecko can easily escape its predators.

Some paragraphs contain more than one cause and effect. In the following paragraph, one cause and its effect are underlined. Find the second cause and its effect.

> <u>Birds have a body covering of feathers.</u> <u>The feathers keep birds warm and dry</u>. Feathers also give a bird's body a smooth surface over which air can easily flow. Another thing that helps birds fly is their bones. A bird's bones are filled with air pockets. As a result, the bird is very light, and this helps it fly.

Skill Practice

Read the following paragraph. Use the Tips for Identifying Cause and Effect to help you answer the questions.

> The viceroy butterfly would be a tasty meal for a bird. However, the viceroy looks a lot like the monarch butterfly. Birds often mistake the viceroy for a monarch, which tastes bad to birds. Therefore, birds usually leave the viceroy alone.

1. What causes birds to not eat the viceroy butterfly?

2. What is the effect of the viceroy's looking like a monarch?

3. Name a signal word that helped you identify a cause or an effect.

Sequence

Some lessons in this science book are written to help you understand the order in which things happen. You can use a graphic organizer like this one to show a sequence.

1. The first thing that happened	→	2. The next thing that happened	→	3. The last thing that happened

Tips for Understanding a Sequence

- Pay attention to the order in which events happen.
- Recall dates and times to help you understand the sequence.
- Look for time-order signal words such as *first, next, then, last,* and *finally.*
- Sometimes it is helpful to add time-order words yourself as you read.

Here is an example.

> Suppose you have a mixture of rice, paper clips, and marbles. You need to separate the parts of the mixture. **First,** you separate the marbles with your hands. **Then,** you use a magnet to separate the paper clips. **Finally,** the rice is left.

Time-order words

Here is what you could record in the graphic organizer.

1. First, you separate the marbles by hand.	→	2. Then, you use the magnet to separate the paper clips.	→	3. Finally, the rice is left.

More About Sequence

Sometimes information is sequenced by dates. Use a graphic organizer like the following to sequence the order in which water in a pond freezes and melts.

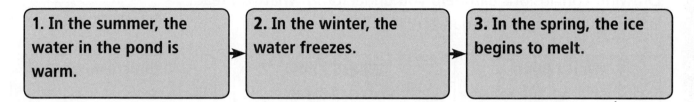

| 1. In the summer, the water in the pond is warm. | → | 2. In the winter, the water freezes. | → | 3. In the spring, the ice begins to melt. |

When time-order words are not given, add your own. Look at the underlined time-order word in the paragraph below. How many more time-order words can you add to help you understand the sequence?

> When you cook food, you make new kinds of matter. <u>First</u>, flour, eggs, milk, and oil are mixed to make pancake batter. The batter is poured on a stove. The batter cooks and turns into pancakes. The pancakes will never be flour, eggs, milk, and oil again.

Skill Practice

Read the following paragraph. Use the Tips for Understanding Sequence to answer the questions.

> A shiny iron bolt was left outdoors. It sat in the rain and moist air. After several days, the bolt began to turn dull. After a week, it turned an orange-brown color. When it was picked up a month later, the orange-brown iron bolt was flaky and soft. The orange-brown material was rust. When a metal turns to rust, it loses some of its strength.

1. What is the first thing that happens in this sequence?

2. About how long did the process take?

3. What three phrases helped you identify the sequence in this paragraph?

Draw Conclusions

Focus Skill

At the end of each lesson in this science book, you will be asked to draw conclusions. To draw conclusions, use information from the text you are reading and what you already know. Drawing conclusions can help you understand what you read. You can use a graphic organizer like this one.

| **What I Read**
List facts from the text. | + | **What I Know**
List related ideas that you already know. | = | **Conclusion:**
Combine what you just read in the text with what you already know. |

Tips for Drawing Conclusions

- To draw conclusions, ask *What do I need to think about from the text?*

- To draw conclusions, ask *What do I really know that could help me draw a conclusion?*

- Be sure your conclusions make sense.

Here is an example.

When astronauts visited the moon, they left footprints. On the moon, there is no water. There is also very little air. Without air, there is no wind or weather. So the footprints that were left on the moon are still there.

Here is what you could record in the graphic organizer.

| **What I Read**
The astronauts left footprints on the moon. The moon has no weather. | + | **What I Know**
Footprints left on earth would be washed away by wind or rain. | = | **Conclusion:**
The footprints on the moon will be there for a long time. |

More About Drawing Conclusions

Sometimes a paragraph does not contain enough information to draw a conclusion that makes sense. Read the paragraph below. Think of one right conclusion you could draw. Then think of a conclusion that would be wrong.

> Venus is the second planet from the sun. It is about the same size as Earth. Venus is dry and covered with thick clouds. The thick clouds trap heat and make the planet's surface very hot.

Text Information

Your Own Experience

What I Read The clouds on Venus trap heat and make the planet very hot.	+	**What I Know**	=	**Conclusion:**

Skill Practice

Read the following paragraph. Use the Tips for Drawing Conclusions to answer the questions.

> The inner planets are Mercury, Venus, Earth, and Mars. They are the four planets in the solar system that are closest to the sun. When you see these planets from space, Earth is the only one that looks blue. None of the other planets have liquid water. People would need special suits to live on the other planets.

1. What conclusion can you draw about the inner planets?

2. What information from your own experience helped you draw the conclusion?

3. What text information did you use to draw the conclusion?

Summarize

Retell what you have just read. Use the main idea and only the most important details.

Tips for Summarizing

- To write a summary, ask—What is the most important idea or the main thing that happened?

- Be sure the details you include are things the reader needs to know.

- Make your summary shorter than what you have read.

- Write a summary in your own words. Be sure to put the events in order.

Here is an example.

Main Idea

Fish are a type of animal group. They live their entire lives in water. Fish have gills that they use to take in oxygen from the water. Fish have a body covering of scales. The scales are small, thin, flat plates that help protect the fish. Fish also have fins they use to move in water.

Detail

Main Idea: Fish are a type of animal group.

| **Detail:** Fish have gills they use to take in oxygen. | **Detail:** They are covered with scales. | **Summary:** Fish are an animal group. They have gills, a body covering of scales, and fins. |

Here is what you could record in the graphic organizer.

Main Idea:		Detail:		Summary:
Fish are a type of animal group.	+	Fish have gills they use to take in oxygen. They are covered with scales.	=	Fish are an animal group. They have gills, a body covering of scales, and fins.

More About Summarizing

Sometimes a paragraph has details that are not important enough to put in a summary. What if the paragraph on page R26 included a sentence about the color and size of a fish's scales? You would leave these details out of the summary. They would not be needed to understand the main idea.

Skill Practice

Read the following paragraph. Use the Tips for Summarizing to answer the questions.

> Amphibians are animals that begin life in the water and move onto land as adults. Amphibians lay eggs in the water. The eggs stay there until they hatch. Young amphibians, such as tadpoles, live in the water. They breathe with gills. As they grow, they develop lungs. Once they have lungs, their gills disappear. Tadpoles also develop other body parts, such as legs. These help them live on land. Most adult amphibians live on land.

1. If a friend asked you what this paragraph is about, what information would you include? What would you leave out?

2. What is the main idea of the paragraph?

3. What two details would you include in a summary of the paragraph?

Using Tables, Charts, and Graphs

As you do investigations in science, you collect, organize, display, and interpret data. Tables, charts, and graphs are good ways to organize and display data so that others can understand and interpret your data.

The tables, charts, and graphs in this Handbook will help you read and understand data. You can also use the information to choose the best ways to display data so that you can use it to draw conclusions and make predictions.

Reading a Table

A third-grade class is studying the lengths of different sea animals. They want to find out how the lengths vary. The table shows some of the data the students have collected.

LENGTHS OF SEA ANIMALS	
Animal	**Length (in feet)**
Whale shark	60
White shark	40
Bottlenose dolphin	10
Giant squid	55
Gray whale	50

Title ← (LENGTHS OF SEA ANIMALS)
Header ← (Length (in feet))
Data ← (40)

How to Read a Table

1. Read the title to find out what the table is about.

2. Read the headings to find out what information is given.

3. Study the data. Look for patterns.

4. **Draw conclusions.** If you display the data in a graph, you might be able to see patterns easily.

By studying the table, you can see the lengths of different sea animals. However, suppose the students want to look for patterns in the data. They might choose to display the data in a different way, such as in a bar graph.

Reading a Bar Graph

The data in this bar graph is the same as in the table. A bar graph can be used to compare the data about different events or groups.

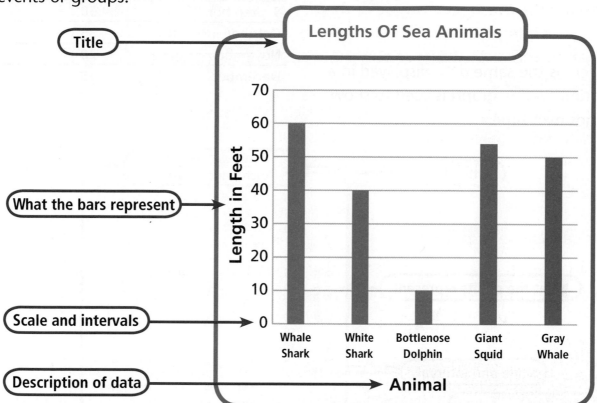

Title

What the bars represent

Scale and intervals

Description of data

Lengths Of Sea Animals

Length in Feet

70
60
50
40
30
20
10
0

Whale Shark | White Shark | Bottlenose Dolphin | Giant Squid | Gray Whale

Animal

How to Read a Bar Graph

1. Look at the graph to determine what kind of graph it is.

2. Read the graph. Use the labels to guide you.

3. Analyze the data. Study the bars to compare the measurements. Look for patterns.

4. Draw conclusions. Ask yourself questions like those on the right.

Skills Practice

1. How long is a gray whale?

2. How much longer is a whale shark than a white shark?

3. Which two sea animals vary in length by 40 feet?

4. Predict Which of these sea animals might you find in an aquarium at an animal park?

5. Was the bar graph a good choice for displaying this data? Explain your answer.

Reading a Line Graph

A scientist collected this data about temperatures in Anchorage, Alaska.

TEMPERATURES IN ANCHORAGE, ALASKA	
Month	**Temperature in Degrees Fahrenheit**
August	55
September	50
October	35
November	20
December	15

Here is the same data displayed in a line graph. A line graph is used to show changes over time.

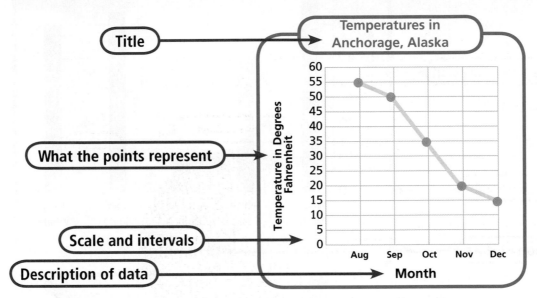

Title → Temperatures in Anchorage, Alaska

What the points represent →

Scale and intervals →

Description of data →

How to Read a Line Graph

1. Look at the graph to determine what kind of graph it is.

2. Read the graph. Use the labels to guide you.

3. Analyze the data. Study the points along the lines. Look for patterns.

4. **Draw conclusions.** Ask yourself questions like those on the right.

Skills Practice

1. In what month is the normal temperature 35 degrees?

2. **Predict** How will the temperature change from December to August?

3. Was the line graph a good choice for displaying this data? Explain why.

Reading a Circle Graph

A family went bird watching on an island. They counted 50 birds on the island. They wanted to know which birds they saw most often. They classified the birds by making a table. Here is the data they collected.

BIRD SIGHTINGS	
Bird	**Number Observed**
Pelican	4
Bald Eagle	1
Osprey	10
Egret	15
Sandpiper	20

The circle graph shows the same data as the table. A circle graph can be used to show data as a whole made up of different parts.

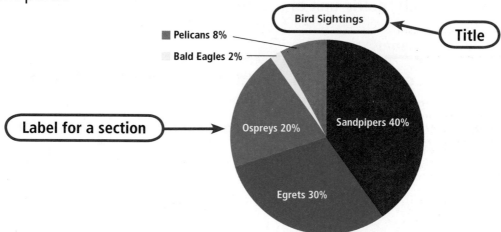

How to Read a Circle Graph

1. Look at the title of the graph to learn what kind of information is shown.

2. Read the graph. Look at the label of each section to find out what information is shown.

3. Analyze the data. Compare the sizes of the sections to determine how they are related.

4. **Draw conclusions.** Ask yourself questions like those on the right.

Skills Practice

1. Which type of bird did they see most often?

2. **Predict** If they return to the island in a month, should they expect to see a bald eagle?

3. Was the circle graph a good choice for displaying this data? Explain why.

Using Metric Measurements

A measurement is a number that represents a comparison of something being measured to a unit of measurement. Scientists use many different tools to measure objects and substances as they work. Scientists almost always use the metric system for their measurements.

Measuring Length in Metric Units

When you measure length, you find the distance between two points. The distance may be in a straight line, along a curved path, or around a circle. The table shows the metric units of length and how they are related.

Equivalent Measures
1 centimeter (cm) = 10 millimeters (mm)
1 decimeter (dm) = 10 centimeters (cm)
1 meter (m) = 1,000 millimeters
1 meter = 10 decimeters
1 kilometer (km) = 1,000 meters

You can use these comparisons to help you learn the size of each metric unit of length:

A millimeter (mm) is about the thickness of a dime.	A centimeter (cm) is about the width of your index finger.	A decimeter (dm) is about the width of an adult's hand.	A meter (m) is about the width of a door.
	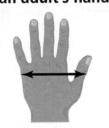		

Sometimes you may need to change units of length. The following diagram shows how to multiply and divide to change to larger and smaller units.

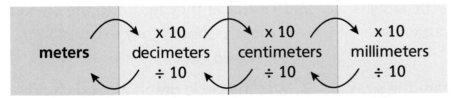

To change larger units to smaller units, you need more of the smaller units. So, multiply by 10, 100, or 1,000.

Example: 500 dm = ___ cm

Measuring Capacity in Metric Units

When you measure capacity, you find the amount a container can hold when it is filled. The table shows the metric units of capacity and how they are related.

A **milliliter (mL)** is the amount of liquid that can fill part of a dropper.

A **liter (L)** is the amount of liquid that can fill this plastic bottle.

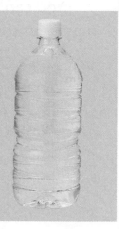

You can use multiplication to change liters to milliliters.

You can use division to change milliliters to liters.

2 L = _____ mL

Think: There are 1,000 mL in 1 L.

2 L = 2 x 1,000 = 2,000 mL

So, 2 L = 2,000 mL.

4,000 mL = _____ L

Think: There are 1,000 mL in 1 L.

4,000 ÷ 1,000 = 4

So, 4,000 mL = 4 L.

Skills Practice

Complete. Tell whether you multiply or divide by 1,000.

1. 4 L = _____ mL

2. 5,000 mL – _____ L

3. 3,000 mL = _____ L

4. 6 L = _____ mL

Measuring Mass

Matter is what all objects are made of. Mass is the amount of matter that is in an object. The metric units of mass are the gram (g) and the kilogram (kg).

You can use these comparisons to help you understand the masses of some everyday objects.

A paper clip is about 1 gram (g).	A slice of wheat bread is about 20 grams.	A box of 12 crayons is about 100 grams.	A large wedge of cheese is 1 kilogram (kg).

You can use multiplication to change kilograms to grams.

You can use division to change grams to kilograms.

2 kg = _____ g Think: There are 1,000 g in 1 kg. 2 kg = 2 x 1,000 = 2,000 g So, 2 kg = 2,000 g.	4,000 g = _____ kg Think: There are 1,000 g in 1 kg. 4,000 ÷ 1,000 = 4 So, 4,000 g = 4 kg.

Skills Practice

Complete. Tell whether you multiply or divide by 1,000.

1. 2,000 g = ___ kg

2. 3,000 g = _____ kg

3. 4 kg = _____ g

4. 7 kg = _____ g

Measurement Systems

SI Measures (Metric)

Temperature
Ice melts at 0 degrees Celsius (°C).
Water freezes at 0°C.
Water boils at 100°C.

Length and Distance
1,000 meters (m) = 1 kilometer (km)
100 centimeters (cm) = 1 m
10 millimeters (mm) = 1 cm

Force
1 newton (N) = 1 kilogram x
    1 meter/second/second (kg-m/s^2)

Volume
1 cubic meter (m^3) = 1 m x 1 m x 1 m
1 cubic centimeter (cm^3) =
    1 cm x 1 cm x 1 cm
1 liter (L) = 1,000 millimeters (mL)
1 cm^3 = 1 mL

Area
1 square kilometer (km^2) =
                1 km x 1 km
1 hectare = 10,000 m^2

Mass
1,000 grams (g) = 1 kilogram (kg)
1,000 milligrams (mg) = 1 g

Rates (Metric and Customary)
kmh = kilometers per hour
m/s = meters per second
mph = miles per hour
A liter (L) is the amount of liquid that
can fill a plastic bottle.

Customary Measures

Volume of Fluids
2 cups (c) = 1 pint (pt)
2 pt = 1 quart (qt)
4 qt = 1 gallon (gal)

Temperature
Ice melts at 32 degrees Fahrenheit (°F).
Water freezes at 32°F.
Water boils at 212°F.

Length and Distance
12 inches (in.) = 1 foot (ft)
3 ft = 1 yard (yd)
5,280 ft = 1 mile (mi)

Weight
16 ounces (oz) = 1 pound (lb)
2,000 pounds = 1 ton (T)

Safety in Science

Doing investigations in science can be fun, but you need to be sure you do them safely. Here are some rules to follow.

1. **Think ahead.** Study the steps of the investigation so you know what to expect. If you have any questions, ask your teacher. Be sure you understand any caution statements or safety reminders.

2. **Be neat.** Keep your work area clean. If you have long hair, pull it back so it doesn't get in the way. Roll or push up long sleeves to keep them away from your experiment.

3. **Oops!** If you spill or break something, or if you get cut, tell your teacher right away.

4. **Watch your eyes.** Wear safety goggles anytime you are directed to do so. If you get anything in your eyes, tell your teacher right away.

5. **Yuck!** Never eat or drink anything during a science activity.

6. **Don't get shocked.** Be especially careful if an electric appliance is used. Be sure that electrical cords are in a safe place where you can't trip over them. Never pull a plug out of an outlet by pulling on the cord.

7. **Keep it clean.** Always clean up when you have finished. Put everything away and wipe your work area. Wash your hands.

Visit the Multimedia Science Glossary to see illustrations of these words and to hear them pronounced.
www.hspscience.com

Every entry in the glossary begins with a term and a *phonetic respelling*. A phonetic respelling writes the word the way it sounds, which can help you pronounce new or unfamiliar words.

The Pronunciation Key below will help you understand the respellings. Syllables are separated by a bullet (•). Small uppercase letters show stressed, or accented, syllables.

The definition of the term follows the respelling. An example of how to use the term in a sentence follows the definition.

The page number in ( ) at the end of the entry tells you where to find the term in your textbook. These terms are highlighted in yellow in the lessons. Every entry has an illustration to help you understand the term.

Pronunciation Key

Sound	As in	Phonetic Respelling	Sound	As in	Phonetic Respelling
a	bat	(BAT)	oh	over	(OH•ver)
ah	lock	(LAHK)	oo	pool	(POOL)
air	rare	(RAIR)	ow	out	(OWT)
ar	argue	(AR•gyoo)	oy	foil	(FOYL)
aw	law	(LAW)	s	cell	(SEL)
ay	face	(FAYS)		sit	(SIT)
ch	chapel	(CHAP•uhl)	sh	sheep	(SHEEP)
e	test	(TEST)	th	that	(THAT)
	metric	(MEH•trik)		thin	(THIN)
ee	eat	(EET)	u	pull	(PUL)
	feet	(FEET)	uh	medal	(MED•uhl)
	ski	(SKEE)		talent	(TAL•uhnt)
er	paper	(PAY•per)		pencil	(PEN•suhl)
	fern	(FERN)		onion	(UHN•yuhn)
eye	idea	(eye•DEE•uh)		playful	(PLAY•fuhl)
i	bit	(BIT)		dull	(DUHL)
ing	going	(GOH•ing)	y	yes	(YES)
k	card	(KARD)		ripe	(RYP)
	kite	(KYT)	z	bags	(BAGZ)
ngk	bank	(BANGK)	zh	treasure	(TREZH•er)

Multimedia Science Glossary: www.hspscience.com

accurate

[AK•yuh•ruht] **Correct:** Mark measured the root twice to make sure his measurement was *accurate.* (8)

adaptation

[ad•uhp•TAY•shuhn] **A feature that helps a living thing survive:** A giraffe's long neck is an *adaptation* for reaching leaves high on a tree. (233)

attract [uh•TRAKT] **To pull toward:** Magnets *attract* iron. (196)

B

balance [BAL•uhns] **Not too many and not too few of a kind of living thing:** When people change the environment, they may change the *balance* among living things. (298)

bar graph [BAR GRAF] **A graph that uses bars to display data:** This *bar graph* can help you see differences in the lengths of animals that live in the sea. (32)

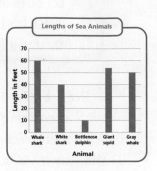

Lengths of Sea Animals

C

Celsius [SEL•see•uhs] **The metric scale for measuring temperature:** The temperature of ice is 0 degrees *Celsius.* (155)

clay [KLAY] **Soil with very, very tiny grains of rock:** Georgia is famous for its red *clay.* (87)

coastal plain

[KOH•stuhl PLAYN] **An area of low, flat land near an ocean:** Most of southern Georgia is part of the *coastal plain.* (282)

conduction
[kuhn•DUHK•shuhn] **The movement of heat between objects that are touching each other:** Heat moves from the hot coils on a stove to a pot by *conduction*. (167)

conductor
[kuhn•DUHK•ter] **An object that heat can move through easily:** Coils on a stove are a good *conductor* of heat. (167)

conservation
[kahn•ser•VAY•shuhn] **The saving of resources by using them wisely:** As a form of *conservation*, car companies develop new cars that use less gas. (340)

D

data table [DAY•tuh TAY•buhl] **A display that organizes data into rows and columns:** A *data table* helps you organize your data as you record it. (32)

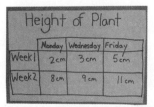

drought [DROWT]
A long period of time with very little rain: A *drought* can be bad for farmers because plants need water to grow. (294)

E

ecosystem
[EE•koh•sis•tuhm] **All the living and nonliving things that interact in an environment:** Air, sunlight, water, soil, and many kinds of plants and animals are part of this marsh *ecosystem*. (268)

electromagnet
[ee•lek•troh•MAG•nit] **A magnet that can be turned on and off by using electricity:** An *electromagnet* can be made with a battery, a wire, and an iron nail. (208)

environment
[en•VY•ruhn•muhnt]
Everything that is around a living thing: Plants and animals must get everything they need to live from their *environment*. (267)

erosion
[uh•ROH•zhuhn]
The movement of weathered rock and soil: When rivers carry away soil, it causes *erosion*. (98)

evidence
[EV•uh•duhns]
Information collected in a scientific inquiry: You must collect *evidence* to prove whether or not your prediction is correct. (23)

experiment
[ek•SPEHR•uh•muhnt]
A test done to find out if a hypothesis is correct: In this *experiment*, the only difference between the cups is the type of soil the plants are growing in. (41)

extinct [ek•STINGT]
Describes a kind of living thing that is no longer found on Earth: Dinosaurs are *extinct*. (132)

F

fossil [FAHS•uhl]
The hardened remains of a plant or an animal that lived long ago: We can learn about living things of long ago by studying *fossils*. (114)

friction [FRIK•shuhn]
A force between two moving objects that slows the objects and produces heat: Rubbing your hands together causes *friction*, which warms your hands. (178)

 G

generator [JEN•er•ayt•er]
A device that uses a magnet to produce a current of electricity: Workers use a *generator* to produce electricity when there is no power after a storm. (209)

 H

habitat [HAB•ih•tat]
The place where a plant or an animal lives: Underground burrows in grasslands are part of a prairie dog's *habitat*. (269)

hardness [HARD•nuhs]
The measure of how difficult it is for a mineral to be scratched: Minerals that can be scratched with a fingernail have a low *hardness*. (60)

heat [HEET]
The movement of thermal energy from hotter to cooler objects: *Heat* is needed to melt a solid object. (156)

hibernate [HY•ber•nayt]
To spend the winter in a kind of deep sleep: When an animal *hibernates*, its breathing and heartbeat rates slow down and its body temperature drops. (248)

humus [HYOO•muhs]
The part of soil made up of broken-down pieces of dead plants and animals: *Humus* helps plants grow. (84)

hypothesis
[hy•PAHTH•uh•sis]
A possible answer to a question in an investigation: The students' *hypothesis* is that a block will slide faster than an eraser on a cooking sheet. (41)

igneous rock
[IG•nee•uhs RAHK]
Rock that was once melted and then cooled and hardened: Granite is one kind of *igneous rock.* (72)

inquiry [IN•kwer•ee]
A question about something or a close study of it: The class grew plants as part of their *inquiry* about greenhouses. (6)

insulation
[in•suh•LAY•shuhn]
Material used to slow the movement of heat: *Insulation* is added to walls of houses to help keep them warm in winter and cool in summer. (169)

insulator
[IN•suh•layt•er] **An object that doesn't conduct heat well:** An oven mitt is a good *insulator* because it does not allow heat from the pan to reach your hands. (168)

investigation
[in•ves•tuh•GAY•shuhn]
A scientific study: The students performed an *investigation* to find out which substances dissolve in water. (40)

L

line graph [LYN GRAF]
A graph that uses lines to display data: You can see how temperature and time of year are related in this *line graph*. (33)

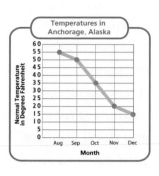

Temperatures in Anchorage, Alaska

loam [LOHM] **Soil that is a mixture of humus, sand, silt, and clay:** Farmers know that *loam* is a good kind of soil for growing many types of plants. (89)

M

magnet [MAG•nit]
An object that is attracted to iron: A *magnet* will pick up objects made of iron. (196)

magnetic [mag•NET•ik]
Attracting objects that have iron in them: *Magnetic* objects will stick to most refrigerators. (198)

metamorphic rock [met•uh•MAWR•fik RAHK] **Rock that has been changed by heat or pressure:** Gneiss is one kind of *metamorphic rock*. (73)

migrate [MY•grayt]
To travel from one place to another and back again: Some kinds of birds *migrate* south for the winter and return north for the summer. (249)

mineral [MIN•er•uhl]
A solid object found in nature that has never been alive: Most gemstones are *minerals*. (58)

mountain

[MOWNT•uhn] **A high, raised part of Earth's surface:** The Blue Ridge is a *mountain* chain in Georgia. (278)

 N

natural resource

[NACH•er•uhl REE•sawrs] **A material that is found in nature and that is used by living things:** Fish are a *natural resource* that people and some other living things use for food. (314)

nonrenewable resource

[nahn•rih•NOO•uh•buhl REE•sawrs] **A resource that, when it is used up, will not exist again during a human lifetime:** Coal, oil, and natural gas are *nonrenewable resources*. (318)

O

opinion

[uh•PIN•yuhn] **A personal belief that is not based on evidence:** Make sure you don't confuse your *opinions* with evidence that comes from an investigation. (23)

Cats are the best pets!

P

piedmont

[PEED•mahnt] **An area, with many hills, between the coastal plain and the mountains:** The soils of the *piedmont* have many rocks, unlike the sandy soils of the coastal plain. (280)

pollution

[puh•LOO•shuhn] **Harmful material that is added to the environment:** Oil spills are a kind of *pollution* that can kill many living things. (328)

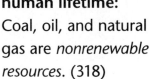

predict [pree•DIKT] **To tell what you think will happen in the future:** You *predict* the outcome of an experiment before you begin the experiment. (20)

 R

recycle [ree•sy•kuhl] **To reuse a resource by breaking it down and making a new product:** When you *recycle* cans and newspaper, you help the environment. (344)

reduce [ree•DOOS] **To use less of a resource:** You can *reduce* how much electricity you use by turning off lights when you leave a room. (342)

renewable resource [rih•NOO•uh•buhl REE•sawrs] **A resource that can be replaced quickly:** If we are careful how we cut and plant trees, forests can be a *renewable resource*. (316)

repel [ree•PEL] **To push away:** The north-seeking poles of two magnets *repel* each other. (197)

reproduce [ree•pruh•DOOS] **To produce new living things:** Living things *reproduce* in many ways, such as by making seeds, laying eggs, or giving birth to live young. (236)

reuse [ree•YOOZ] **To use a resource again and again:** You can *reuse* a tire by turning it into a swing. (343)

rock [RAHK] A naturally formed solid made of grains of one or more minerals: *Rocks* come in many shapes, colors, textures, and sizes. (62)

sand [SAND] Soil with grains of rock that you can see with your eyes alone: When rocks are broken down into small pieces, they become *sand*. (87)

scientific method [sy•uhn•TIF•ik METH•uhd] An organized plan that scientists use to conduct an investigation: This student is using the *scientific method* to design an experiment. (40)

sedimentary rock [sed•uh•MEN•ter•ee RAHK] Rock made when materials settle into layers and get squeezed until they harden into rock: Sandstone is one kind of *sedimentary rock*. (73)

silt [SILT] Soil with grains of rock that are too small to see with your eyes alone: You can find *silt* at the bottom of a river. (87)

survive [ser•VYV] To stay alive: Plants and animals have features that help them *survive*. (232)

T

temperature
[TEM•per•uh•cher]
The measure of how hot or cold something is: In winter, the *temperature* is usually colder than it is in summer. (154)

temporary magnet
[TEM•puh•rair•ee MAG•nit] **A magnet made by passing an iron object near a magnet:** A *temporary magnet* will not always be magnetic. (210)

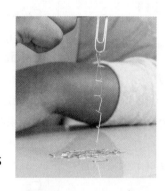

thermal energy
[THER•muhl EN•er•jee]
The form of energy that moves particles of matter: *Thermal energy* from the sun will melt a snowman and warm the ground. (156)

thermometer
[ther•MAHM•uh•ter]
A tool that measures how hot or cold something is: Many *thermometers* have two scales—degrees Celsius and degrees Fahrenheit. (9)

trait [TRAYT]
A characteristic, or feature, of a plant or animal: The different *traits* of these flowers help you tell them apart. (232)

W

weathering
[WETH•er•ing] **The breaking down of rocks into smaller pieces:** *Weathering* has formed a hole in this sandstone, making an arch. (96)

wetland [WET•land]
Land that is covered with water most of the time: Ducks, alligators, and many kinds of frogs live in *wetlands*. (285)

Index

CHARACTERISTICS Bobcats have good senses of sight and smell. They use their whiskers to feel.

YOUNG A young bobcat stays with its mother for the first year of its life.

HUNTING Bobcats have sharp claws and teeth for catching rabbits and other small animals.

CAMOUFLAGE A bobcat's color and markings help it blend in with its surroundings and sneak up on its prey.

MOVEMENT A bobcat's strong back legs are longer than its front legs.